The Wretched of the Earth

OTHER WORKS BY FRANTZ FANON
PUBLISHED BY GROVE PRESS

Black Skin, White Masks
A Dying Colonialism
Toward the African Revolution

THE WRETCHED OF THE EARTH

Frantz Fanon

*Translated from the French
by Richard Philcox*

*with commentary by
Jean-Paul Sartre
and
Homi K. Bhabha
and
Cornel West*

60th Anniversary Edition

Grove Press
New York

Originally published in the French language by François Maspero éditeur, Paris, France, under the title *Les damnés de la terre*, copyright © 1961 by François Maspero éditeur S.A.R.L.

Revised sixtieth anniversary edition first published in October 2021.

Published simultaneously in Canada
Printed in Canada

ISBN: 978-0-8021-5863-5
eISBN: 978-0-8021-9885-3

Library of Congress Cataloging-in-Publication Data is available for this title.

Grove Press
an imprint of Grove Atlantic
154 West 14th Street
New York, NY 10011

Distributed by Publishers Group West

groveatlantic.com

23 24 25 26   10 9 8 7 6 5 4

Contents

Introduction to the Sixtieth Anniversary Edition by Cornel West

Frantz Fanon is the greatest revolutionary intellectual of the mid-twentieth century. He also is the most relevant for the twenty-first century. His theoretical genius, literary artistry, and political courage are undeniable. And his personal integrity, wholesale honesty, and self-critical tenacity are indisputable. Like Charlie Parker's bebop revolution in modern music, Frantz Fanon's works and witness disrupted and shattered prevailing paradigms in modern philosophy, culture, and politics. Similar to Nina Simone's subversive sonic intellect, Frantz Fanon made confronting the historical realities of decolonization inescapable. In short, he is a towering figure in our neo-liberal and neo-colonial time because he cast a light on the terrifying and terroristic underside of white supremacist European imperialism—a light that enables us to keep track of how those chickens have come home to roost around the world.

The Wretched of the Earth (1961) was Fanon's last testament—at the tender age of thirty-six—to his prophetic vocation. This calling was motivated by a profound love of colonized people and grounded in a deep love of the truth of their doings and sufferings. In the first moments of this perennial classic book, he writes, "decolonization, therefore, implies the urgent need to thoroughly challenge the colonial situation. Its definition can, if we want to describe it accurately, be summed up in the well-known words: 'The last shall be first.' Decolonization is verification of this."[1] His biblical allusion to Jesus (Matthew 20:16) and revolutionary declaration of a "murderous and decisive struggle" between the colonizer and colonized, occupier and occupied, makes us confront the naked violence and raw force of the asymmetric power of the dominating over the dominated. Fanon will not allow us to begin our discussion with the counter-violence of the oppressed, but rather with longstanding and often overlooked terror and trauma of the structural violence and everyday horror shot through the colonial realities for precious ordinary people.

When Fanon states, "the colonial world is a compartmentalized world,"[2] he compels us to acknowledge colonialism is a sustained barbaric war waged against colonized people sanctioned by Western values. "Now it so happens that when the colonized hear a speech on Western culture they draw their machetes or at least check to see they are close to hand . . . In the period of decolonization the colonized masses thumb their noses at these very values, shower them with insults and vomit them up."[3] Fanon's indictment of European colonialism is more than a fancy epistemic rejection of Eurocentrism or a mere Nietzschean moment of opposition against a dialectical vision of deliverance. Rather, Fanon is deepening, refining, and "slightly stretching" Marxist analysis by wedding an unrelenting critique of predatory capitalism and its imperial tentacles with an Empire-driven analysis of a war-like white supremacy that permeates the very souls of colonial subjects as well as shapes every sphere of colonial society. Like a great jazz musician, Fanon enacts and embodies modes of counterpoint that creatively fuse Karl Marx's critique of capitalist economies, Carl von Clausewitz's philosophy of war (with Mao Zedong's guerrilla warfare addition), François Tosquelles's (and

---

[1] Frantz Fanon, *The Wretched of the Earth* (WE), 2.
[2] WE, 3.
[3] WE, 8.

to some degree Jacques Lacan's) rich notions of sociogeny and milieu therapy, and, above all, the inimitable examples of Aimé Césaire (Fanon's teacher, mentor, and fellow Martiniquean freedom fighter) and Jean-Paul Sartre.

Fanon is first and foremost a revolutionary whose artistry in language, speech, and political praxis bids us to resist and overthrow all forms of dogma and domination that subjugate oppressed peoples. (Note his "final prayer" in *Black Skin, White Masks* [1952]: "O my body, always make me a man who questions!"[4]). This intense Socratic energy—aligned with what he calls "African self-criticism"—yields a thoroughgoing internationalism that passes through a genuine national consciousness. "Self-awareness does not mean closing the door on communication. Philosophy teaches us on the contrary that it is its guarantee. National consciousness, which is not nationalism, is alone capable of giving us an international dimension . . . It is at the heart of national consciousness that international consciousness establishes itself and thrives."[5] Fanon's revolutionary internationalism—like that of Karl Marx, C. L. R. James, Rosa Luxemburg, Ella Baker, Albizu Campos, B. R. Ambedkar, Emma Goldman, or his comrade Ali Shariati—never reduced the intellectual richness of European history solely to the vicious European crimes against humanity, especially against Third World peoples. He even goes further,

All the elements for a solution to the major problems of humanity existed at one time or another in European thought. But the Europeans did not act on the mission that was designated them . . . [6]

The Third World must start over a new history of man which takes account of not only the occasional prodigious theses maintained by Europe but also its crimes . . . [7]

---

[4] Frantz Fanon, *Black Skin, White Masks*, (New York: Grove Press), 206.
[5] WE, 179–180.
[6] WE, 237.
[7] WE, 238.

Moreover, if we want to respond to the expectations of the Europeans we must not send them back a reflection, however ideal, of their society and their thought that periodically sickens even them.

For Europe, for ourselves and for humanity, comrades, we must make a new start, develop a new way of thinking, and endeavor to create a new man.[8]

For Fanon, revolutionary internationalism — anti-imperialist, anti-capitalist, anti-colonialist, anti-patriarchal, and anti-white-supremacist — yields a new humanism that puts a premium on the psychic, social, and political needs of poor and working peoples — a solidarity and universality from below.

Women shall be given equal importance to men . . . in daily life, at the factory, in the schools, and in assemblies.[9]

If the national government wants to be national it must govern by the people and for the people, for the disinherited and by the disinherited. No leader . . . can replace the will of the people, and the national government, before concerning itself with international prestige, must first restore dignity to all citizens, furnish their minds, fill their eyes with human things and develop a human landscape for the sake of its enlightened and sovereign inhabitants.[10]

Yet Fanon's revolutionary internationalism and new humanism were betrayed by new national bourgeoisies from every corner of the globe. In his famous and still highly relevant chapter, "The Trials and Tribulations of National Consciousness" (a favorite I recall in our intense discussions with Black Panther Party comrades in the sixties and seventies), he rightly predicted, the "fight for democracy against man's oppression gradually emerges from a universalist, neoliberal confusion to arrive, sometimes laboriously, at a demand for nationhood. But the unpreparedness of

---

[8] WE, 239.
[9] WE, 142.
[10] WE, 144.

the elite, the lack of practical ties between them and the masses, their apathy, and, yes, their cowardice at the crucial moment in the struggle, are the cause of tragic trials and tribulations."[11]

In our time—our Obama moment and its aftermath—this neoliberal tragic mishap has become a neoliberal fascist backlash. Big Money—Wall Street, Silicon Valley, and Big Tech (as well as Big Militarism), filtered through the Pentagon and State Department—is in the driver's seat. Ugly white supremacy is the public face. And patriarchy, homophobia, and transphobia run amok.

The most well-known sentence in Fanon's canonical work is the first line of "On National Culture": "Each generation must discover its mission, fulfill it or betray it, in relative opacity."[12] Let it be said again—surely and strongly—that the national bourgeoisies of the past sixty years since Fanon's book appeared have indeed betrayed their revolutionary mission. Their "neoliberal universalism" can no longer hide and conceal their capitulation to Big Money, Big Militarism—and political centrism. Furthermore, their levels of corruption, lack of accountability, greed, narcissism, and repression of those who threaten their power have trumped any fundamental transformation.

Fanon's Algerian context led to his fascinating yet sometimes objectionable formulations about the revolutionary potential of the lumpenproletariat, the peasantry, or even the cathartic effect of armed struggle for colonized people. Yet his crucial claims about the need for strong mechanisms of accountability for leaders, the necessity of self-critical political education for citizens, and the civic institutions that attend to trauma and mental disorders are irrefutable. Like his teacher, Maurice Merleau-Ponty, Frantz Fanon is one of the few great revolutionary intellectuals who always connected the psychic and the political, the existential

---

[11] WE, 97.
[12] WE, 145.

and the economic, the spiritual and the social.

In our present-day moment of imperial decay and capitalist decrepitude (be it in the USA, China, or Russia)—including our ecological emergency, escalating neo-fascism, and pervasive xenophobia (against Muslims, Arabs, Jews, and LGBTQ+ peoples) as well as deep white supremacy—the spirit of Fanon is most manifest in my American imperialist context in the revolutionary internationalist wings of the Black Lives Matter movement and the Palestinian Lives Matter movement aligned with the Boycott, Divestment, and Sanctions efforts. Yet the task of full-fledged decolonization and wholesale democratization with genuine socialist options remains unfinished. Let us not betray our mission—just as Frantz Fanon never sold his soul nor betrayed his prophetic vocation!

—Cornel West
May 2021

Foreword: Framing Fanon
by Homi K. Bhabha

The colonized, underdeveloped man is a political creature in the most global sense of the term.

Frantz Fanon: *The Wretched of the Earth*

And once, when Sartre had made some comment, he [Fanon] gave an explanation of his egocentricity: a member of a colonised people must be constantly aware of his position, his image; he is being threatened from all sides; impossible to forget for an instant the need to keep up one's defences.

Simone de Beauvoir, *The Force of Circumstance*

Frantz Fanon's legend in America starts with the story of his death in Washington on December 6, 1961. Despite his reluctance to be treated "in that country of lynchers",[1] Fanon was advised that his only chance of survival lay in seeking the leukemia treatment available at the National Institutes of Health in Bethesda, Maryland. Accompanied by a CIA case officer provided by the American Embassy in Tunis, Fanon flew to Washington, changing planes in Rome, where he met Jean-Paul Sartre but was too

---

For my brother Sorab: doctor of my soul; healer of my mind. —HKB

[1] Simone de Beauvoir, *The Force of Circumstance, Vol. II: The Autobiography of Simone de Beauvoir*, trans. Peter Green (New York: Paragon House, 1992), 317.

enfeebled to utter a single word. A few days later, on October 3, Fanon was admitted to the hospital as Ibrahim Fanon, a supposedly "Libyan" nom de guerre he had assumed to enter a hospital in Rome after being wounded in Morocco during a mission for the Algerian National Liberation Front.

His body was stricken, but his fighting days were not quite over; he resisted his death "minute by minute," a friend reported from his bedside, as his political opinions and beliefs turned into the delirious fantasies of a mind raging against the dying of the light. His hatred of racist Americans now turned into a distrust of the nursing staff, and he awoke on his last morning, having probably had a blood transfusion through the night, obsessed with the idea that "they put me through the washing machine last night."[2] His death was inevitable. "We did everything we could," his doctor reported later, "but in 1961 there wasn't much you could do . . . especially when he came to us so late."[3] Perhaps it was the writing of *The Wretched of the Earth* in a feverish spurt between April and July of 1961 that contributed to this fatal delay; when his wife, Josie Fanon, read him the enthusiastic early reviews of the book, he could only say, "That won't give me back my bone marrow."[4] On the day of his death, the French police seized copies of *The Wretched of the Earth* from the Paris bookshops.[5] After his death, Simone de Beauvoir remembered seeing Fanon's photograph all over Paris for a couple of weeks, "on the cover of *Jeune Afrique*, in the window of the Maspero bookstore, younger, calmer than I had ever seen him, and very handsome."[6]

❖   ❖   ❖

---

[2] Claude Lanzmann, as cited by David Macey in *Frantz Fanon: A Life* (London: Granta Books, 2000), 489–90. Much of the biographical detail and personal incident comes from Simone de Beauvoir's account of Fanon in *The Force of Circumstance*, and from David Macey's remarkably informed biography.

[3] Joseph Alsop, "Passing of New Left's Hero an Odd Facet of U.S. History," in *Washington Post*, February 21, 1969, A21.

[4] Macey, 489.

[5] Ibid.

[6] de Beauvoir, 329.

A colonized person must constantly be aware of his image, jealously protect his position, Fanon said to Sartre. The defenses of the colonized are tuned like anxious antennae waiting to pick up the hostile signals of a racially divided world. In the process, the colonized acquire a peculiar visceral intelligence dedicated to the survival of body and spirit. Fanon's two most influential texts, *Black Skin, White Masks* and *The Wretched of the Earth*, evoke the concrete and contrasting worlds of colonial racism as experienced in metropolitan France in the 1950s and during the anticolonial Algerian war of liberation a decade later. Is his work lost in a time warp? Is his impassioned plea that "the Third World must start over a new history of man"[7] merely a vain hope? Does such a lofty ideal represent anything more than the lost rhetorical baggage of that daunting quest for a nonaligned postcolonial world inaugurated at the Bandung Conference in 1955. Who can claim that dream now? Who still waits in the antechamber of history? Did Fanon's ideas die with the decline and dissolution of the black power movement in America, buried with Steve Biko in South Africa, or were they born again when the Berlin Wall was dismembered and a new South Africa took its place on the world's stage? Questions, questions. ...

As we catch the religiosity in Fanon's language of revolutionary wrath — "the last shall be the first," "the almighty body of violence rearing up ..."[8] — and run it together with his description of the widening circle of national unity as reaching the "boiling point" in a way that "is reminiscent of a religious brotherhood, a church or a mystical doctrine,"[9] we find ourselves both forewarned and wary of the ethnonationalist religious conflicts of our own times. When we hear Fanon say that "for the people only fellow nationals are ever owed the truth,"[10] we furiously object

---

[7] Frantz Fanon, *The Wretched of the Earth* (WE), 238.
[8] *WE*, 2, 50.
[9] *WE*, 84.
[10] *WE*, 14.

to such a narrow and dangerous definition of "the people" and "the truth." To have Fanon uphold the view that the building of national consciousness demands cultural homogeneity and the disappearance or dissolution of differences is deeply troubling. Is he not dangerously outdated? Fanon's best hopes for the Algerian revolution were taken hostage and summarily executed, first by a bureaucratized military rule that violated his belief "that an army is never a school for war, but a school for civics ... ,"[11] and then by the rise of fundamentalist groups like the Islamic Salvation Front. Josie Fanon looked out of her window in the El Biar district of Algiers in October 1988 only to find scenes of carnage. In violently quelling a demonstration in the street below, the army had enflamed the passions of Algerian youths, who responded by torching police cars before they were felled by a barrage of bullets. Speaking to her friend the Algerian writer Assia Djebar on the telephone, Josie sighed: "Oh Frantz, the wretched of the earth again."[12] The legacy of Fanon leaves us with questions; his virtual, verbal presence among us only provokes more questions. And that is as it should be. "O my body, make of me always a man who questions!" was Fanon's final, unfinished prayer at the end of *Black Skin, White Masks*.

The time is right to reread Fanon, according to David Macey, his most brilliant biographer, because "Fanon was angry," and without the basic political instinct of anger there can be no hope for "the wretched of the earth [who] are still with us."[13] What hope does Fanon's anger hold for us today? Although times have changed, and history never appears twice in the emperor's new clothes, *mais plus ça change*. ... New global empires rise to enforce their own civilizing missions in the name of democracy and free markets where once progress and development

---

[11] WE, 141.
[12] Assia Djebar, *Le blanc de l'Algérie* (Paris: Albin Michel, 1995), 106–7, cited in Macey, 506.
[13] Macey, 503.

were seen as the shibboleths of a modernized, westernized salvation. As if such civic, public goods were exportable commodities; as if these "other" countries and cultures were innocent of
the leavening spirit of freedom; as if the deplorable tyrannies
and dictatorships of our day, which must be destroyed, were not
themselves part of the intricate negotiations, and internecine
histories, of world powers and their political interests; as if any
civilizing mission, despite its avowed aims, had ever been free
of psychological terror, cultural arrogance, and even physical
torture. "The colonized, underdeveloped man is today a political
creature in the most global sense of the term,"[14] Fanon writes
in *The Wretched of the Earth*, and it is my purpose, almost half
a century later, to ask what might be saved from Fanon's ethics
and politics of decolonization to help us reflect on globalization
in our sense of the term.

It must seem ironic, even absurd at first, to search for associations
and intersections between decolonization and globalization—
parallels would be pushing the analogy—when decolonization
had the dream of a "Third World" of free, postcolonial nations
firmly on its horizon, whereas globalization gazes at the nation
through the back mirror, as it speeds toward the strategic de-
nationalization of state sovereignty. The global aspirations of
Third World "national" thinking belonged to the internationalist traditions of socialism, Marxism, and humanism, whereas the
dominant forces of contemporary globalization tend to subscribe
to free-market ideas that enshrine ideologies of neoliberal tech-
nocractic elitism. And finally, while it was the primary purpose of
decolonization to repossess land and territoriality in order to ensure the security of national polity and global equity, globalization
propagates a world made up of virtual transnational domains and
wired communities that live vividly through webs and connectivi-
ties "on line." In what way, then, can the once colonized woman

---

[14] *WE*, 40.

or man become figures of instruction for our global century?

To this end, there is an immediate argument to be made that suggests that the economic "solutions" to inequality and poverty subscribed to by the IMF and the World Bank, for instance, have "the feel of the colonial ruler," according to Joseph Stiglitz, once senior vice president and chief economist of the World Bank. "They help to create a dual economy in which there are pockets of wealth. ... But a dual economy is not a developed economy."[15] It is the reproduction of dual, unequal economies as effects of globalization that render poorer societies more vulnerable to the "culture of conditionality," through which what is purportedly the granting of loans turns, at times, into the peremptory enforcement of policy. These dual economies claim to sustain diverse worlds of opportunity, consisting of global villages, silicon valleys, and oases of outsourcing dotted across the North and the South. The landscape of opportunity and "choice" has certainly widened in scope, but the colonial shadow falls across the successes of globalization. Dual economies create divided worlds in which uneven and unequal conditions of development can often mask the ubiquitous, underlying factors of persistent poverty and malnutrition, caste and racial injustice, the hidden injuries of class, the exploitation of women's labor, and the victimization of minorities and refugees. For instance, "India shining," the 2004 election slogan of the "high tech" Hindu nationalist BJP government, failed to mention the darker, daily reality of the 63 percent of rural households that do not have electricity and the ten to fifteen hours of blackouts and brownouts that afflict those that do on any given day.[16]

Global duality should be put in the historical context of Fanon's

---

[15] Joseph E. Stiglitz, *Globalization and Its Discontents* (New York: W. W. Norton, 2003), 40.

[16] Anil K. Rajvanshi, "Key Issues in Rural Electrification," published in Projects Monitor, 16 October 2003, http://pune.sancharnet.in/nariphaltan/ruralelec.htm.

founding insight into the "geographical configuration" of colonial governance,[17] his celebrated description of the Manichaean or compartmentalized structure of colonial society. The generic duality that spans the global world of colonized societies is "a world divided in two ... inhabited by different species."[18] Spatial compartmentalization, Macey acutely argues, is typical of the social structure of settler societies like Algeria, but demographic duality is also found in other colonial societies that were divided between the club and the bazaar or the cantonment and the civil lines. Fanon's emphasis on the racialization of inequality does not, of course, apply uniformly to the inequities of contemporary global underdevelopment. However, the racial optic—if seen as a symbolic stand-in for other forms of social difference and discrimination—does clarify the role played by the obscuring and normalizing discourses of progress and civility, in both East and West, that only "tolerate" differences they are able to culturally assimilate into their own *singular* terms, or appropriate within their own *untranslated* traditions. As Fanon puts it in what is perhaps the most quoted (and quarreled over) passage in *The Wretched of the Earth*:

The singularity of the colonial context lies in the fact that economic reality, inequality, and enormous disparities in lifestyles never manage to mask the human reality. Looking at the immediacies of the colonial context, it is clear that what divides this world is first and foremost what species, what race one belongs to. In the colonies the economic infrastructure is also a superstructure.[19]

In my view, *The Wretched of the Earth* does indeed allow us to look well beyond the immediacies of its anticolonial context—the Algerian war of independence and the African continent—toward

---

[17] WE, 3.
[18] WE, 5.
[19] Ibid.

a critique of the configurations of contemporary globalization. This is not because the text prophetically transcends its own time, but because of the peculiarly grounded, historical stance it takes toward the future. The critical language of duality—whether colonial or global—is part of the *spatial* imagination that seems to come so naturally to geopolitical thinking of a progressive, postcolonial cast of mind: margin and metropole, center and periphery, the global and the local, the nation and the world. Fanon's famous trope of colonial compartmentalization, or Manichaeanism, is firmly rooted within this anticolonial spatial tradition. But there is another time frame at work in the narrative of *The Wretched of the Earth* that introduces a *temporal* dimension into the discourse of decolonization. It suggests that the *future* of the decolonized world—"The Third World must start over a new history of Man ..."—is imaginable, or achievable, only in the process of resisting the peremptory and polarizing choices that the superpowers impose on their "client" states. Decolonization can truly be achieved only with the destruction of the Manichaeanism of the cold war; and it is this belief that enables the insights of *The Wretched of the Earth* to be effective beyond its publication in 1961 (and the death of its author in that year), and to provide us with salient and suggestive perspectives on the state of the decompartmentalized world after the dismemberment of the Berlin Wall in 1989.

Fanon is resolute that the Third World should follow the socialist path, "based on the principle that man is the most precious asset."[20] But he is equally insistent that the Third World "must not be content to define itself in relation to values which *preceded* it. ... The basic issue with which we are faced is not the *unequivocal choice* between socialism and capitalism such as they have been defined by men from different continents and different periods of time" (my emphasis).[21] If decolonization

---

[20] WE, 56.
[21] WE, 55.

can be achieved only through the destruction of the "compart-mentalized" colonial system, then the "new humanism" of the Third World cannot properly emerge until the bipolar tensions, contradictions, and dependencies of the cold war are brought to an end. There are two histories at work in *The Wretched of the Earth*: the Manichaean history of colonialism and decolonization embedded in text and context, against which the book mounts a major political and ethical offensive; and a history of the coercive "univocal choices" imposed by the cold warriors on the rest of the world, which constitute the ideological conditions of its writing. In attempting to think proleptically of questions of freedom and fairness beyond the cold war, Fanon intriguingly projects unfinished business and unanswered questions related to the mid-twentieth century and the "end" of empire into the uncertain futures of the fin de siècle and the end of the cold war. It is in this sense that his work provides a genealogy for globalization that reaches back to the complex problems of decolonization (rather than the simpler story of the death of communism and the triumph of free-market neoliberalism), and it could be said, both factually and figuratively, that *The Wretched of the Earth* takes us back to the future. Reflect, for instance, on Fanon's far-reaching wariness about the national consciousness of "young" nations, then absent it from his wider critique of the "underdeveloped" nationalist bourgeoisie of postcolonial countries and listen to his statement as a weather report on our own day:

National consciousness is nothing but a crude, empty fragile shell. The cracks in it explain how easy it is for young independent countries to switch back from nation to ethnic group and from state to tribe—a regression which is so terribly detrimental and prejudicial to the development of the nation and national unity."[22]

It is, of course, one of the most significant lessons of the

---

[22] WE, 97.

postcolonial experience that no nation is simply young or old, new or ancient, despite the date of its independence. "New" national, international, or global emergences create an unsettling sense of transition, as if history is at a turning point; and it is in such *incubational* moments—Antonio Gramsci's word for the perceived "newness" of change—that we experience the palimpsestical imprints of past, present, and future in peculiarly contemporary figures of time and meaning. Fanon's description of the "crude, empty fragile shell" of emergent national histories quickens the long shadows cast by the ethnonationalist "switchbacks" of our own times, the charnel houses of ethnic cleansing: Bosnia, Rwanda, Kosovo, Gujarat, Sudan. Less spectacular, but no less tragic, are the regressions that lead to the "tribalisms" of religious fundamentalism. And then there are those deeply disabling theses of "the clash of civilizations" once turned against Islam and now targeting migrants, refugees, and minorities more generally.

Fanon's vision of the global future, *post* colonialism and after decolonization, is an ethical and political *project*—yes, a plan of action as well as a projected aspiration—that must go beyond "narrow-minded nationalism" or bourgeois nationalist formalism because "if nationalism is not explained, enriched, and deepened, if it does not very quickly turn into a social and political consciousness, into humanism, then it leads to a dead-end."[23] Now many readers have held that The Wretched of the Earth is long on prophecy and polemics and short on policy and planning—a deliberately universalized level of analysis that has led The Wretched of the Earth to become, as Stuart Hall has remarked, the "Bible of decolonisation."[24] It has also been justly argued that Fanon's Third World is an iconic evocation of Africa, a symbol of Pan-African solidarity composed of his syncretic experiences of the

---

[23] WE, 144.
[24] Interview with Stuart Hall in *Frantz Fanon: Black Skin, White Masks.* dir. Isaac Julien (UK: Arts Council of England, 1996).

Maghreb, West Africa, South Africa, and the Antilles, with scant awareness of Latin America (with the exception of Cuba), Asia, or the Middle East.[25]

These fine historical readings have greatly enhanced our understanding of the universalizing, generalizing tendency in Fanon's writings. There is more to be said, however, about Fanon's universalism if it is read, as I have proposed, in relation to a concept of the Third World as a project marked by a double temporality. Decolonization demands a sustained, quotidian commitment to the struggle for national liberation, for when the high, heady wind of revolution loses its velocity, there is no "question of bridging the gap in one giant stride. The epic is played out on a difficult day to day basis and the suffering endured far exceeds that of the colonial period."[26] But the coming into being of the Third World is also a *project of futurity* conditional upon being freed from the "univocal choice" presented by the cold war. Fanon's invocation of a new humanism — "Let us endeavour to invent a man in full, something which Europe has been incapable of achieving"[27] — is certainly grounded in a universalist ontology that informs both its attitude to human consciousness and social reality. The historical agency of the discourse of Third Worldism, however, with its critical, political stance against the *imposed* univocal choice of "capitalism vs. socialism," makes it less universalist in temper and more strategic, activist, and aspirational in character:

The basic confrontation which seemed to be colonialism versus anti-colonialism, indeed capitalism versus socialism, is already losing its importance. What matters today, the issue which blocks the horizon, is the need for a redistribution of wealth. Humanity will have to address this question, no matter how devastating the consequences may be.[28]

---

[25] Macey, 469.
[26] WE, 90.
[27] WE, 236.
[28] WE, 55.

Fanon's call for a redistribution of wealth and technology beyond the rhetorical pieties of "moral reparation"[29] is a timely reminder of the need for something like a "right" to equitable development (controversial though it may be) at a time when dual economies are celebrated as if they were global economies. And coming to us from the distances of midcentury decolonization, Fanon's demand for a fair distribution of rights and resources makes a timely intervention in a decade-long debate on social equity that has focused perhaps too exclusively on the culture wars, the politics of identity, and the politics of recognition. Fanon's call has certainly been heard by popular movements and social institutions committed to debt relief or forgiveness; it has led to health initiatives that see the availability of generic drugs for HIV-AIDS as an economic necessity for the "right" to life and human capability; and his influence is felt amongst reformist bodies that seek to restructure international trade and tariffs, and democratize the governance of global financial institutions, in favor of equitable assistance and redistribution.

The actors and agents of these global initiatives of an international civil society *in the making*, whether they are NGOs, human rights organizations, international legal or educational bodies, or national and transnational popular movements, have done their best to resist the coercive cultures of univocal choice. Sometimes they succeed; often they fail; most likely they survive uncertainly between success and failure. By seeing the need for equitable distribution as part of a humanistic project, Fanon transforms its economic terms of reference; he places the problem of development in the context of those forceful and fragile "psycho-affective" motivations and mutilations that drive our collective instinct for survival, nurture our ethical affiliations and ambivalences, and nourish our political desire for freedom.

---

[29] WE, 40.

I want to turn now to Fanon's exploration of the psycho-affective realm, which is neither subjective nor objective, but a place of social and psychic mediation, and—if I may quote Fanon out of context—"the glowing focal point where citizen and individual develop and grow. ..."[30] It is Fanon's great contribution to our understanding of ethical judgment and political experience to insistently frame his reflections on violence, decolonization, national consciousness, and humanism in terms of the psycho-affective realm—the body, dreams, psychic inversions and displacements, phantasmatic political identifications. A psycho-affective relation or response has the semblance of universality and timelessness because it involves the emotions, the imagination or psychic life, but it is only ever mobilized into social meaning and historical effect through an embodied and embedded action, an engagement with (or resistance to) a given reality, or a performance of agency in the present tense.

The nervous conditions and political agitations of psycho-affectivity compose and decompose the compartmentalized worlds of colonialism and metropolitan racism. In *Black Skin, White Masks*, Fanon dramatically explores the psycho-affective predicament of the Antillean Negro as he is assailed by the depersonalizing, discriminatory gaze of racist recognition: "*Look, a Negro ... !*" The black person, a free French citizen from an overseas department of the republic, is assailed on a public thoroughfare in Lyon or Paris. He is forced to inhabit an alienating and fragmented reality as soon as "the white man's eyes" calls forth this "other" being who is "battered down by tom-toms, cannibalism, intellectual deficiency, fetishism, racial defects. ..."[31] Black citizens are fixed as dyes in the personae of stereotypes whose persecutory force creates a sense of social death; or they are vaporized into a more general "climate of opinion" where

---

[30] WE, 40.
[31] Frantz Fanon, *Black Skin, White Masks* (New York: Grove Press), 116.

the racialized person is seen as a threat, an infection, a symptom of social decline: "overdetermined from without ... dissected under white eyes ... I am fixed ... and my long antennae pick up the catch phrases strewn over the surface of things. ..."[32] It is the peculiarity of regimes of racial oppression that they make immediately visible and vivid the more mediated and abstract practices of power such as class division, the exploitation of labor, and social hierarchies of status. "Looking at the immediacies of the colonial context," Fanon writes, "it becomes clear that what divides this world is first and foremost what species, what race one belongs to. In the colonies the economic infrastructure is also a superstructure. The cause is effect: you are rich because you are white, you are white because you are rich."[33]

It is the Manichaean mentality that goes with such racial-cultural discriminations, and the economic divisions set up to accommodate and authorize them, that create the violent psycho-affective conditions that Fanon describes in *The Wretched of the Earth*. The colonial vocabulary is shot through with arrogance, antagonism, and anxiety: *those* hysterical masses; *their* blank faces; *this* vegetative existence.[34] The colonized, who are often devoid of a public voice, resort to dreaming, imagining, acting out, embedding the reactive vocabulary of violence and retributive justice in their bodies, their psyches: "To blow the colonial world to smithereens is henceforth a clear image within the grasp and imagination of every colonized subject. To dislocate the colonial world. ... To destroy the colonist's sector. ... Challenging the colonial world is not a rational confrontation of viewpoints. It is not a discourse on the universal, but the impassioned claim by the colonized that their world is fundamentally different."[35]

---

[32] Ibid.
[33] WE, 5.
[34] WE, 7.
[35] WE, 6.

There is more to the psycho-affective realm than the subject of violence, which has become the cause célèbre of the first chapter of *The Wretched of the Earth,* "On Violence." Hannah Arendt's assault on the book in the late sixties was an attempt at staunching the wildfire it spread across university campuses, while she readily acknowledged that it was really Sartre's preface that glorified violence beyond Fanon's words or wishes. Sartre fanned the flames — "We have certainly sown the wind; they are the whirlwind. Sons of violence, at every instant they draw their humanity from it"[36] — while arguing that despite the doctrine of liberatory violence, Fanon, "the man, deep down hated it."[37] It is difficult to do justice to Fanon's views on violence, or to appreciate his passionate approach to the phenomenology of decolonization, without acknowledging a profound internal dissonance, in French colonial thought, between the free standing of the citizen and the segregated status of the subject — the double political destiny of the same colonized person. Indeed, I want to argue that the troubled traffic between the psychic body and the body politic — the subjective experience of objective reality[38] so typical of Fanon's style — suggests that the psycho-affective relation is also "the glowing focal point where citizen and individual develop and grow. ..."[39] When Fanon insists that the colonized's impassioned claim to difference is a challenge to the discourse of rational confrontation and universality, he is both using and opposing the very words and values — rationality, universalism — upon which the French *mission civilisatrice* founded its governmental practices of colonial assimilation, associationism, and integration.

---

[36] Jean-Paul Sartre, *Colonialism and Neocolonisalism,* trans. Haddour, Brewer, and McWilliams (London: Routledge, 2001), 149.

[37] Ibid., 158.

[38] Robert J. C. Young, *Postcolonialism: An Historical Introduction* (Oxford: Blackwells, 2001), 274. Young provides a most cogent and clarifying introductory account of Fanon's life and work.

[39] WE, 40.

The originality of the French phenomenological approach
to colonialism and decolonization lies in its awareness of the
abiding instability of the system, however stable its institutions
may appear. "If one chooses to understand the colonial system,"
Albert Memmi writes in *The Coloniser and the Colonized*, "he
must admit that it is unstable and its equilibrium constantly
threatened."[40] The civilizing mission is grounded in a profound sense of instability—not a surmountable or sublatable
"contradiction"—as the French Republic gazes anxiously upon
its own mirror image as a world power. On the one hand, France
is the supreme bearer of universal Rights and Reason—"bearer
even of a new category of time for the indigenous populations";[41]
on the other, its various administrative avatars—assimilation,
association, integration—deny those same populations the right
to emerge as "French citizens" in a public sphere of their own
ethical and cultural making. The principle of citizenship is held
out; the *poesis* of free cultural choice and communal participation is withheld.

The fear of instability and disequilibrium between freedom
and fealty, as I have described it, is evident in the history of colonial Algeria. Citizenship becomes the unstable, unsustainable
psycho-affective site in the conflict between political and legal
assimilation, and the respect for, and recognition of, Muslim
ethical and cultural affiliations. Between 1865 and 1936, fewer
than three thousand Algerian Muslims had availed themselves
of Napoleon's *senatus consulte*, which extended French citizenship to those Muslims who agreed to divest themselves of civil
status under Islamic law.[42] Again, the Algerian statute of 1947

---

[40] Albert Memmi, *The Coloniser and the Colonised* (Boston: Beacon Press,
1967) 120.

[41] James D. LeSueur, *Uncivil War: Intellectuals and Identity Politics During
the Decolonization of Algeria* (Philadelphia: University of Pennsylvania Press,
2001), 22.

[42] Ibid., 20. I am indebted to this excellent work for historical information
on the civilizing mission.

made a "grand" gesture, which was no more than a sleight of hand. The electoral system was divided into two colleges: one for Europeans and a small number of Muslims who were granted full political rights, the other for the majority of the Muslim population. Fearful of the increase in the Muslim vote, the statute allotted half the seats in the Algerian assembly to the first college, and in 1948 and subsequent years, the colonial administration rigged the ballots to prevent further Muslim participation.[43] Such widespread disenfranchisement bred a deep distrust in the Muslim population, leading a number of dissident groups to amalgamate in 1954 to form the Front de Libération Nationale (FLN). Hussein Bulhan describes the process: "Gradually those who for decades sought assimilation into French society and the traditional nationalists joined forces in the FLN."[44] When "inte-gration" was proposed by the last governor-general, Jacques Soustelle (after the Algerian War of Independence began in 1954), the "Algerian fact" of diverse regional cultures, languages, and ethnicities was recognized, so long as these "provincial"—provisional?—French citizens could be kept "secure" under the surveillant eye of the paternalistic colonial power that deeply distrusted what it saw as the regressive zealotry of Islam.[45] Such a threatened equilibrium leads to a phenomenological condition of nervous adjustment, narcissistic justification, and vain, even vainglorious, proclamations of progressive principles on the part of the colonial state; and it is these very psycho-affective symptoms that reveal the injustices and disequilibrium that haunts the colonial historical record. Fanon was quick to grasp the psycho-affective implications of a subtly punishing and disabling paternalistic power:

---

[43] Paul Clay Sorum, *Intellectuals and Decolonization in France* (Chapel Hill: University of North Carolina Press, 1977), 60.

[44] Hussein Abdilahi Bulhan, "Revolutionary Psychiatry of Fanon," in *Rethinking Fanon: The Continuing Dialogue*, ed. Nigel Gibson (Amherst, NY: Humanity Books, 1999), 155.

[45] LeSueur, 23–27.

At the level of the unconscious, therefore, colonialism was not seeking to be perceived as a sweet, kind-hearted mother who protects her child from a hostile environment, but rather a mother who constantly prevents her basically perverse child from committing suicide or giving free rein to its malevolent instincts. The colonial mother is protecting the child from itself, from its ego, its physiology, its biology, and its ontological misfortune.[46]

French colonial policy acknowledges the naked right of the colonized *as individual*—divested of cultural differences—to be identified as a citizen of the republic. But there exists, at the same time, a discriminatory denial or disavowal of the colonized citizen's right to be represented and recognized as a culturally clothed subject who may not conform to the norms and practices of French civil society. Without the rights of representation and participation, in the *public* sphere, can the subject ever be a citizen in the true sense of the term? If the colonized citizen is prevented from exercising his or her collective and communal agency as a full and equal member of civil society, what kind of shadow does that throw on the public virtue of the French republic? This does not merely make an ass of the law of assimilationist colonialism; it creates profound ethical and phenomenological problems of racial injustice at the heart of the psycho-affective realm of the colonial relation. As Sartre perceived the problem, "One of the functions of racism is to compensate the latent universalism of bourgeois liberalism: since all human beings have the same rights, the Algerian will be made a subhuman."[47] It is this anomalous and ambivalent situation of universality-with-racism, and formal citizenship-without-equality, that is an unresolvable embarrassment within the ideals and ideologies of the civilizing mission. I use the word *embarrassment* advisedly, to return to the question of colonial "instability" and my discussion of the psycho-affective sphere in *The Wretched of the Earth*.

---

[46] WE, 149.
[47] Sartre, 45.

"On Violence" describes the struggle between brute realities and resistant bodies in a prose that rises off the page to take you by the hand, "to touch my reader affectively, or in other words irrationally or sensually. For me words have a charge. I find myself incapable of escaping the bite of a word, the vertigo of a question-mark."[48] The colonialist declares the native to be "a corrosive element ... distorting everything which involves aesthetics or morals ... an unconscious and incurable instrument of blind forces."[49] Such an ontological obliteration of the "other" results in "the colonised's affectivity [being put] on edge like a running sore flinching from a caustic agent,"[50] as the psyche retreats into muscular spasms and hysterical symptoms. Treating the natives as some*thing* less than human — settler vigilante groups called their wanton killing of Muslim Algerians "rat-hunts"[51] — results in a process of depersonalization that creates a sense of bodily memory and a violent corporeal agency: "The shanty-town is the consecration of the colonised's *biological* decision to invade the enemy citadel at all costs, and if need be, by the most underground channels" (my emphasis).[52] These violent aspects of the realm of psycho-affective conflict and defense do not, however, tell the whole story to be found in *The Wretched of the Earth*.

Much of the book is devoted to exploring the processes by which decolonization turns into the project of nation building; and by delving into the "bubbling trepidation"[53] that exists in the moment of transition, *The Wretched of the Earth* opens up possibilities for positive and productive psycho-affective relations. "Reclaiming the past does not only rehabilitate or justify the promise of a national culture," Fanon writes, "it triggers a change of

---

[48] Macey, 159.
[49] WE, 6.
[50] WE, 19.
[51] Bulhan, in Gibson, 155.
[52] WE, 81.
[53] WE, 161.

fundamental importance in the colonised's psycho-affective equilibrium."[54] The psycho-affective equilibrium achieved through the creation of a national culture passes through a "national stage" on its way to constructing a world-system based on the ideals of global equity. "This cold war ... gets us nowhere," Fanon argues repeatedly. "The nuclear arms race must be stopped and the underdeveloped regions must receive generous investments and technical aid. The fate of the world depends on the response given to this question."[55] If the anticolonial movement aims at establishing national sovereignty and cultural independence, the visionary goal of decolonization is to dismantle the "either-or" of the cold war that dictates ideological options and economic choices to Third World nations as an integral part of the supra-national, xenophobic struggle for world supremacy. Cold war internationalism, with its dependent states and its division of the spoils, repeats the Manichaean structure of possession and dispossession experienced in the colonial world. The unraveling of the Soviet system saw the rapid emergence of ethnoregional patriotisms and nationalisms of a fissionary kind that destroyed the existence of the very possibility of civil society in the midst of civil war and ethnic cleansing.

Fanon was committed to creating a world-system of Third World nations that fostered a postcolonial consciousness based on a "dual emergence" of national sovereignty and international solidarity, for "it is at the heart of national consciousness that international consciousness establishes itself and thrives."[56] The hopeful symmetry of Fanon's dual emergence was based not on a "metaphysical principle" of cultural authenticity or geopolitical exceptionalism (the African "tradition," the Asian "temperament," the Latin American "spirit") but on the political and ethical principles of independence and security—a regional

---

[54] WE, 148.
[55] WE, 61.
[56] WE, 180.

solidarity extended to any nation that seems to be internally vulnerable to antidemocratic governance or externally threatened by hegemonic, quasi-colonial powers.[57] In many ways, Fanon's cherished ideals of regional integration and economic collaboration on broad socialist principles of urban and agrarian development were sullied by the corrupt and nepotistic practices of the colonial bourgeoisie that he despised for its hedonistic appropriation of the role of the settler, its small-time racketeering, its lack of the "pioneering aspect, the inventive, discoverer-of-new-worlds aspect" of a progressive national bourgeoisie. (According to a World Bank Working Report, almost 40 percent of South African private wealth is held outside the country.)[58] But Fanon's belief in the critical importance of economic and technological support for "underdeveloped regions"—"the fate of the world depends on the response given to this question"—is a troubling issue that returns each time a new famine occurs, or a developing country is shackled by unredeemable debt, and these problems have had no satisfactory solution across the half century from his day to ours.

With a few exceptions, the cartography of the global south follows the contours of the Third World. The unanswered call for "development as freedom,"[59] to use Amartya Sen's excellent phrase, has a long history of failure (for which national governments must share responsibility with the international community). However, Fanon's proleptic proposal that the postcolonial narrative of independent nation building could enter its international phase only after the end of the Cold War telescopes that long history of neglect into our times, whence it reveals the poignant proximity of the incomplete project of decolonization to

---

[57] WE, 179.

[58] Paul Collier, Anke Hoeffler, and Catherine Pattillo, "Flight Capital as a Portfolio Choice," *World Bank Policy Research Working Paper* no. 2066 (February 1999).

[59] See Amartya Sen, *Development as Freedom* (New York: Anchor Books), (see Oxford UP, 1999).

the dispossessed subjects of globalization. Caught up in this spiral of history, the wretched of the earth, in our time and Fanon's, enter the zone of psycho-affectivity and echo the horrifying call to violence. Fanon for our times.

And Fanon for other times and places ...

❊   ❊   ❊

In 1966, Bobby Seale and Huey Newton read *The Wretched of the Earth* in a house in Oakland, and—so the story goes[60]—when they were arrested some months later for "blocking the sidewalk," the text provided foundational perspectives on neocolonialism and nationalism that inspired the founding of the Black Nationalist Party. In *A Panther Is a Black Cat*, written in 1971, Reginald Major (Kelley) acknowledges Fanon's influence on the Panthers. With a sexist swagger that was part of the macho style of the times, Major praises Fanon's analysis of the colonial mentality in understanding the yardstick of "whiteness" that devalues black consciousness and results in a "cultural and psychic genocide"[61] that leads to the inadequacy of black manhood. Gillo Pontecorvo's *Battle of Algiers* became a cult film among the Bay Area Panthers because it was "Fanon-linked," and young revolutionaries attentively watched its depiction of terrorist acts and the organization of covert cells. "They found satisfaction in the flick. The natives won."[62]

❊   ❊   ❊

In the early seventies, Steve Biko's room in the student residence at the University of Natal became the meeting place for members of the South African Students Association; it was also the intellectual center of the black consciousness movement. That dorm room in Durban was the place where Biko, "the person

---

[60] Sandra Adell, ed., *African American Culture* (Detroit, MI: Gale Research, 1996), 50–51.

[61] Reginold Major, *A Panther Is a Black Cat* (New York: William Morrow, 1971), 138–39.

[62] Ibid.

who brought ideas,"[63] first circulated *The Wretched of the Earth* to his friends and comrades—writers, activists, community workers, actors, students—who were also conversant with the poetry and the politics of the Black Panther movement. Fanon's singular contribution to the theoretical understanding of the black consciousness movement lay in his extension of the economistic theories of Marxism toward a greater emphasis on the importance of psychological and cultural liberation—the psycho-affective realm of revolutionary activism and emancipation.

*   *   *

In a prison cell in the notorious H-Block of Belfast prison, sometime after 1973, a young apprentice coach builder and member of the Irish Republican Army, Bobby Sands, first read Fanon's *The Wretched of the Earth*, of which there were multiple copies on the H-Block shelves. A historian of the IRA[64] suggests that Fanon's incendiary spirit may have set alight IRA passions because of passages like this:

"The last shall be first and the first last." Decolonisation is the putting into practice of this sentence. ... For if the last shall be first, this will only come to pass after a murderous and decisive struggle between the two protagonists. That affirmed intention to place the last at the head of things ... can only triumph if we use all means to turn the scale, including, of course, that of violence.

*   *   *

The Shiite revival of the 1960s and 1970s, which developed into the Iranian revolution led by Ayatollah Khomeini, was based on a revision of Shiite doctrine influenced by Marxism

---

[63] N. Barney Pityana, M. Ramphele, M. Mpumiwana, and L. Wilson, eds., *Bounds of Possibility: The Legacy of Steve Biko and Black Consciousness* (Cape Town, South Africa: David Phillip, 1991), 28–29, 109, 147.

[64] Richard English, *Armed Struggle: The History of the IRA* (New York: Oxford University Press, 2003), 197–99, 234–35.

and committed to the ideology of Third World liberation.[65] No scholar or intellectual was more respected among the student militants who followed the People's Mujahideen than Ali Shariati, who had read Fanon during his student days in Paris and translated *The Wretched of the Earth* into Persian. According to Giles Keppel, a historian of political Islam, "Shariati rendered the difference between 'oppressors' and 'oppressed' with the Koranic terms *mostakbirnie* (the arrogant) and *mostadafine* (the weakened or disinherited), thus transposing the theory of class struggle into the terminology of Islam."[66] This "translated," hybrid term crept into Khomeini's political rhetoric—via Shariati's translation of Fanon—after 1978, in his attempt to broaden the appeal of his message and address a more diverse audience.

* * *

Finally, on September 19, 2001, Richard Perle, former U.S. assistant secretary of defense (1981–87), wrote the following three passages:

> There is an air of Vichyite defeatism about some of the commentary on the current war on terrorism.

> We constantly hear the reiteration of such themes as "We don't know who the enemy is," "We don't know where to strike them" ... and that the "Wretched of the Earth" (to use the title of Frantz Fanon's famous anti-colonial tract) are so desperate that they would not fear honorable death at the hands of what they see as the Great Satan.

> The U.S. Defense Secretary, Donald Rumsfeld ... [is] quite right to say that it is a totally new kind of war which the Free World now faces.[67]

---

[65] Gilles Keppel, *Jihad: The Trail of Political Islam*, trans. Anthony F. Roberts (Cambridge, MA: Harvard University Press, 2002). My account derives from this book.

[66] Ibid.

[67] Richard Perle, "Get Governments out of Terrorism Business," *National Post*, September 19, 2001, A16.

*   *   *

Fanon acknowledges the enormous significance of this phenomenological level of life when he opens his essay "On National
Culture" with one of his most enigmatic and inspiring pronounce-
ments: "Each generation must discover its mission, fulfill it or
betray it, in relative opacity."[68] I turn to that issue by first return-
ing to my beginning: What forms of unhappy consciousness
prevail among the colonized who feel threatened from all sides?
How does the body speak in extremis, how does the mind with-
stand? "Colonialism forces the colonized to constantly ask the
question: '*Who am I in reality?*'"[69] Fanon writes in *The Wretched
of the Earth*. From where does the spirit of revolt arise in the midst
of the confusion of "myriad signs of the colonial world"?[70] How
do the oppressed discover the enduring strength to found a free
and just society, a national consciousness, if they are continuously
aware of their own anxiety and fragility?

The Wretched of the Earth emerges, year after year, in Oakland, Natal, Belfast, Tehran, Washington, Paris, to say nothing
of Bombay, where I first read it, or wherever you may be today as
this book falls into your hands. Fanon is invoked repeatedly by
liberal students, radical activists, human rights workers, cultural
historians, literary scholars, journalists, even a former U.S. assistant defense secretary. It could be said that Fanon's street fighting
days came to an end in the 1970s and 1980s, and that he now
takes his place on the bookshelves alongside CLR James, Sartre,
Memmi, Marcuse, Guevara, Angela Davis. . . . Those who claim
to follow in Fanon's footsteps, it is often said, only absorb his abstract arguments and stirring sentiments; they fail to understand
his selfless engagement with the Algerian War of Independence
and turn a blind eye to his failure to consider the possibility that
a state built on the revolutionary violence of the FLN could slide

---

[68] WE, 145.
[69] WE, 182.
[70] WE, 16.

more easily into state terror and religious fanaticism. Marxists have traditionally distanced themselves from Fanon's emphasis on psycho-affective factors in political reasoning while criticizing his refusal to prioritize the role of the organized proletariat in the anticolonial revolution.

The insurgent energies of the Algerian peasantry and lumpen-proletariat, Fanon believed, would guard against the corruption and cooptation of "westernized" nationalist parties led by urban elites. But in the opinion of some of his FLN comrades, Fanon displayed a naïve *nostalgie de la boue* in championing a peasantry that had become fragmented and displaced through the 1950s, some of them confined to refugee or resettlement camps in Tunisia and Morocco, others having migrated to cities in Algeria or France.[71] It was in the late 1950s that Fanon's commitment to the Algerian cause seemed to turn from a political commitment into a more inward identification, a consummate self-fashioning of himself as an Algerian. This radical indigeniza-tion of identity, like his overestimation of the peasantry, could be seen as his avoidance or enhancement of his own natal and psychic reality—a compensatory family romance that would dis-avow his Martinican origins,[72] through a phantasmatic denial of the "unheroic assimilation" of the Antillean heritage in favor of the "virile and decolonised fraternity" of the FLN.[73] Simone de Beauvoir's memories of her conversations with Fanon flesh out this poignant and problematic predicament. "Above all I don't want to become a professional revolutionary,"[74] Fanon anxiously observed of himself, as he lamented his exilic existence as an Antillean fighting for Algerian independence.

---

[71] Mohamed Harbi, quoted in Macey, 481.

[72] See Albert Memmi's remarkable essay, "The Impossible Life of Frantz Fanon," in *Massachusetts Review* (Winter 1973), 9–39, and *Dominated Man: Notes Toward a Portrait* (New York: Orion Press. 1968).

[73] François Vergès, *Monsters and Revolutionaries: Colonial Family Romances and Métissage* (Durham: Duke University Press), 211.

[74] de Beauvoir, 317.

Fanon's involvement in the Algerian revolution was primarily as witness, doctor, diplomat, writer—or as he was once known in Tunisia, "the pamphleteer from Martinique." (This moniker refers to his frequent contributions to *El Mujahid*, the Algerian nationalist newspaper, after he took up residence in Tunis, having been expelled from Algeria by the French administration in 1957.) During his tenure at the psychiatric hospital at Blida (1953–56), there were occasions on which he covertly trained the *fidayine* (village militias) to cope with their own attacks of terror and anxiety while they were carrying out assassination attempts; he also taught them psychological ways and physiological means of withstanding torture and resisting interrogation.[75] In 1960, Fanon was involved in exploring the possibility of establishing a Saharan front in southern Algeria, to be accessed from Mali, which could provide a line of supply and support for FLN forces.[76]

The years leading up to the composition of *The Wretched of the Earth* in 1961 were fraught with the violence and uncertainty of the Algerian War of Independence, which the French state pursued as if it were no more than the "pacification" of a civil uprising. French left-wing intellectuals came together under the banner of the "Manifesto of the 121" to support the Algerian nationalists, and compared the French military presence in Algeria to the "Hitlerite order": "Does it have to be recalled that fifteen years after the destruction of the Hitlerite order, French militarism has, because of the demands of a war of this kind, succeeded in reintroducing torture and has once more institutionalised it in Europe?"[77]

Simone de Beauvoir, one of the staunchest supporters of the Manifesto, expressed a shared sense of disgust and despair: "Ten thousand Algerians had been herded into the Vel' d'Hiv' like the Jews at Drancy once before. Again I loathed it all—this country,

---

[75] de Beauvoir, 315.

[76] Macey, 437–44. Once again, Macey provides the definitive account of the Mali expedition.

[77] *Manifesto*, quoted in Macey, 449.

myself, the whole world."[78] During a particularly brutal offensive in July 1959 named Operation Binoculars, General René Challe's troops sought to root out the insurgents of the Armée de Libération Nationale (ALN) hiding in the high Kabylia mountains by annihilating local villages that offered support to the nationalists. The policy of *regroupement*, or resettlement, moved the rural population to barbed-wire compounds resembling concentration camps —fifteen thousand people sequestered in a space meant for three thousand and surrounded by bleak torched fields "without water, without sewage or sanitation of any kind, without land to cultivate and for the most part without work. ...."[79] A couple of years earlier, in 1957, the southern edge of the Kabylia had been the site of the appalling massacre of Melouza. The rivalry between the FLN and the MNA (Mouvement Nationaliste Algérienne), which had centered on territorial control and tribal affiliation, exploded into a bloodbath when the FLN leadership ordered its operatives to "exterminate this vermin"[80]—a chilling, uncanny echo, half a century later, of Kurtz's command, "Exterminate the brutes," in Joseph Conrad's classic tale of colonial turpitude in the Belgian Congo, *Heart of Darkness*. The FLN herded all males above the age of fifteen, Alistair Horne writes, "into houses and into the mosque and slaughtered them with rifles, pick-axes and knives: a total of 301."[81]

Fanon forged his thinking on violence and counterviolence in these conditions of dire extremity, when everyday interactions were turned into exigent events of life and death—incendiary relations between colonizer and colonized, internecine feuds between revolutionary brotherhoods,[82] terrorist attacks in Paris

---

[78] de Beauvoir, 321.

[79] Jules Roy in Alistair Horne, *A Savage War of Peace: Algeria 1954–1962* (New York: Penguin Books, 1987), 338.

[80] My account is based on Alistair Horne, *A Savage War of Peace*, 221–22. For the discursive representation of the event, and the implications of its various ideological interpretations and manifestations, see LeSueur, "Massacre at Melouza: The 'Whodunit' of the French-Algerian War?" 166ff.

[81] Horne, 222.

[82] WE, 18.

and Algiers by the ultra right-wing OAS (Organisation Armée Secrète) and their *pieds noirs* supporters (European settlers in Algeria). As a locus classicus of political resistance and the rhetoric of retributive violence, *The Wretched of the Earth* captures the tone of those apocalyptic times:

> The colonized subject discovers reality and transforms it through his praxis, his deployment of violence and his agenda for liberation.[83]

> But how do we get from violence to setting violence in motion? What blows the lid?[84]

> When the Algerians reject any method which does not include violence … they know that such madness alone can deliver them from colonial oppression. A new type of relationship is established in the world. The peoples of the Third World are in the process of shattering their chains, and what is extraordinary is that they succeed.[85]

Hannah Arendt's objection to *The Wretched of the Earth* has less to do with the occurrence of violence than with Fanon's teleological belief that the whole process would end in a new humanism, a new planetary relation to freedom defined by the Third World. Collective violence engenders close political kinships like suicide squads and revolutionary brotherhoods, she wrote, but "No body politic I know was ever founded on equality before death and its actualisation in violence."[86] Arendt is, at best, only half right in her reading of Fanon. He is cautious about the celebration of spontaneous violence—"where my blood calls for the blood of the other"—because "hatred is not an agenda" capable of maintaining the unity of party organization once violent revolt breaks down into the difficult day-to-day strategy of

---

[83] WE, 21.
[84] WE, 31.
[85] WE, 34.
[86] Hannah Arendt, *On Violence* (New York: Harcourt, Brace and World, 1970), 69.

fighting a war of independence.[87] On the other hand, Sartre's preface to *The Wretched of the Earth* (the nub of Arendt's attack on Fanon's ideas) is committed to bringing the colonial dialectic to its conclusion by carrying home— to metropolitan France—the lessons and the lesions of anticolonial violence.[88] Those who adhere to principles of nonviolence in the face of colonial oppression are taunted with the ethical *impossibility* of their positions—"even your non-violent thoughts are a condition born of an age-old oppression. ..."[89] Sartre pares away the pieties and vanities of Enlightenment universalism to reveal its tolerance of racist ideas and practices. He confronts his compatriots with a spectacular "striptease of our humanism"[90] while justifying the uses of violence to recover an ontological claim to humanity for those who have been treated as subhuman: "Sons of violence, at every instant they draw their humanity from it: we were human beings at their expense, they are making themselves human beings at ours."[91]

For Arendt, Fanon's violence leads to the death of politics; for Sartre, it draws the fiery, first breath of human freedom. I propose a different reading. Fanonian violence, in my view, is part of a struggle for psycho-affective survival and a search for human agency in the midst of the agony of oppression. It does not offer a clear choice between life and death or slavery and freedom, because it confronts the colonial condition of life-in-death. Fanon's phenomenology of violence conceives of the colonized—body, soul, culture, community, history—in a process of "continued agony [rather] than a total disappearance."[92] He describes this

---

[87] WE, 89.

[88] I have slightly altered Sartre's phrase "to bring the dialectic to its conclusion." See Sartre, *Colonialism and Neocolonialism*, 150.

[89] Sartre, 151.

[90] Ibid., 150.

[91] Ibid., 149–50.

[92] I have adapted this phrase from Frantz Fanon, "Racism and Culture" in *Towards an African Revolution*, 35.

state of political consciousness and psychic being with a harrowing accuracy:

> Exploitation, tortures, raids, racism, collective liquidations ... [all] make of the native an object in the hands of the occupying nation. This object man, without means of existing, without a raison d'être, is broken in the very depth of his substance. The desire to live, to continue, becomes more and more indecisive, more and more phantom-like. It is at this stage that the well-known guilt complex appears.[93]

Does the "guilt complex" lie at the very origins of violence, or does the struggle for liberation have to violently free itself of guilt in order to be effective? The double-edged nature of this question—guilt as a stimulant, or an obstacle to freedom, or possibly both—fulfills Fanon's wish (expressed to Sartre and Beauvoir) that "all political leaders should be psychiatrists as well."[94] Fanon's style of thinking and writing operates by creating repeated disjunctions—followed by proximate juxtapositions—between the will of the political agent and the desire of the psycho-affective subject. His discourse does not privilege the subjective over the objective, or vice versa, nor does his argument prescribe a hierarchy of relations between material reality and mental or corporeal experience. The double figure of the politician-psychiatrist, someone like Frantz Fanon himself, attempts to decipher the changing *scale* (measure, judgment) of a problem, event, identity, or action as it comes to be represented or framed in the shifting ratios and relations that exist between the realms of political and psycho-affective experience.

The connections between guilt and violence are part of such a delicate balance:

> The colonized subject is always on his guard: *confused by the myriad signs of the colonial world he never knows whether he is out of line.*

---

[93] Ibid.
[94] de Beauvoir, 318.

Confronted with a world configured, the colonized subject is always presumed guilty. *The colonized does not accept his guilt, but rather considers it a kind of curse*, a sword of Damocles. But deep down the colonized subject knows no authority. *He is dominated but not domesticated.* He is made to feel inferior, but by no means convinced of his inferiority. He patiently waits for the colonist to let down his guard and then jumps on him. The muscles of the colonized are always tensed. ... The symbols of society such as the police force, bugle calls in the barracks, military parades, and the flag flying aloft, serve not only as inhibitors but also stimulants. They do not signify: "Stay where you are." But rather "Get ready to do the right thing." ... This impulse to take the colonist's place maintains a constant muscular tonus. It is a known fact that under certain emotional circumstances an obstacle usually escalates action (my emphasis).[95]

It seems, at first, that this is a straightforward spectacle of Fanonian retributive violence. The origins of violence lie in a presumptive "false guilt," which the colonized has to assume because of his powerless position; but it is a guilt that he does not accept or interiorize — "He is made to feel inferior, but by no means convinced of his inferiority." The eruption of violence is a manifestation of this anxious act of masking, from which the colonized emerges as a guerrilla in camouflage waiting for the colonist to let down his guard so that he might jump; each obstacle encountered is a stimulant to action and a shield to hide the insurgent's intention to take the colonist's place. Because he is dominated by military power and yet not fully domesticated by the hegemonic persuasions of assimilation and the civilizing mission, the anticolonial nationalist is able to decipher the double and opposed meanings emitted by the sounding symbols of society, the bugle calls or police sirens: "They do not signify: 'Stay where you are.' But rather 'Get ready to do the right thing.'" From the torqued mind and muscle of the colonized subject "on guard" emerges

---

[95] WE, 16.

the nationalist agent as mujahid (FLN soldier) or *fidayine* (FLN guerrilla).

There is, however, another scenario that runs through this narrative of violence and is somewhat unsettling to its progress, although not unraveled by it. Here the psycho-affective imagination of violence is a desperate act of survival on the part of the "object man," a struggle to keep alive. The "false" or masked guilt complex (as I have called it) emerges, Fanon tells us in the preceding quotation, when the very desire to live becomes faint and attenuated, "more and more indecisive, more and more phantom-like."[96] At this point, the splitting, or disjunction, between being dominated and being domesticated—the irresolvable tension between the colonized as both subject and citizen from which anticolonial violence emerges—is experienced as a psychic and affective *curse* rather than, primarily, as a political "cause" (in both senses of the term). The native may not accept the authority of the colonizer, but his complex and contradictory fate—where rejected guilt begins to *feel* like shame—hangs over him like a Damoclean sword; it threatens him with an imminent disaster that may collapse both the internal life and the external world. At this moment, the political agent may be shadowed—rather than stimulated—by the psycho-affective subject who also inhabits his bodily space. The colonizer's constant muscular tension may turn into a hysterical rigid limb, just as Fanon observes that "the colonist is an exhibitionist."[97] The mujahid may hear the double call of siren and bugle and yet be caught "in the tightly-knit web of colonialism,"[98] psychically split and politically paralyzed between the command to "Stay where you are" and the desire to "Get ready to do the right thing." There

---

[96] In a larger version of this essay to be published in *A Global Measure* (Harvard University Press), I develop the concept of "false-guilt" in the direction of an understanding of shame.

[97] WE, 17.

[98] Ibid.

is every possibility, as Fanon writes, "that the colonist keeps the colonized in a state of rage, which he prevents from boiling over ... [and this] periodically erupts into bloody fighting between tribes, clans, and individuals."[99] The aspiration to do the right thing might be felled by the fragility of the individual, by ata-vistic animosities, by the iron hand of history, or by indecision and uncertainty, but these failures do not devalue the ethical and imaginative act of reaching out toward rights and freedoms.

Fanon, the phantom of terror, might be only the most intimate, if intimidating, poet of the vicissitudes of violence. But poetic jus-tice can be questionable even when it is exercised on behalf of the wretched of the earth. And if, as I have argued, the lesson of Fanon lies in his fine adjustment of the balance between the politician and the psychiatrist, his skill in altering the "scale" between the social dimension and the psycho-affective relation, then we have to admit that he is in danger of losing his balance when, for instance, he writes: "Violence can thus be understood to be the perfect media-tion. The colonized man liberates himself in and through violence. The praxis enlightens the militant because it shows him the means and the end."[100] Knowing what we now know about the double destiny of violence, must we not ask: Is violence ever a *perfect* mediation? Is it not simply rhetorical bravura to assert that *any* form of secular, material mediation can provide a transparency of political action (or ethical judgment) that reveals "the means *and* the end"? Is the clear mirror of violence not something of a mirage in which the dispossessed see their reflections but from which they cannot slake their thirst?

Fanon has a rich variety of readers who do not come to his work to seek the "perfect mediation" of violence. They turn to *The Wretched of the Earth*, generation after generation, for a more obscure reason, armed only with an imperfect sense of obligation toward the ideals they want to serve and the values they seek to

---

[99] Ibid.
[100] WE, 44.

preserve. The message they take away from Fanon's book is a quieter, more contemplative one: "*Each generation must discover its mission, fulfill it or betray it, in relative opacity.*"[101]

According to his friends, Fanon was somewhat opaque in person. There was a dark and hesitant air about him that infused his speech and writing with "an enigmatic quality, as though they contained obscure, disturbing prophecies."[102] His publisher, Francis Jeanson, called it the "bodily aspect of his intellectual approach."[103] Jean Daniel, the editor of *Le Nouvel Observateur*, remembers that the handshake of the dying Fanon became "more urgent and always seemed to have a message."[104] The deeper messages of poet-politicians are never as easy to decipher as the myths offered up in their names. It is for this reason that I have tried, in this essay, to trace the prophecies of Fanon's living hand as it rises again to beckon enigmatically toward our own times, in this new translation of *The Wretched of the Earth*.

Each age has its peculiar opacities and its urgent missions. The parts we play in the design and direction of historical transformations are shadowed by the contingency of events and the quality of our characters. Sometimes we break the mold; at others, our will is broken. What enables us to aspire to the fraught and fervent desire for freedom is the belief that human beings are capable of imagining what Fanon once described as a "time [that] must no longer be that of the moment or the next harvest but rather of the rest of the world."[105]

I would like to thank Mark Jerng and David Mulrooney for invaluable assistance with this essay, and Lia Brozgal for her excellent translations.

---

[101] WE, 132.
[102] de Beauvoir, 317.
[103] Francis Jeanson, quoted in Macey, 159.
[104] Macey, 433.
[105] WE, 122.

Preface
by Jean-Paul Sartre

Not so long ago the Earth numbered 2 billion inhabitants, i.e., 500 million men and 1.5 billion "natives." The first possessed the Word, the others borrowed it. In between, an array of corrupt petty kings, feudal lords, and a fake, fabricated bourgeoisie served as go-betweens. In the colonies, truth displayed its nakedness; the metropolises preferred it clothed; they had to get the "natives" to love them. Like mothers, of sorts. The European elite decided to fabricate a native elite; they selected adolescents, branded the principles of Western culture on their foreheads with a red-hot iron, and gagged their mouths with sounds, pompous awkward words that twisted their tongues. After a short stay in the metropolis they were sent home, fully doctored. These walking lies had nothing more to say to their brothers; from Paris, London, and Amsterdam we yelled, "Parthenon! Fraternity!" and somewhere in Africa and Asia mouths echoed "... thenon!... nity!" It was a golden age.

Then it was over: the mouths opened of their own accord; the black and yellow voices still talked of our humanism, but it was to blame us for our inhumanity. We quite happily listened to these polite displays of bitterness. At first we were amazed and proud: "What? They can chat away all on their own? Look what we did with them!" There was no doubt in our minds they accepted our ideal since they were accusing us of not respecting it. Europe then really believed in its mission: it had Hellenized the Asians and created this new species, the Greco-Roman blacks. Pragmatic as ever, we added, quite among ourselves, "Oh let them shout, it will get it out of their system; their bark is worse than their bite."

Then came another generation, which shifted the question. Its writers and poets took enormous pains to explain to us that our values poorly matched the reality of their lives and that they could neither quite reject them nor integrate them. Roughly, this meant: You are making monsters out of us; your humanism wants us to be universal and your racist practices are differentiating us. We listened to them, very nonchalantly. Colonial administrators are not paid to read Hegel, so he's seldom on their reading list, but they don't need this philosopher to tell them that unhappy consciences get tangled up in their contradictions. Ultimate end result: nil. So let us perpetuate their misfortune; nothing will come out of it but hot air. If, the experts told us, there were the slightest hint of a demand in their lamentations, it would be for integration. Consenting to it, of course, would be out of the question: we would ruin the system, which, as you know, relies on gross exploitation. All we need do is dangle a carrot in front of their eyes and they will come running. As for anything like a revolt, we had absolutely nothing to worry about: what lucid "native" would set about massacring the dashing sons of Europe with the sole intention of becoming Europeans like them? In short, we encouraged their melancholic moods, and we thought it would not be bad, for once, to award the Goncourt Prize to a black. That was before 1939.

1961. Listen: "Let us not lose time in useless laments and sickening mimicry. Let us leave this Europe which never stops talking of man yet massacres him at every one of its street corners, at every corner of the world. For centuries it has stifled virtually the whole of humanity in the name of a so-called 'spiritual adventure.'" The tone is new. Who dares voice it? An African, a man from the Third World, a former colonized subject. "Europe," he adds, "has gained such a mad and reckless momentum ... that it is heading toward the brink from which we would be advised to remove ourselves." In other words, Europe is done for. A truth that is hard to swallow, but of which all of us are—are we not, fellow Europeans?—convinced deep down.

We must make one reservation, however. When one Frenchman, for example, says to another: "We're done for!"—which, to my knowledge, has happened practically every day since 1930— it's a passionate discourse, burning with rage and love, where the speaker puts himself in the same boat as his fellow countrymen. And then as a rule he adds: "Unless ..." Everyone gets the message: one cannot afford to make a single mistake. If his recommendations are not followed to the letter, then and only then will the country be done for. In short, it's a threat, followed by a piece of advice, and such remarks shock even less because they spring from a national intersubjectivity. When Fanon, on the contrary, says that Europe is heading for ruin, far from uttering a cry of alarm, he is offering a diagnostic. Dr. Fanon claims he neither considers it to be a hopeless case—miracles have been known to exist—nor is he offering to cure it. He is stating the fact that it is in its death throes. As an outsider, he bases his diagnostic on the symptoms he has observed. As for treating it, no: he has other things to worry about. Whether it survives or perishes, that's not his problem. For this reason his book is scandalous. And if you mumble, sniggering awkwardly: "He's really got it in for us!" you have missed the true nature of the scandal, for Fanon has got nothing "in for you" at all; his book, which is such a hot issue for others, leaves you out in the cold. It often talks *about* you, but never *to* you. Gone are the black Goncourts and the yellow Nobels: the days of the colonized prizewinners are over. A "French-speaking" ex-native bends the language to new requirements, fashions it for his own use, and speaks to the colonized alone: "Natives of all the underdeveloped countries unite!" What a downfall. For the fathers, we were the only interlocutors; for the sons, we no longer count: we are the object of their discourse. Of course, Fanon mentions in passing our infamous crimes at Sétif, Hanoi, and Madagascar, but he does not waste time condemning them: he makes use of them. He demolishes the tactics of colonialism, the complex play of relations uniting and opposing the colonists and the "metropolitans." *For the sake of his brothers*, his aim is to teach them how to outwit us.

In short, the Third World discovers *itself* and speaks to *itself* through this voice. We know it is not a uniform world, and it still contains subjected peoples, some of whom have acquired a false independence, others who are fighting to conquer their sovereignty, and yet others who have won their freedom, but who live under the constant threat of imperialist aggression. These differences are born out of colonial history, in other words, oppression. In some places the metropolis makes do with paying a clique of feudal overlords; in others, it has fabricated a fake bourgeoisie of colonized subjects in a system of divide and rule; elsewhere, it has killed two birds with one stone: the colony is both settlement and exploitation. Europe, therefore, has hardened the divisions and conflicts, forged classes, and in some cases, racism, and endeavored by every means to generate and deepen the stratification of colonized societies. Fanon hides nothing. In order to wage the struggle against us, the former colony must wage a struggle against itself. Or rather it is one and the same thing. In the heat of combat, all domestic barriers must be torn down, the powerless bourgeoisie of racketeers and *compradores*, the still privileged urban proletariat and the lumpenproletariat of the shanty towns, must all align with the positions of the rural masses, the true reservoir for the national and revolutionary army. In countries where colonialism has deliberately halted development, the peasantry, when it decides to revolt, very quickly emerges as the *radical* class. It is all too familiar with naked oppression, suffers far worse than the urban workers, and to prevent it from dying of hunger, nothing less will do than the demolition of every existing structure. If it triumphs, the national revolution will be socialist; if it is stopped in its momentum, if the colonized bourgeoisie takes over power, the new state, despite its official sovereignty, will remain in the hands of the imperialists. The case of Katanga illustrates this fairly well. The unity of the Third World, therefore, is not complete: it is a work in progress that begins with all the colonized in every pre- or post-independent country, united under the leadership of the peasant class. This is what Fanon explains to his brothers in Africa, Asia, and Latin America: we shall achieve revolutionary socialism everywhere and all together or we shall be beaten one by one by our former tyrants. He hides nothing: neither the weaknesses nor the disagreements nor the mystification. In some places the government gets off to a bad start; in others, after a stunning success, it loses momentum; elsewhere, it has come to a halt. In order to revive it the peasants must drive their bourgeoisie into the ocean. The reader is sharply warned of the most dangerous types of alienation: the leader, the personality cult, Western culture, and equally so, the revival of African culture from a distant past. The true culture is the revolution, meaning it is forged while the iron is hot. Fanon speaks out loud and clear. We Europeans, we can hear him. The proof is you are holding this book. Isn't he afraid that the colonial powers will take advantage of his sincerity?

No. He is not afraid of anything. Our methods are outdated: they can sometimes delay emancipation, but they can't stop it. And don't believe we can readjust our methods: neocolonialism, that lazy dream of the metropolises, is a lot of hot air; the "Third Force" does not exist or if it does it is the phony bourgeoisie to which colonialism has already handed over power. Our Machiavellianism has little hold on this world, which is wide awake and hot on the trail of every one of our lies. The colonist has but one recourse: force or whatever is left of it. The "native" has but one choice: servitude or sovereignty. What does Fanon care if you read or don't read his book? It is for his brothers he denounces our old box of mischief, positive we don't have anything else up our sleeve. It is to them he says: Europe has got its claws on our continents, they must be severed until she releases them. The moment is right for us. Nothing can happen in Bizerta, Elizabethville, or the Algerian *bled* without the whole world knowing about it. The rival blocs take up opposite sides, they keep each other at bay, let us take advantage of this paralysis, let us enter history, and as we burst in let us make it universal for the first time. Let us fight. Failing other weapons, the patience of the knife will suffice.

Europeans, open this book, look inside. After taking a short walk in the night you will see strangers gathered around a fire, get closer and listen. They are discussing the fate reserved for your trading posts and for the mercenaries defending them. They might see you, but they will go on talking among themselves without even lowering their voices. Their indifference strikes home: their fathers, creatures living in the shadows, *your* creatures, were dead souls; you afforded them light, you were their sole interlocutor, you did not take the trouble to answer the zombies. The sons ignore you. The fire that warms and enlightens them is not yours. You, standing at a respectful distance, you now feel eclipsed, nocturnal, and numbed. It's your turn now. In the darkness that will dawn into another day, you have turned into the zombie.

In that case, you say, let's throw this book out of the window. Why bother to read it since it is not meant for us? For two reasons: first, because Fanon analyzes you for his brothers and demolishes for them the mechanism of our alienations. Take advantage of it to discover your true self as an object. Our victims know us by their wounds and shackles: that is what makes their testimony irrefutable. They only need to know what we have done to them for us to realize what we have done to ourselves. Is this necessary? Yes, because Europe is doomed. But, you will say once again, we live in the metropolis, and we disapprove of extremes. It's true, you are not colonists, but you are not much better. They were your pioneers, you sent them overseas, they made you rich. You warned them: if they shed too much blood you would pretend to disown them; the same way a State—no matter which one—maintains a mob of agitators, provocateurs, and spies abroad whom it disowns once they are caught. You who are so liberal, so humane, who take the love of culture to the point of affectation, you pretend to forget that you have colonies where massacres are committed in your name. Fanon reveals to his comrades—especially to those who remain a little too Westernized—the solidarity of the metropolitans with their colonial agents. Have the courage to read it, primarily because it will make you feel ashamed, and shame, as Marx said, is a revolutionary feeling. You see I, too, cannot lose my subjective illusion. I, too, say to you: "All is lost unless. . . ." I, a European, am stealing my enemy's book and turning it into a way of healing Europe. Make the most of it.

And this is the second reason: aside from Sorel's fascist chatter, you will find that Fanon is the first since Engels to focus again on the midwife of history. And don't be led into believing that hotheadedness or an unhappy childhood gave him some odd liking for violence. He has made himself spokesman for the situation, nothing more. But that is all he needs to do in order to constitute, step by step, the dialectic that liberal hypocrisy hides from you and that has produced us just as much as it has produced him.

In the last century, the bourgeoisie considered the workers an envious lot, unhinged by their uncouth appetites, but it was careful to include these great brutes in the human race. Unless they were men and free, how could they possibly sell their manpower? In France and England humanism claims to be universal.

Forced labor is quite the opposite: there is no contract; in addition it requires intimidation; the oppression, therefore, is visible. By rejecting metropolitan universalism, our soldiers overseas apply the *numerus clausus* to the human species: since none can rob, enslave, or kill his fellow man without committing a crime, they lay down the principle that the colonized subject is not a fellow man. Our military forces have received orders to change this abstract certainty into reality: orders are given to reduce the inhabitants of the occupied territory to the level of a superior ape in order to justify the colonist's treatment of them as beasts of burden. Colonial violence not only aims at keeping these enslaved men at a respectful distance, it also seeks to dehumanize them. No effort is spared to demolish their traditions, to substitute our language for theirs, and to destroy their culture without giving them ours. We exhaust them into a mindless state. Ill fed and sick, if they resist, fear will finish the job: guns are pointed at the peasants; civilians come and settle on their land and force them to work for them under the whip. If they resist, the soldiers fire, and they are dead men; if they give in and degrade themselves, they are no longer men. Shame and fear warp their character and dislocate their personality. Such a business is conducted briskly by experts: psychological warfare was not born yesterday. Nor was brainwashing. And yet despite all their efforts, nowhere have they achieved their aim; no more in the Congo where they cut off the hands of the blacks than in Angola where quite recently they pierced the lips of the malcontents in order to padlock them. And I am not saying it is impossible to change a man into an animal. I am saying they can't do it without weakening him considerably: beating is never enough, pressure has to be brought by undernourishing him. That's the problem with servitude: when you domesticate a member of our species, you lower his productivity, and however little you give him, a barnyard being ends up costing more than he's worth. For this reason the colonists are forced to stop breaking him in halfway. The result: neither man nor beast, but the "native." Beaten, underfed, sick, and frightened, but only up to a certain point, yellow, black, or white he always has the same character traits — lazy, sly, and thieving, who lives on nothing and understands only the language of violence.

Poor colonist: his contradiction has been unmasked. He ought to kill those he plunders, like they say the *djinns* do. But that is now out of the question. Doesn't he have to exploit them as well? Failing to carry the massacre to the point of genocide, and servitude to a state of mindlessness, he cracks up, the situation is reversed, and an implacable logic leads to decolonization.

Not right away. First of all the European reigns: he has already lost but doesn't realize it; he does not yet know that the "natives" are false "natives." He has to make them suffer, he claims, in order to destroy or repress the evil they have inside them; after three generations, their treacherous instincts will be stamped out. What instincts? Those that drive the slaves to massacre their masters? How come he cannot recognize his own cruelty now turned against him? How come he can't see his own savagery as a colonist in the savagery of these oppressed peasants who have absorbed it through every pore and for which they can find no cure? The answer is simple: this arrogant individual, whose power of authority and fear of losing it has gone to his head, has difficulty remembering he was once a man; he thinks he is a whip or a gun; he is convinced that the domestication of the "inferior races" is obtained by governing their reflexes. He disregards the human memory, the indelible reminders; and then, above all, there is this that perhaps he never knew: we only become what we are by radically negating deep down what others have done to us. Three generations? As early as the second, hardly had the sons opened their eyes than they saw their fathers being beaten. In psychiatric terms, they were "traumatized." For life. But these constant acts of repeated aggression, far from forcing them into submission, plunge them into an intolerable contradiction, which sooner or later the European will have to pay for. After that, when it is their turn to be broken in, when they are taught shame, pain, and hunger, we will only be fueling in their bodies a volcanic fury whose power matches the pressure applied to them. They only understand the language of violence, you were saying? Of course; at first the only violence they understand is the colonist's, and then their own, reflecting back at us like our reflection bouncing back at us from a mirror. Don't be mistaken; it is through this mad rage, this bile and venom, their constant desire to kill us, and the permanent contraction of powerful muscles, afraid to relax, that they become men. It is *through* the *colonist*, who wants to turn them into beasts of burden, and against him. Still blind and abstract, hatred is their only asset. The master provokes it because he seeks to deaden their minds; he fails to break it because his interests stop him halfway. The false "natives," therefore, are still humans owing to the power and powerlessness of the oppressor that are transformed into the natives' stubborn rejection of their animal condition. As for the rest, the message is clear. They are lazy, of course they are: it's a form of sabotage. Sly and thieving: What did you expect? Their petty thieving marks the start of a still unorganized resistance. And if that is not enough there are those who assert themselves by hurling themselves with their bare hands against the guns; these are their heroes; and others turn into men by killing Europeans. They are shot: the sacrifice of these outlaws and martyrs exalts the terrified masses.

Terrified, yes. At this new stage colonial aggression is internalized by the colonized as a form of terror. By that I mean not only the fear they feel when faced with our limitless means of repression, but also the fear that their own fury inspires in them. They are trapped between our guns, which are pointing at them, and those frightening instincts, those murderous impulses, that emerge from the bottom of their hearts and that they don't always recognize. For it is not first of all *their* violence, it is ours, on the rebound, that grows and tears them apart; and the first reaction by these oppressed people is to repress this shameful anger that is morally condemned by them and us, but that is the only refuge they have left for their humanity. Read Fanon: you will see that in a time of helplessness, murderous rampage is the collective unconscious of the colonized.

This repressed rage, never managing to explode, goes round in circles and wreaks havoc on the oppressed themselves. In order to rid themselves of it they end up massacring each other, tribes battle one against the other since they cannot confront the real enemy—and you can count on colonial policy to fuel rivalries; the brother raising his knife against his brother believes he is destroying once and for all the hated image of their common debasement. But these expiatory victims do not satisfy their thirst for blood, and the only way to stop themselves from marching against the machine guns is to become our accomplices: the very dehumanization process they are rejecting will be speeded up by their own initiative. Under the amused gaze of the colonist, they protect themselves with supernatural safeguards, sometimes reviving awesome old myths, at other times tying themselves to meticulous rituals. The colonized, therefore, in his obsession, shuns his deep desires by inflicting on himself odd rites that monopolize him at every moment. They dance: that keeps them occupied; it relaxes their painfully contracted muscles, and what's more, the dance secretly mimes, often unbeknownst to them, the No they dare not voice, the murders they dare not commit. In some regions they use the last resort: possession. What was once quite simply a religious act, an exchange between the believer and the sacred, has been turned into a weapon against despair and humiliation: the *zars*, the *loas*, the Saints of Santeria possess them, take control of their violence and squander it in trances ending in exhaustion. At the same time their idols protect them: in other words the colonized protect themselves from colonial alienation by going one step better with religious alienation, with the ultimate end result of having accumulated two alienations, each of which reinforces the other. In certain psychoses, therefore, tired of being insulted day in and day out, the hallucinating individual suddenly gets it into his head to hear an angel's voice complimenting him; this doesn't stop the jeering, but at least it gives him a break. It is a means of defense and the end of their story: the personality dislocates and the patient is a case for dementia. For a few rigorously selected unfortunates, there is that other possession I mentioned earlier: Western culture. In their shoes, you might say, I would prefer my *zars* to the

Acropolis. Okay: you've got the message. Not quite, however, because you are not in their shoes. Not yet. Otherwise you'd know they have no choice: they accumulate. Two worlds, that makes two possessions: you dance all night long, at dawn you hurry to church to attend mass. Day by day the crack widens. Our enemy betrays his brothers and becomes our accomplice; his brothers do the same. The status of "native" is a neurosis introduced and maintained by the colonist in the colonized *with their consent.*

Demanding yet denying the human condition makes for an explosive contradiction. And explode it does, as you and I know. And we live in an age of conflagration: it only needs the rising birth rate to worsen the food shortage, it only needs the newly born to fear living a little more than dying, and for the torrent of violence to sweep away all the barriers. In Algeria and Angola, Europeans are massacred on sight. This is the age of the boomerang, the third stage of violence: it flies right back at us, it strikes us and, once again, we have no idea what hit us. The "liberals" remain stunned: they admit we had not been polite enough to the "natives," that it would have been wiser and fairer to grant them certain rights, wherever possible; they would have been only too happy to admit them in batches without a sponsor to that exclusive club—the human species; and now this barbaric explosion of madness is putting them in the same boat as the wretched colonists. The metropolitan Left is in a quandary: it is well aware of the true fate of the "natives," the pitiless oppression they are subjected to, and does not condemn their revolt, knowing that we did everything to provoke it. But even so, it thinks, there are limits: these guerrillas should make every effort to show some chivalry; this would be the best way of proving they are men. Sometimes the Left berates them: "You're going too far; we cannot support you any longer." They don't care a shit for its support; it can shove it up its ass for what it's worth. As soon as the war began, they realized the harsh truth: we are all equally as good as each other. We have all taken advantage of them, they have nothing to prove, they won't give anyone preferential treatment. A single duty, a single objective: drive out colonialism by *every* means. And the most liberal among us would be prepared to accept this, at a pinch, but they cannot help seeing in this trial of strength a perfectly inhuman method used by subhumans to claim for themselves a charter for humanity: let them acquire it as quickly as possible, but in order to merit it, let them use nonviolent methods. Our noble souls are racist.

They would do well to read Fanon; he shows perfectly clearly that this irrepressible violence is neither a storm in a teacup nor the reemergence of savage instincts nor even a consequence of resentment: it is man reconstructing himself. I believe we once knew, and have since forgotten, the truth that no indulgence can erase the marks of violence: violence alone can eliminate them. And the colonized are cured of colonial neurosis by driving the colonist out by force. Once their rage explodes, they recover their lost coherence, they experience self-knowledge through reconstruction of themselves; from afar we see their war as the triumph of barbarity; but it proceeds on its own to gradually emancipate the fighter and progressively eliminates the colonial darkness inside and out. As soon as it begins it is merciless. Either one must remain terrified or become terrifying—which means surrendering to the dissociations of a fabricated life or conquering the unity of one's native soil. When the peasants lay hands on a gun, the old myths fade, and one by one the taboos are overturned: a fighter's weapon is his humanity. For in the first phase of the revolt killing is a necessity: killing a European is killing two birds with one stone, eliminating in one go oppressor and oppressed: leaving one man dead and the other man free; for the first time the survivor feels a *national* soil under his feet. In that moment the nation does not forsake him: it is there wherever he goes and wherever he is—always by his side, it merges with his freedom. But after the initial surprise the colonial army responds: one must unite or be massacred. Tribal conflicts diminish and tend to disappear: firstly, because they jeopardize the revolution, and more precisely because they had no other purpose but to shift the violence onto false enemies. When they persist—like in the Congo—it is because they are fueled by the agents of colonialism. The nation moves forward: every comrade in arms represents the nation for every other comrade. Their brotherly love is the reverse side of the hatred they feel for you: linked as brothers by the fact that each of them has killed and can at any moment kill again. Fanon shows his readers the limits of "spontaneity," the need for and the risks of "organization." But however immense the task, at each new stage of the undertaking, the revolutionary consciousness deepens. The last complexes are swept away: just let them try and talk about a "dependency complex" in an ALN soldier. Freed from his blinkers, the peasant becomes aware of his needs: these were killing him, but he tried to ignore them; now he discovers their infinite demands. In this atmosphere of mass violence—in order to hold out five or eight years, as the Algerians have done—the military, social, and political demands are indistinguishable. The war—if only the question of command and responsibilities—establishes new structures that will be the first institutions of peace. Here then is man instated in new traditions even, future daughters of a horrible present; here he is legitimized by a right about to be born or born every day in the heat of combat: with the last of the colonists killed, re-embarked or assimilated, the minority species disappears, giving way to socialist brotherhood. And this is still not enough: the fighter takes short cuts; you don't think he is risking his life to turn himself into an old "metropolitan." Look how patient he is: perhaps he dreams sometimes of another Dien Bien Phu; but don't believe he is really counting on it: he is a beggar who in his wretchedness is fighting the rich and their military might. In expectation of decisive victories, and very often expecting nothing, he works his enemies to distraction. This is not without terrifying losses; the colonial army turns savage: police checks, search operations, roundups, and punitive raids; they massacre women and children. This new man knows that his life as a man begins with death; he considers himself a potential candidate for death. He will be killed: it is not just that he accepts the risk of being killed, he is certain of it. This walking dead man has lost his wife and his sons; he has seen so much agony he prefers victory to survival; others will profit from the victory, not him; he is too weary. But this weariness of heart is the reason behind his incredible courage. We find our humanity this side of death and despair; he finds it on the other side of torture and death. We have sown the wind; he is the hurricane. Offspring of violence, he draws every moment of his humanity from it: we were men at his expense, he becomes a man at ours. Another man: a man of higher quality.

Here Fanon stops. He has shown the way: as spokesman for the fighters, he has called for union, the unity of the African continent against every discord and every idiosyncrasy. He has achieved his purpose. If he had wanted to describe fully the historical phenomenon of colonization, he would have had to talk about us—which was certainly not his intention. But when we have closed the book, it continues to haunt us, in spite of its author: for we sense the force of these peoples waging a revolution and our only response is violence. A new moment in violence, therefore, occurs, and this time it involves us because it is in the process of changing us to the same extent it changes the false "native." Everyone can think what he likes, provided however that he thinks: in a Europe stunned by the blows it is receiving these days, the slightest distraction of thought in France, Belgium, and England amounts to a criminal complicity with colonialism. This book had certainly no need for a preface. Especially as it is not addressed to us. I have written one, however, to carry the dialectic through to its conclusion: we, too, peoples of Europe, we are being decolonized: meaning the colonist inside every one of us is surgically extracted in a bloody operation. Let's take a good look at ourselves, if we have the courage, and let's see what has become of us.

First of all we must confront an unexpected sight: the striptease of our humanism. Not a pretty sight in its nakedness:

nothing but a dishonest ideology, an exquisite justification for plundering; its tokens of sympathy and affectation, alibis for our acts of aggression. The pacifists are a fine sight: neither victims nor torturers! Come now! If you are not a victim when the government you voted for and the army your young brothers served in, commits "genocide," without hesitation or remorse, then, you are undoubtedly a torturer. And if you choose to be a victim, risking one or two days in prison, you are simply trying to take the easy way out. But you can't; there is no way out. Get this into your head: if violence were only a thing of the future, if exploitation and oppression never existed on earth, perhaps displays of nonviolence might relieve the conflict. But if the entire regime, even your nonviolent thoughts, is governed by a thousand-year-old oppression, your passiveness serves no other purpose but to put you on the side of the oppressors.

You know full well we are exploiters. You know full well we have taken the gold and minerals and then oil from the "new continents," and shipped them back to the old metropolises. Not without excellent results in the shape of palaces, cathedrals, and centers of industry; and then when crisis loomed, the colonial markets were there to cushion the blow or divert it. Stuffed with wealth, Europe granted humanity *de jure* to all its inhabitants: for us, a man means an accomplice, for we have *all* profited from colonial exploitation. This pale, bloated continent ended up by lapsing into what Fanon rightly calls "narcissism." Cocteau was irritated by Paris, "this city that never stops talking about herself." And Europe, what else is it doing? And that super-European monster, North America? What empty chatter: liberty, equality, fraternity, love, honor, country, and what else? This did not prevent us from making racist remarks at the same time: dirty nigger, filthy Jew, dirty Arab. Noble minds, liberal and sympathetic — neocolonialists, in other words — claimed to be shocked by this inconsistency, since the only way the European could make himself man was by fabricating slaves and monsters. As long as the status of "native" existed, the imposture remained unmasked. We saw in the human species an abstract premise of universality that served as a pretext for concealing more concrete practices: there was a race of subhumans overseas who, thanks to us, might, in a thousand years perhaps, attain our status. In short, we took the human race to mean elite. Today the "native" unmasks his truth; as a result, our exclusive club reveals its weakness: it was nothing more and nothing less than a minority. There is worse news: since the others are turning into men against us, apparently we are the enemy of the human race; the elite is revealing its true nature—a gang. Our beloved values are losing their feathers; if you take a closer look there is not one that isn't tainted with blood. If you need proof, remember those noble words: How generous France is. Generous? Us? And what about Sétif? And what about those eight years of fierce fighting that have cost the lives of over a million Algerians? And the torture by electricity? But you must understand we are not being blamed for having betrayed some mission or other: for the good reason we don't have any. It is our very generosity that is being challenged; such a beautiful, melodious word means only one thing: status granted. For the new men on the other side who have been set free, nobody has the power or the privilege to deny anybody anything. Everyone has every right. Over everything. And the day when our human race has fully matured, it will not define itself as the sum of the inhabitants of the globe, but as the infinite unity of their reciprocities. I shall stop here; you won't have trouble finishing the job; for the first and last time you only need to look our aristocratic virtues in the face: they are doomed; how could they survive the aristocracy of subhumans who engendered them? A few years back, a bourgeois, and colonialist, commentator had only this to say in defense of the West: "We are no angels. But at least we have remorse." What an admission! In the past our continent had other life buoys: the Parthenon, Chartres, the Rights of Man, and the swastika. We know now what they are worth. And now the only thing they claim can save us from shipwreck is the very Christian feeling of guilt. It's the end; as you can see, Europe leaks like a sieve. What then has happened? Quite simply this: we were the subjects of history, and now we are the objects. The power struggle has been reversed, decolonization is in progress; all our mercenaries can try and do is delay its completion.

But in order to do that, the former metropolises would have to pull out all the stops and commit all their forces to a battle lost in advance. That old colonial brutality that made Bugeaud a dubious hero, here it is at the end of the colonial venture applied tenfold yet still insufficient. The troops are dispatched to Algeria where they have held out for seven years with no result. The violence has changed direction; victorious, we enforced it without it ever seeming to affect us; it dislocated the other, whereas our humanism as men remained intact. United by profit, the metropolitans baptized their commonwealth of crimes Fraternity and Love. Today, the very same violence, blockaded everywhere, comes back to us through our soldiers, internalizes itself and possesses us. Involution begins: the colonized reintegrate themselves, and we, the reactionaries and the liberals, the colonists and the metropolitans, disintegrate. Fury and fear are already stripped naked: they are laid bare in the brutal punitive raids in Algiers. Where are the savages now? Where is the barbarity? Nothing is missing, not even the drums: the car horns hammer out, "Algeria for the French," while the Europeans burn the Muslims alive. Not so long ago, Fanon recalls, a congress of psychiatrists deplored Algerian criminality: these people are killing themselves, they said, it's not normal; the cortex of the Algerian must be underdeveloped. In Central Africa others established that "the African uses his frontal lobes very little." These scientists would do well to pursue their research in Europe, and especially among the French. For we, too, must be affected by frontal idleness for some time now: our patriots have been assassinating their fellow countrymen, and if they find no one home, they blow up the concierge and the house. This is only the beginning; civil war is predicted for autumn or next spring. Our lobes, however, seem perfectly normal: couldn't the reason be rather that, powerless to crush the "native," violence turns inward, bottles itself up deep inside us, and seeks an outlet? The unity of the Algerian people produces the disunity of the French: throughout the territories of the ex-metropolises the tribes are dancing and preparing to fight. Terror has left Africa to settle here; for there are raving fanatics who want to make us pay with our blood for the shame of having been beaten by the "native," and then there are the others, all the others, the liberals, the hardliners of the spineless Left who are just as guilty (after Bizerta, after the September lynchings, who took to the streets to shout "Enough is enough"?), but more composed. The fever is mounting in them, too, as well as spiteful anger. But they're scared stiff! They conceal their rage behind myths and complicated rituals. In order to delay the final reckoning and the hour of truth, they have given us a Grand Magician as our leader whose function is to keep us in the dark at any cost. To no effect; hailed by some, rejected by others, violence goes round in circles: one day it explodes in Metz, the next day in Bordeaux; now it's here, then it's there, like the game of pass the slipper. Slowly but surely it is our turn to head down the road to "native" status. But in order to become genuine "natives" our territory would have to be occupied by the formerly colonized and we would have to be starving to death. This will not be the case; no, it is the demise of colonialism that possesses us; we shall soon be mounted by it in all its arrogance and senility; that is our *zar*, that is our *loa*. And you will be convinced on reading Fanon's last chapter that it is better to be a "native" in the pit of misery than an erstwhile colonist. It is not right that a police officer should be obliged to torture ten hours a day: at that rate his nerves will go to pieces, unless torturers are forbidden to work overtime in their own interest. When you want to safeguard the morale of the nation and the army under the rigor of the law, it is not right for the latter to systematically demoralize the former. Nor for a country with a republican tradition to entrust its young men by the hundreds of thousands to putschist officers. It is not right, my fellow countrymen, you who know all the crimes committed in our name, it is really not right not to breathe a word about them to anybody, not even to your own soul, for fear of having to pass judgment on yourselves. At first you had no idea, I am prepared to believe it, then you suspected, and now you know, but you still keep silent. Eight years of silence have a damaging effect. And in vain: the blinding glare of torture is high in the sky, flooding the entire country; under this blaze of light, not a single laugh rings true any longer, not a single face that is not painted to mask the anger and the fear, no longer a single act that does not betray our disgust and our complicity. Today whenever two Frenchmen meet, there is a dead body between them. And did I say one ...? France was once the name of a country; be careful lest it become the name of a neurosis in 1961.

Will we recover? Yes. Violence, like Achilles' spear, can heal the wounds it has inflicted. Today we are in chains, humiliated, sick with fear: at our lowest ebb. Fortunately for us, this is still not enough for the colonialist aristocracy: it cannot accomplish its rearguard mission in Algeria until it has first finished colonizing the French. Every day we shrink back from the fight, but rest assured it will be inevitable. The killers, they need it; they will swoop down on us and lash out haphazardly. The time for illusionists and wizardry is over: either you fight or rot in the camps. This is the last stage of the dialectic: you condemn this war but you don't yet dare declare your support for the Algerian fighters; have no fear, you can count on the colonists and mercenaries to help you make up your mind. Perhaps, then, with your back to the wall, you will finally unleash this new violence aroused in you by old, rehashed crimes. But, as they say, that is another story. The history of man. The time is coming, I am convinced, when we shall join the ranks of those who are making it.

September 1961

On Violence

National liberation, national reawakening, restoration of the nation to the people or Commonwealth, whatever the name used, whatever the latest expression, decolonization is always a violent event. At whatever level we study it—individual encounters, a change of name for a sports club, the guest list at a cocktail party, members of a police force or the board of directors of a state or private bank—decolonization is quite simply the substitution of one "species" of mankind by another. The substitution is unconditional, absolute, total, and seamless. We could go on to portray the rise of a new nation, the establishment of a new state, its diplomatic relations and its economic and political orientation. But instead we have decided to describe the kind of tabula rasa which from the outset defines any decolonization. What is singularly important is that it starts from the very first day with the basic claims of the colonized. In actual fact, proof of success lies in a social fabric that has been changed inside out. This change is extraordinarily important because it is desired, clamored for, and demanded. The need for this change exists in a raw, repressed, and reckless state in the lives and consciousness of colonized men and women. But the eventuality of such a change is also experienced as a terrifying future in the consciousness of another "species" of men and women: the *colons*, the colonists.

*   *   *

Decolonization, which sets out to change the order of the world, is clearly an agenda for total disorder. But it cannot be accomplished by the wave of a magic wand, a natural cataclysm, or a gentleman's agreement. Decolonization, we know, is an historical process: In other words, it can only be understood, it can only find its significance and become self coherent insofar as we can discern the history-making movement which gives it form and substance. Decolonization is the encounter between two congenitally antagonistic forces that in fact owe their singularity to the kind of reification secreted and nurtured by the colonial situation. Their first confrontation was colored by violence and their cohabitation—or rather the exploitation of the colonized by the colonizer—continued at the point of the bayonet and under cannon fire. The colonist and the colonized are old acquaintances. And consequently, the colonist is right when he says he "knows" them. It is the colonist who *fabricated* and *continues to fabricate* the colonized subject. The colonist derives his validity, i.e., his wealth, from the colonial system.

Decolonization never goes unnoticed, for it focuses on and fundamentally alters being, and transforms the spectator crushed to a nonessential state into a privileged actor, captured in a virtually grandiose fashion by the spotlight of History. It infuses a new rhythm, specific to a new generation of men, with a new language and a new humanity. Decolonization is truly the creation of new men. But such a creation cannot be attributed to a supernatural power: The "thing" colonized becomes a man through the very process of liberation.

Decolonization, therefore, implies the urgent need to thoroughly challenge the colonial situation. Its definition can, if we want to describe it accurately, be summed up in the well-known words: "The last shall be first." Decolonization is verification of this. At a descriptive level, therefore, any decolonization is a success.

* * *

In its bare reality, decolonization reeks of red-hot cannonballs and bloody knives. For the last can be the first only after a murderous and decisive confrontation between the two protagonists. This determination to have the last move up to the front, to have them clamber up (too quickly, say some) the famous echelons of an organized society, can only succeed by resorting to every means, including, of course, violence.

You do not disorganize a society, however primitive it may be, with such an agenda if you are not determined from the very start to smash every obstacle encountered. The colonized, who have made up their mind to make such an agenda into a driving force, have been prepared for violence from time immemorial. As soon as they are born it is obvious to them that their cramped world, riddled with taboos, can only be challenged by out and out violence.

The colonial world is a compartmentalized world. It is obviously as superfluous to recall the existence of "native" towns and European towns, of schools for "natives" and schools for Europeans, as it is to recall apartheid in South Africa. Yet if we penetrate inside this compartmentalization we shall at least bring to light some of its key aspects. By penetrating its geographical configuration and classification we shall be able to delineate the backbone on which the decolonized society is reorganized.

The colonized world is a world divided in two. The dividing line, the border, is represented by the barracks and the police stations. In the colonies, the official, legitimate agent, the spokesperson for the colonizer and the regime of oppression, is the police officer or the soldier. In capitalist societies, education, whether secular or religious, the teaching of moral reflexes handed down from father to son, the exemplary integrity of workers decorated after fifty years of loyal and faithful service, the fostering of love for harmony and wisdom, those aesthetic forms of respect for the status quo, instill in the exploited a mood of submission and inhibition which considerably eases the task of the agents of law and order. In capitalist countries a multitude of sermonizers, counselors, and "confusion-mongers" intervene between the exploited and the authorities. In colonial regions, however, the proximity and frequent, direct intervention by the police and the military ensure the colonized are kept under close scrutiny, and contained by rifle butts and napalm. We have seen how the government's agent uses a language of pure violence. The agent does not alleviate oppression or mask domination. He displays and demonstrates them with the clear conscience of the law enforcer, and brings violence into the homes and minds of the colonized subject.

The "native" sector is not complementary to the European sector. The two confront each other, but not in the service of a higher unity. Governed by a purely Aristotelian logic, they follow the dictates of mutual exclusion: There is no conciliation possible, one of them is superfluous. The colonist's sector is a sector built to last, all stone and steel. It's a sector of lights and paved roads, where the trash cans constantly overflow with strange and wonderful garbage, undreamed-of leftovers. The colonist's feet can never be glimpsed, except perhaps in the sea, but then you can never get close enough. They are protected by solid shoes in a sector where the streets are clean and smooth, without a pothole, without a stone. The colonist's sector is a sated, sluggish sector, its belly is permanently full of good things. The colonist's sector is a white folks' sector, a sector of foreigners.

The colonized's sector, or at least the "native" quarters, the shanty town, the Medina, the reservation, is a disreputable place inhabited by disreputable people. You are born anywhere, anyhow. You die anywhere, from anything. It's a world with no space, people are piled one on top of the other, the shacks squeezed tightly together. The colonized's sector is a famished sector, hungry for bread, meat, shoes, coal, and light. The colonized's sector is a sector that crouches and cowers, a sector on its knees, a sector that is prostrate. It's a sector of niggers, a sector of towelheads. The gaze that the colonized subject casts at the colonist's sector is a look of lust, a look of envy. Dreams of possession. Every type of possession: of sitting at the colonist's table and sleeping in his bed, preferably with his wife. The colonized man is an envious man. The colonist is aware of this as he catches the furtive glance, and constantly on his guard, realizes bitterly that: "They want to take our place." And it's true there is not one colonized subject who at least once a day does not dream of taking the place of the colonist.

This compartmentalized world, this world divided in two, is inhabited by different species. The singularity of the colonial context lies in the fact that economic reality, inequality, and enormous disparities in lifestyles never manage to mask the human reality. Looking at the immediacies of the colonial context, it is clear that what divides this world is first and foremost what species, what race one belongs to. In the colonies the economic infrastructure is also a superstructure. The cause is effect: You are rich because you are white, you are white because you are rich. This is why a Marxist analysis should always be slightly stretched when it comes to addressing the colonial issue. It is not just the concept of the precapitalist society, so effectively studied by Marx, which needs to be reexamined here. The serf is essentially different from the knight, but a reference to divine right is needed to justify this difference in status. In the colonies the foreigner imposed himself using his cannons and machines. Despite the success of his pacification, in spite of his appropriation, the colonist always remains a foreigner. It is not the factories, the estates, or the bank account which primarily characterize the "ruling class." The ruling species is first and foremost the outsider from elsewhere, different from the indigenous population, "the others."

The violence which governed the ordering of the colonial world, which tirelessly punctuated the destruction of the indigenous social fabric, and demolished unchecked the systems of reference of the country's economy, lifestyles, and modes of dress, this same violence will be vindicated and appropriated when, taking history into their own hands, the colonized swarm into the forbidden cities. To blow the colonial world to smithereens is henceforth a clear image within the grasp and imagination of every colonized subject. To dislocate the colonial world does not mean that once the borders have been eliminated there will be a right of way between the two sectors. To destroy the colonial world means nothing less than demolishing the colonist's sector, burying it deep within the earth or banishing it from the territory.

Challenging the colonial world is not a rational confrontation of viewpoints. It is not a discourse on the universal, but the impassioned claim by the colonized that their world is fundamentally different. The colonial world is a Manichaean world. The colonist is not content with physically limiting the space of the colonized, i.e., with the help of his agents of law and order. As if to illustrate the totalitarian nature of colonial exploitation, the colonist turns the colonized into a kind of quintessence of evil.[1] Colonized society is not merely portrayed as a society without values. The colonist is not content with stating that the colonized world has lost its values or worse never possessed any. The "native" is declared impervious to ethics, representing not only the absence of values but also the negation of values. He is, dare we say it, the enemy of values. In other words, absolute evil. A corrosive element, destroying everything within his reach, a corrupting element, distorting everything which involves aesthetics or morals, an agent of malevolent powers, an unconscious and incurable instrument of blind forces. And Monsieur Meyer could say in all seriousness in the French National Assembly that we

---

[1] We have demonstrated in *Black Skin, White Masks* the mechanism of this Manichaean world.

should not let the Republic be defiled by the penetration of the Algerian people. Values are, in fact, irreversibly poisoned and infected as soon as they come into contact with the colonized. The customs of the colonized, their traditions, their myths, especially their myths, are the very mark of this indigence and innate depravity. This is why we should place DDT, which destroys parasites, carriers of disease, on the same level as Christianity, which roots out heresy, natural impulses, and evil. The decline of yellow fever and the advances made by evangelizing form part of the same balance sheet. But triumphant reports by the missions in fact tell us how deep the seeds of alienation have been sown among the colonized. I am talking of Christianity and this should come as no surprise to anybody. The Church in the colonies is a white man's Church, a foreigners' Church. It does not call the colonized to the ways of God, but to the ways of the white man, to the ways of the master, the ways of the oppressor. And as we know, in this story many are called but few are chosen.

Sometimes this Manichaeanism reaches its logical conclusion and dehumanizes the colonized subject. In plain talk, he is reduced to the state of an animal. And consequently, when the colonist speaks of the colonized he uses zoological terms. Allusion is made to the slithery movements of the yellow race, the odors from the "native" quarters, to the hordes, the stink, the swarming, the seething, and the gesticulations. In his endeavors at description and finding the right word, the colonist refers constantly to the bestiary. The European seldom has a problem with figures of speech. But the colonized, who immediately grasp the intention of the colonist and the exact case being made against them, know instantly what he is thinking. This explosive population growth, those hysterical masses, those blank faces, those shapeless, obese bodies, this headless, tailless cohort, these children who seem not to belong to anyone, this indolence sprawling under the sun, this vegetating existence, all this is part of the colonial vocabulary. General de Gaulle speaks of "yellow multitudes," and Monsieur Mauriac of the black, brown, and yellow hordes that will soon invade our shores. The colonized know all that and roar with laughter every time they hear themselves called an animal by the other. For they know they are not animals. And at the very moment when they discover their humanity, they begin to sharpen their weapons to secure its victory.

As soon as the colonized begin to strain at the leash and to pose a threat to the colonist, they are assigned a series of good souls who in the "Symposiums on Culture" spell out the specificity and richness of Western values. But every time the issue of Western values crops up, the colonized grow tense and their muscles seize up. During the period of decolonization the colonized are called upon to be reasonable. They are offered rock-solid values, they are told in great detail that decolonization should not mean regression, and that they must rely on values which have proved to be reliable and worthwhile. Now it so happens that when the colonized hear a speech on Western culture they draw their machetes or at least check to see they are close to hand. The supremacy of white values is stated with such violence, the victorious confrontation of these values with the lifestyle and beliefs of the colonized is so impregnated with aggressiveness, that as a counter measure the colonized rightly make a mockery of them whenever they are mentioned. In the colonial context the colonist only quits undermining the colonized once the latter have proclaimed loud and clear that white values reign supreme. In the period of decolonization the colonized masses thumb their noses at these very values, shower them with insults and vomit them up.

Such an occurrence normally goes unseen because, during decolonization, certain colonized intellectuals have established a dialogue with the bourgeoisie of the colonizing country. During this period the indigenous population is seen as a blurred mass. The few "native" personalities whom the colonialist bourgeois have chanced to encounter have had insufficient impact to alter their current perception and nuance their thinking. During the period of liberation, however, the colonialist bourgeoisie frantically seeks contact with the colonized "elite." It is with this elite that the famous dialogue on values is established. When the colonialist bourgeoisie realizes it is impossible to maintain its domination over the colonies it decides to wage a rearguard campaign in the fields of culture, values, and technology, etc. But what we should never forget is that the immense majority of colonized peoples are impervious to such issues. For a colonized people, the most essential value, because it is the most meaningful, is first and foremost the land: the land, which must provide bread and, naturally, dignity. But this dignity has nothing to do with "human" dignity. The colonized subject has never heard of such an ideal. All he has ever seen on his land is that he can be arrested, beaten, and starved with impunity; and no sermonizer on morals, no priest has ever stepped in to bear the blows in his place or share his bread. For the colonized, to be a moralist quite plainly means silencing the arrogance of the colonist, breaking his spiral of violence, in a word ejecting him outright from the picture. The famous dictum which states that all men are equal will find its illustration in the colonies only when the colonized subject states he is equal to the colonist. Taking it a step further, he is determined to fight to be more than the colonist. In fact, he has already decided to take his place. As we have seen, it is the collapse of an entire moral and material universe. The intellectual who, for his part, has adopted the abstract, universal values of the colonizer is prepared to fight so that colonist and colonized can live in peace in a new world. But what he does not see, because precisely colonialism and all its modes of thought have seeped into him, is that the colonist is no longer interested in staying on and coexisting once the colonial context has disappeared. It is no coincidence that, even before any negotiation between the Algerian government and the French government, the so-called "liberal" European minority has already made its position clear: it is clamoring for dual citizenship, nothing less. By sticking to the abstract the colonist is being forced to make a very substantial leap into the unknown. Let us be honest, the colonist knows perfectly well that no jargon is a substitute for reality.

The colonized subject thus discovers that his life, his breathing and his heartbeats are the same as the colonist's. He discovers that the skin of a colonist is not worth more than the "native's." In other words, his world receives a fundamental jolt. The colonized's revolutionary new assurance stems from this. If, in fact, my life is worth as much as the colonist's, his look can no longer strike fear into me or nail me to the spot and his voice can no longer petrify me. I am no longer uneasy in his presence. In reality, to hell with him. Not only does his presence no longer bother me, but I am already preparing to waylay him in such a way that soon he will have no other solution but to flee.

The colonial context, as we have said, is characterized by the dichotomy it inflicts on the world. Decolonization unifies this world by a radical decision to remove its heterogeneity, by unifying it on the grounds of nation and sometimes race. To quote the biting words of Senegalese patriots on the maneuvers of their president, Senghor: "We asked for the Africanization of the top jobs and all Senghor does is Africanize the Europeans." Meaning that the colonized can see right away if decolonization is taking place or not: The minimum demand is that the last become the first.

But the colonized intellectual introduces a variation on this demand and in fact, there seems to be no lack of motivation to fill senior positions as administrators, technicians, and experts. The colonized, however, equate this nepotism with acts of sabotage and it is not unusual to hear them declare: "What is the point of being independent then . . . ?"

Wherever an authentic liberation struggle has been fought, wherever the blood of the people has been shed and the armed phase has lasted long enough to encourage the intellectuals to withdraw to their rank and file base, there is an effective eradication of the superstructure borrowed by these intellectuals from the colonialist bourgeois circles. In its narcissistic monologue the colonialist bourgeoisie, by way of its academics, had implanted in the minds of the colonized that the essential values—meaning Western values—remain eternal despite all errors attributable to man. The colonized intellectual accepted the cogency of these ideas and there in the back of his mind stood a sentinel on duty guarding the Greco-Roman pedestal. But during the struggle for liberation, when the colonized intellectual touches base again with his people, this artificial sentinel is smashed to smithereens. All the Mediterranean values, the triumph of the individual, of enlightenment and Beauty turn into pale, lifeless trinkets. All those discourses appear a jumble of dead words. Those values which seemed to ennoble the soul prove worthless because they have nothing in common with the real-life struggle in which the people are engaged.

And first among them is individualism. The colonized intellectual learned from his masters that the individual must assert himself. The colonialist bourgeoisie hammered into the colonized mind the notion of a society of individuals where each is locked in his subjectivity, where wealth lies in thought. But the colonized intellectual who is lucky enough to bunker down with the people during the liberation struggle, will soon discover the falsity of this theory. Involvement in the organization of the struggle will already introduce him to a different vocabulary. "Brother," "sister," "comrade" are words outlawed by the colonialist bourgeoisie because in their thinking my brother is my wallet and my comrade, my scheming. In a kind of auto-da-fé, the colonized intellectual witnesses the destruction of all his idols: egoism, arrogant recrimination, and the idiotic, childish need to have the last word. This colonized intellectual, pulverized by colonialist culture, will also discover the strength of the village assemblies, the power of the people's commissions and the extraordinary productiveness of neighborhood and section committee meetings. Personal interests are now the collective interest because in reality *every-one* will be discovered by the French legionnaires and consequently massacred or else *everyone* will be saved. In such a context, the "every man for himself" concept, the atheist's form of salvation, is prohibited.

Self-criticism has been much talked about recently, but few realize that it was first of all an African institution. Whether it be in the *djemaas* of North Africa or the palavers of West Africa, tradition has it that disputes which break out in a village are worked out in public. By this I mean collective self-criticism with a touch of humor because everyone is relaxed, because in the end we all want the same thing. The intellectual sheds all that calculating, all those strange silences, those ulterior motives, that devious thinking and secrecy as he gradually plunges deeper among the people. In this respect then we can genuinely say that the community has already triumphed and exudes its own light, its own reason.

But when decolonization occurs in regions where the liberation struggle has not yet made its impact sufficiently felt, here are the same smart alecks, the sly, shrewd intellectuals whose behavior and ways of thinking, picked up from their rubbing shoulders with the colonialist bourgeoisie, have remained intact. Spoiled children of yesterday's colonialism and today's governing powers, they oversee the looting of the few national resources. Ruthless in their scheming and legal pilfering they use the poverty, now nationwide, to work their way to the top through import-export holdings, limited companies, playing the stock market, and nepotism. They insist on the nationalization of business transactions, i.e., reserving contracts and business deals for nationals. Their doctrine is to proclaim the absolute need for nationalizing the theft of the nation. In this barren, national phase, in this so-called period of austerity, their success at plundering the nation swiftly sparks anger and violence from the people. In the present international and African context, the poverty-stricken and independent population achieves a social consciousness at a rapidly accelerating pace. This, the petty individualists will soon find out for themselves.

In order to assimilate the culture of the oppressor and venture into his fold, the colonized subject has had to pawn some of his own intellectual possessions. For instance, one of the things he has had to assimilate is the way the colonialist bourgeoisie thinks. This is apparent in the colonized intellectual's inaptitude to engage in dialogue. For he is unable to make himself inessential when confronted with a purpose or idea. On the other hand, when he operates among the people he is constantly awestruck. He is literally disarmed by their good faith and integrity. He is then constantly at risk of becoming a demagogue. He turns into a kind of mimic man who nods his assent to every word by the people, transformed by him into an arbiter of truth. But the fellah, the unemployed and the starving do not lay claim to truth. They do not say they represent the truth because they are the truth in their very being.

During this period the intellectual behaves objectively like a vulgar opportunist. His maneuvering, in fact, is still at work. The people would never think of rejecting him or cutting the ground from under his feet. What the people want is for everything to be pooled together. The colonized intellectual's insertion into this human tide will find itself on hold because of his curious obsession with detail. It is not that the people are opposed to analysis. They appreciate clarification, understand the reasoning behind an argument, and like to see where they are going. But at the start of his cohabitation with the people the colonized intellectual gives priority to detail and tends to forget the very purpose of the struggle—the defeat of colonialism. Swept along by the many facets of the struggle, he tends to concentrate on local tasks, undertaken zealously but almost always too pedantically. He does not always see the overall picture. He introduces the notion of disciplines, specialized areas and fields into that awesome mixer and grinder called a people's revolution.

Committed to certain frontline issues he tends to lose sight of the unity of the movement and in the event of failure at the local level he succumbs to doubt, even despair. The people, on the other hand, take a global stance from the very start. "Bread and land: how do we go about getting bread and land?" And this stubborn, apparently limited, narrow-minded aspect of the people is finally the most rewarding and effective working model.

The question of truth must also be taken into consideration. For the people, only fellow nationals are ever owed the truth. No absolute truth, no discourse on the transparency of the soul can erode this position. In answer to the lie of the colonial situation, the colonized subject responds with a lie. Behavior toward fellow nationalists is open and honest, but strained and indecipherable toward the colonists. Truth is what hastens the dislocation of the colonial regime, what fosters the emergence of the nation. Truth is what protects the "natives" and undoes the foreigners. In the colonial context there is no truthful behavior. And good is quite simply what hurts *them* most.

We have seen therefore that the Manichaeanism that first governed colonial society is maintained intact during the period of decolonization. In fact the colonist never ceases to be the enemy, the antagonist, in plain words public enemy number 1. The oppressor, ensconced in his sector, creates the spiral, the spiral of domination, exploitation and looting. In the other sector, the colonized subject lies coiled and robbed, and fuels as best he can the spiral which moves seamlessly from the shores of the colony to the palaces and docks of the metropolis. In this petrified zone, not a ripple on the surface, the palm trees sway against the clouds, the waves of the sea lap against the shore, the raw materials come and go, legitimating the colonist's presence, while more dead than alive the colonized subject crouches for ever in the same old dream. The colonist makes history. His life is an epic, an odyssey. He is invested with the very beginning:

"We made this land." He is the guarantor for its existence: "If we leave, all will be lost, and this land will return to the Dark Ages." Opposite him, listless beings wasted away by fevers and consumed by "ancestral customs" compose a virtually petrified background to the innovative dynamism of colonial mercantilism.

The colonist makes history and he knows it. And because he refers constantly to the history of his metropolis, he plainly indicates that here he is the extension of this metropolis. The history he writes is therefore not the history of the country he is despoiling, but the history of his own nation's looting, raping, and starving to death. The immobility to which the colonized subject is condemned can be challenged only if he decides to put an end to the history of colonization and the history of despoliation in order to bring to life the history of the nation, the history of decolonization.

A world compartmentalized, Manichaean and petrified, a world of statues: the statue of the general who led the conquest, the statue of the engineer who built the bridge. A world cocksure of itself, crushing with its stoniness the backbones of those scarred by the whip. That is the colonial world. The colonial subject is a man penned in; apartheid is but one method of compartmentalizing the colonial world. The first thing the colonial subject learns is to remain in his place and not overstep its limits. Hence the dreams of the colonial subject are muscular dreams, dreams of action, dreams of aggressive vitality. I dream I am jumping, swimming, running, and climbing. I dream I burst out laughing, I am leaping across a river and chased by a pack of cars that never catches up with me. During colonization the colonized subject frees himself night after night between nine in the evening and six in the morning.

The colonized subject will first train this aggressiveness sedimented in his muscles against his own people. This is the period when black turns on black, and police officers and magistrates don't know which way to turn when faced with the surprising surge of North African criminality. We shall see later what should be made of this phenomenon.[2] Confronted with the colonial order the colonized subject is in a permanent state of tension. The colonist's world is a hostile world, a world which excludes yet at the same time incites envy. We have seen how the colonized always dream of taking the colonist's place. Not of becoming a colonist, but of replacing him. This hostile, oppressive and aggressive world, bulldozing the colonized masses, represents not only the hell they would like to escape as quickly as possible but a paradise within arm's reach guarded by ferocious watchdogs.

The colonized subject is constantly on his guard: Confused by the myriad signs of the colonial world he never knows whether he is out of line. Confronted with a world configured by the colonizer, the colonized subject is always presumed guilty. The colonized does not accept his guilt, but rather considers it a kind of curse, a sword of Damocles. But deep down the colonized subject acknowledges no authority. He is dominated but not domesticated. He is made to feel inferior, but by no means convinced of his inferiority. He patiently waits for the colonist to let his guard down and then jumps on him. The muscles of the colonized are always tensed. It is not that he is anxious or terrorized, but he is always ready to change his role as game for that of hunter. The colonized subject is a persecuted man who is forever dreaming of becoming the persecutor. The symbols of society such as the police force, bugle calls in the barracks, military parades, and the flag flying aloft, serve not only as inhibitors but also as stimulants. They do not signify: "Stay where you are." But rather "Get ready to do the right thing." And in fact if ever the colonized subject begins to doze off or forget, the colonist's arrogance and preoccupation with testing the solidity of the colo-

---

[2] *Colonial Wars and Mental Disorders*, chapter 5.

nial system will remind him on so many occasions that the great showdown cannot be postponed indefinitely. This impulse to take the colonist's place maintains a constant muscular tonus. It is a known fact that under certain emotional circumstances an obstacle actually escalates action.

The relationship between colonist and colonized is one of physical mass. Against the greater number the colonist pits his force. The colonist is an exhibitionist. His safety concerns lead him to remind the colonized out loud: "Here I am the master." The colonist keeps the colonized in a state of rage, which he prevents from boiling over. The colonized are caught in the tightly knit web of colonialism. But we have seen how on the inside the colonist achieves only a pseudo-petrification. The muscular tension of the colonized periodically erupts into bloody fighting between tribes, clans, and individuals.

At the individual level we witness a genuine negation of common sense. Whereas the colonist or police officer can beat the colonized subject day in and day out, insult him and shove him to his knees, it is not uncommon to see the colonized subject draw his knife at the slightest hostile or aggressive look from another colonized subject. For the colonized subject's last resort is to defend his personality against his fellow countryman. Internecine feuds merely perpetuate age-old grudges entrenched in memory. By throwing himself muscle and soul into his blood feuds, the colonized subject endeavors to convince himself that colonialism has never existed, that everything is as it used to be and history marches on. Here we grasp the full significance of the all too familiar "head-in-the-sand" behavior at a collective level, as if this collective immersion in a fratricidal bloodbath suffices to mask the obstacle and postpone the inevitable alternative, the inevitable emergence of the armed struggle against colonialism. So one of the ways the colonized subject releases his muscular tension is through the very real collective self-destruction of these internecine feuds. Such behavior represents a death wish in the face of danger, a suicidal conduct which reinforces the colonist's existence and domination and reassures him that such men are not rational. The colonized subject also manages to lose sight of the colonist through religion. Fatalism relieves the oppressor of all responsibility since the cause of wrong-doing, poverty, and the inevitable can be attributed to God. The individual thus accepts the devastation decreed by God, grovels in front of the colonist, bows to the hand of fate, and mentally readjusts to acquire the serenity of stone.

In the meantime, however, life goes on and the colonized subject draws on the terrifying myths that are so prolific in underdeveloped societies as inhibitions for his aggressiveness: malevolent spirits who emerge every time you put one foot wrong, leopard men, snake men, six-legged dogs, zombies, a whole never-ending gamut of animalcules or giants that encircle the colonized with a realm of taboos, barriers, and inhibitions far more terrifying than the colonialist world. This magical superstructure that permeates the indigenous society has a very precise function in the way the libido works. One of the characteristics, in fact, of underdeveloped societies is that the libido is primarily a matter for the group and family. Anthropologists have amply described societies where the man who dreams he has sexual intercourse with a woman other than his own must publicly confess his dream and pay the penalty in kind or in several days' work to the husband or the injured family party—which proves, by the way, that so-called prehistorical societies attach great importance to the unconscious.

In scaring me, the atmosphere of myths and magic operates like an undeniable reality. In terrifying me, it incorporates me into the traditions and history of my land and ethnic group, but at the same time I am reassured and granted a civil status, an identification. The secret sphere in underdeveloped countries is a collective sphere that falls exclusively within the realm of magic. By entangling me in this inextricable web where gestures are repeated with a secular limpidity, my very own world, our very own world, thus perpetuates itself. Zombies, believe me, are more terrifying than colonists. And the problem now is not whether to fall in line with the armor-plated world of colonialism, but to think twice before urinating, spitting, or going out in the dark. The magical, supernatural powers prove to be surprisingly ego boosting. The colonist's powers are infinitely shrunk, stamped by foreignness. There is no real reason to fight them because what really matters is that the mythical structures contain far more terrifying adversaries. It is evident that everything is reduced to a permanent confrontation at the level of phantasy.

In the liberation struggle, however, this people who were once relegated to the realm of the imagination, victims of unspeakable terrors, but content to lose themselves in hallucinatory dreams, are thrown into disarray, re-form, and amid blood and tears give birth to very real and urgent issues. Giving food to the mujahideen, stationing lookouts, helping deprived families and taking over from the slain or imprisoned husband—such are the practical tasks the people are asked to undertake in the liberation struggle.

In the colonial world, the colonized's affectivity is kept on edge like a running sore flinching from a caustic agent. And the psyche retracts, is obliterated, and finds an outlet through muscular spasms that have caused many an expert to classify the colonized as hysterical. This overexcited affectivity, spied on by invisible guardians who constantly communicate with the core of the personality, takes an erotic delight in the muscular deflation of the crisis.

Another aspect of the colonized's affectivity can be seen when it is drained of energy by the ecstasy of dance. Any study of the colonial world therefore must include an understanding of the phenomena of dance and possession. The colonized's way of relaxing is precisely this muscular orgy during which the most brutal aggressiveness and impulsive violence are channeled, transformed, and spirited away. The dance circle is a permissive circle. It protects and empowers. At a fixed time and a fixed date men and women assemble in a given place, and under the solemn gaze of the tribe launch themselves into a seemingly disarticulated, but in fact extremely ritualized, pantomime where the exorcism, liberation, and expression of a community are grandiosely and spontaneously played out through shaking of the head, and back and forward thrusts of the body. Everything is permitted in the dance circle. The hillock, which has been climbed as if to get closer to the moon, the river bank, which has been descended whenever the dance symbolizes ablution, washing, and purification, are sacred places. Everything is permitted, for in fact the sole purpose of the gathering is to let the supercharged libido and the stifled aggressiveness spew out volcanically. Symbolic killings, figurative cavalcades, and imagined multiple murders, everything has to come out. The ill humors seep out, tumultuous as lava flows.

One step further and we find ourselves in deep possession. In actual fact, these are organized seances of possession and dispossession: vampirism, possession by djinns, by zombies, and by Legba, the illustrious god of voodoo. Such a disintegration, dissolution or splitting of the personality, plays a key regulating role in ensuring the stability of the colonized world. On the way there these men and women were stamping impatiently, their nerves "on edge." On the way back, the village returns to serenity, peace, and stillness.

During the struggle for liberation there is a singular loss of interest in these rituals. With his back to the wall, the knife at his throat, or to be more exact the electrode on his genitals, the colonized subject is bound to stop telling stories.

After years of unreality, after wallowing in the most extraordinary phantasms, the colonized subject, machine gun at the ready, finally confronts the only force which challenges his very being: colonialism. And the young colonized subject who grows up in an atmosphere of fire and brimstone has no scruples mocking zombie ancestors, two-headed horses, corpses woken from the dead, and djinns who, taking advantage of a yawn, slip inside the body. The colonized subject discovers reality and transforms it through his praxis, his deployment of violence and his agenda for liberation.

We have seen that this violence throughout the colonial period, although constantly on edge, runs on empty. We have seen it channeled through the emotional release of dance or possession. We have seen it exhaust itself in fratricidal struggles. The challenge now is to seize this violence as it realigns itself. Whereas it once reveled in myths and contrived ways to commit collective suicide, a fresh set of circumstances will now enable it to change directions.

From the point of view of political tactics and History, the liberation of the colonies poses a theoretical problem of crucial importance at the current time: When can it be said that the situation is ripe for a national liberation movement? What should be the first line of action? Because decolonization comes in many shapes, reason wavers and abstains from declaring what is a true decolonization and what is not. We shall see that for the politically committed, urgent decisions are needed on means and tactics, i.e., direction and organization. Anything else is but blind voluntarism with the terribly reactionary risks this implies.

What are the forces in the colonial period which offer new channels, new agents of empowerment for the violence of the colonized? First and foremost, the political parties and the intellectual and business elite. However, what is characteristic of certain political groups is that they are strong on principles but abstain from issuing marching orders. During the colonial period the activities of these nationalist political parties are purely for electioneering purposes and amount to no more than a series of philosophic-political discourses on the subject of the rights of peoples to self-determination, the human rights of dignity and freedom from hunger, and the countless declarations of the principle "one man, one vote." The nationalist political parties never insist on the need for confrontation precisely because their aim is not the radical overthrow of the system. Pacifist and lawabiding, partisans, in fact, of order, the new order, these political groups bluntly ask of the colonialist bourgeoisie what to them is essential: "Give us more power." On the specific issue of violence, the elite are ambiguous. They are violent in their words and reformist in their attitudes. While the bourgeois nationalist political leaders say one thing, they make it quite clear it is not what they are really thinking.

This characteristic of the nationalist political parties must be attributed to the nature of their leaders and their supporters. The supporters of the nationalist parties are urban voters. These workers, elementary school teachers, small tradesmen, and shopkeepers who have begun to profit from the colonial situation—in a pitiful sort of way of course—have their own interests in mind. What these supporters are demanding is a better life and improved wages. The dialogue between these political parties and colonialism has continued uninterrupted. Discussions focus on improvements, electoral representation, freedom of the press, and freedom of association. Reforms are discussed. It should come as no surprise therefore that a good many colonial subjects are active members in branches of metropolitan political parties. These colonial subjects are militant activists under the abstract slogan: "Power to the proletariat," forgetting that in their part of the world slogans of national liberation should come first. The colonized intellectual has invested his aggression in his barely veiled wish to be assimilated to the colonizer's world. He has placed his aggression at the service of his own interests, his interests as an individual. The result is the ready emergence of a kind of class of individually liberated slaves, of freed slaves. The intellectual calls for ways of freeing more and more slaves and ways of organizing a genuine class of the emancipated. The masses, however, have no intention of looking on as the chances of individual success improve. What they demand is not the status of the colonist, but his place. In their immense majority the colonized want the colonist's farm. There is no question for them of competing with the colonist. They want to take his place.

The peasantry is systematically left out of most of the nationalist parties' propaganda. But it is obvious that in colonial countries only the peasantry is revolutionary. It has nothing to lose and everything to gain. The underprivileged and starving peasant is the exploited who very soon discovers that only violence pays. For him there is no compromise, no possibility of concession. Colonization or decolonization: it is simply a power struggle. The exploited realize that their liberation implies using every means available, and force is the first. When Monsieur Guy Mollet capitulated to the French settlers in Algeria in 1956, the Front de la Libération Nationale (FLN) in a famous tract stated that colonialism only loosens its hold when the knife is at its throat. No Algerian really thought these terms too violent. The tract merely expressed what every Algerian felt deep down: colonialism is not a machine capable of thinking, a body endowed with reason. It is naked violence and only gives in when confronted with greater violence.

At the critical, deciding moment the colonialist bourgeoisie, which had remained silent up till then, enters the fray. They introduce a new notion, in actual fact a creation of the colonial situation: nonviolence. In its raw state this nonviolence conveys to the colonized intellectual and business elite that their interests are identical to those of the colonialist bourgeoisie and it is therefore indispensable, a matter of urgency, to reach an agreement for the common good. Nonviolence is an attempt to settle the colonial problem around the negotiating table before the irreparable is done, before any bloodshed or regrettable act is committed. But if the masses, without waiting for the chairs to be placed around the negotiating table, take matters into their own hands and start burning and killing, it is not long before we see the "elite" and the leaders of the bourgeois nationalist parties turn to the colonial authorities and tell them: "This is terribly serious! Goodness knows how it will all end. We must find an answer, we must find a compromise."

This notion of compromise is very important in the case of decolonization, for it is far from being a simple matter. Compromise, in fact, involves both the colonial system and the burgeoning national bourgeoisie. The adherents of the colonial system discover that the masses might very well destroy everything. The sabotage of bridges, the destruction of farms, repression and war can severely disrupt the economy. Compromise is also on the agenda for the national bourgeoisie who, unable to foresee the possible consequences of such a whirlwind, fear in fact they will be swept away, and hasten to reassure the colonists: "We are still capable of stopping the slaughter, the masses still trust us, act quickly if you do not want to jeopardize everything." If events go one step further, the leader of the nationalist party distances himself from the violence. He loudly claims he has nothing to do with these Mau-Mau, with these terrorists, these butchers. In the best of cases, he barricades himself in a *no-man's-land* between the terrorists and the colonists and offers his services as "mediator"; which means that since the colonists cannot negotiate with the Mau-Mau, he himself is prepared to begin negotiations. Thus the rear guard of the national struggle, that section of the people who have always been on the other side, now find themselves catapulted to the forefront of negotiations and compromise—precisely because they have always been careful not to break ties with colonialism.

Before holding negotiations, most of the nationalist parties are content in the best of cases to explain and excuse this "savagery." They distance themselves from the people's struggle and can often be heard in private condemning those spectacular acts that have been decreed heinous by the metropolitan press and public opinion. Their preoccupation with objectivity constitutes the legitimate excuse for their failure to act. But this classic attitude of the colonized intellectual and the leaders of the nationalist parties is by no means objective. In fact they are not sure that this reckless violence is the most effective way of defending their own interests. Another thing is that they are convinced violent methods are ineffective. For them, there can be no doubt, any attempt to smash colonial oppression by force is an act of despair, a suicidal act. Because the colonizer's tanks and fighter planes are constantly on their minds. When they are told *we must act*, they imagine bombs being dropped, armored cars rumbling through the streets, a hail of bullets, the police—and they stay put. They are losers from the start. Their incapacity to triumph by violence needs no demonstration; they prove it in their daily life and their maneuvering. They have remained in the puerile position which Engels adopted in his famous argument with that mountain of puerility, Monsieur Dühring:

"Just as Crusoe could procure a sword for himself, we are equally entitled to assume that one fine morning Friday might appear with a loaded revolver in his hand, and then the whole 'force' relationship is inverted. Friday commands and it is Crusoe who has to drudge . . . So, then, the revolver triumphs over the sword; and this will probably make even the most childish axiomatician comprehend that force is no mere act of the will, but requires very real preliminary conditions before it can come into operation, that is to say, instruments, the more perfect of which vanquish the less perfect; moreover, that these instruments have to be produced, which also implies that the producer of more perfect instruments of force, *vulgo* arms, vanquishes the producer of the less perfect instrument, and that, in a word, the triumph of force is based on the production of arms, and this in turn on production in general—therefore on 'economic power', on the 'economic order', on the material means which force has at its disposal."[3]

---

[3] Friedrich Engels, *Anti-Dühring*. trans. Emile Burns (New York International Publishers), pt. 2, chap. III (*The Force Theory*), 184.

In fact the reformist leaders say the same thing: "What do you expect to fight the colonists with? With your knives? With your shotguns?"

Yes, instruments are important in the field of violence since in the end everything is based on the allocation of these instruments of force. But in this respect it so happens that the liberation of colonial territories sheds new light on the matter. For example during the Peninsular War, which was an authentic colonial war, Napoleon was forced to retreat, despite having mustered the massive figure of 400,000 men during the 1810 spring offensive. Yet the French army's instruments of war, the bravery of its soldiers, and the military genius of its leaders made the whole of Europe tremble. Confronted with the enormous resources of the Napoleonic army, the Spanish, buoyed by an unshakeable national fervor, discovered guerrilla warfare, which twenty-five years earlier the American militia had tested on the British troops. But guerrilla warfare, that instrument of violence of the colonized, would amount to nothing if it did not count as a new factor in the global competition between cartels and monopolies.

At the start of colonization, a single military column could occupy a vast amount of territory—from the Congo and Nigeria to the Ivory Coast, etc. But today the national struggle of the colonized is part and parcel of an entirely new situation. Capitalism, in its expansionist phase, regarded the colonies as a source of raw materials which once processed could be unloaded on the European market. After a phase of capital accumulation, capitalism has now modified its notion of profitability. The colonies have become a market. The colonial population is a consumer market. Consequently, if the colony has to be constantly garrisoned, if trade slumps, in other words if manufactured and industrial goods can no longer be exported, this is proof that the military solution must be ruled out. A blind domination on the model of slavery is not economically profitable for the metropolis.

The monopolistic fraction of the metropolitan bourgeoisie will not support a government whose policy is based solely on the power of arms. What the metropolitan financiers and industrialists expect is not the devastation of the colonial population but the protection of their "legitimate interests" using economic agreements.

Capitalism therefore objectively colludes with the forces of violence that erupt in colonial territories. Moreover, the colonized subject is not alone in the face of the oppressor. There is, of course, the political and diplomatic aid of the progressive countries and their peoples. But above all there is the competition and the pitiless war waged by the financial groups. The Conference of Berlin was able to carve up a mutilated Africa among three or four European flags. Currently, the issue is not whether an African region is under French or Belgian sovereignty but whether the economic zones are safeguarded. Artillery shelling and scorched earth policy have been replaced by an economic dependency. The crackdown against a rebel sultan is a thing of the past. Matters have become more subtle, less bloody; plans are quietly made to eliminate the Castro regime. Guinea is held in a stranglehold, Mossadegh is liquidated. The national leader who is afraid of violence is very much mistaken if he thinks colonialism will "slaughter us all." The military, of course, continue to play tin soldiers dating back to the conquest, but the financial interests soon bring them back to earth.

The moderate nationalist political parties are therefore requested to clearly articulate their claims and to calmly and dispassionately seek a solution with the colonialist partner respecting the interests of both sides. When this nationalist reformist movement, often a caricature of trade unionism, decides to act, it does so using extremely peaceful methods: organizing work stoppages in the few factories located in the towns, mass demonstrations to cheer a leader, and a boycott of the buses or imported commodities. All these methods not only put pressure on the colonial authorities but also allow the people to let off steam. This hibernation therapy, this hypnotherapy of the people, sometimes succeeds. From the negotiating table emerges then the political agenda that authorizes Monsieur M'ba, president of the Republic of Gabon, to very solemnly declare on his arrival for an official visit to Paris: "Gabon is an independent country, but nothing has changed between Gabon and France, the status quo continues." In fact the only change is that Monsieur M'ba is president of the Republic of Gabon, and he is the guest of the president of the French Republic.

The colonialist bourgeoisie is aided and abetted in the pacification of the colonized by the inescapable powers of religion. All the saints who turned the other cheek, who forgave those who trespassed against them, who, without flinching, were spat upon and insulted, are championed and shown as an example. The elite of the colonized countries, those emancipated slaves, once they are at the head of the movement, inevitably end up producing an ersatz struggle. They use the term *slavery of their brothers* to shame the slave drivers or to provide their oppressors' financial competitors with an ideology of insipid humanitarianism. Never in fact do they actually appeal to the slaves, never do they actually mobilize them. On the contrary, at the moment of truth—for them, the lie—they brandish the threat of *mass mobilization* as a decisive weapon that would as if by magic put "an end to the colonial regime." There are revolutionaries obviously within these political parties, among the cadres, who deliberately turn their backs on the farce of national independence. But their speeches, their initiatives, and their angry outbursts very soon antagonize the party machine. These factions are gradually isolated, then removed altogether. At the same time, as if there were a dialectical concomitance, the colonial police swoops down upon them. Hounded in the towns, shunned by the militants, rejected by the party leaders, these undesirables with their inflammatory attitude end up in the countryside. It is then they realize in a kind of intoxication that the peasant masses latch on to their every word and do not hesitate to ask them the question for which they are not prepared: "When do we start?"

This encounter between the revolutionaries from the towns and the peasant population will be dealt with later on. For the time being our attention should focus on the political parties in order to demonstrate the nevertheless progressive nature of their action. In their speeches, the political leaders "name" the nation. The demands of the colonized are thus formulated. But there is no substance, there is no political and social agenda. There is a vague form of national framework, what might be termed a minimal demand. The politicians who make the speeches, who write in the nationalist press, raise the people's hopes. They avoid subversion but in fact stir up subversive feelings in the consciousness of their listeners or readers. Often the national or ethnic language is used. Here again, expectations are raised and the imagination is allowed to roam outside the colonial order. Sometimes even these politicians declare: "We blacks, we Arabs," and these terms charged with ambivalence during the colonial period take on a sacred connotation. These nationalist politicians are playing with fire. As an African leader recently told a group of young intellectuals: "Think before speaking to the masses, they are easily excitable." There is therefore a cunning of history which plays havoc with the colonies.

When the political leader summons the people to a meeting, there could be said to be blood in the air. Yet very often the leader is mainly preoccupied with a "show" of force—so as not to use it. The excitement that is fostered, however—the comings and goings, the speech making, the crowds, the police presence, the military might, the arrests and the deportation of leaders—all this agitation gives the people the impression the time has come for them to do something. During these times of unrest the political parties multiply the calls for calm to the left, while to the right they search the horizon endeavoring to decipher the liberal intentions of the colonial authorities.

In order to maintain their stamina and their revolutionary capabilities, the people also resort to retelling certain episodes in the life of the community. The outlaw, for example, who holds the countryside for days against the police, hot on his trail, or who succumbs after killing four or five police officers in single-handed combat or who commits suicide rather than "give up" his accomplices, all constitute for the people role models, action schemas, and "heroes." And there is no point, obviously, in saying that such a hero is a thief, a thug, or a degenerate. If the act for which this man is prosecuted by the colonial authorities is an act exclusively directed against a colonial individual or colonial asset, then the demarcation line is clear and manifest. The process of identification is automatic.

In this maturation process we should also underscore the historical role of national resistance to the colonial conquest. The major figures in the history of the colonized are always those who led the national resistance against foreign invasion. Behanzin, Sundiata, Samory, and Abdel Kader are revived with particular fervor during the period preceding the actual struggle. This is proof that the people are preparing to march again, to break the lull introduced by colonialism and make History.

The emergence of the new nation and the demolition of the colonial system are the result of either a violent struggle by the newly independent people or outside violence by other colonized peoples, which has an inhibiting effect on the colonial regime.

Colonized peoples are not alone. Despite the efforts of colonialism, their frontiers remain permeable to news and rumors. They discover that violence is atmospheric, it breaks out sporadically, and here and there sweeps away the colonial regime. The success of this violence plays not only an informative role but also an operative one. The great victory of the Vietnamese people at Dien Bien Phu is no longer strictly speaking a Vietnamese victory. From July 1954 onward the colonial peoples have been asking themselves: "What must we do to achieve a Dien Bien Phu? How should we go about it?" A Dien Bien Phu was now within reach of every colonized subject. The problem was mustering forces, organizing them and setting a date for action. This pervading atmosphere of violence affects not just the colonized but also the colonizers who realize the number of latent Dien Bien Phu's. The colonial governments are therefore gripped in a genuine wholesale panic. Their plan is to make the first move, to turn the liberation movement to the right and disarm the people: Quick, let's decolonize. Let's decolonize the Congo before it turns into another Algeria. Let's vote a blueprint for Africa, let's create the Communauté for Africa, let's modernize it but for God's sake let's decolonize, let's decolonize. They decolonize at such a pace that they force independence on Houphouët-Boigny. In answer to the strategy of a Dien Bien Phu defined by the colonized, the colonizer replies with the strategy of containment—respecting the sovereignty of nations.

But let us return to this atmospheric violence, this violence rippling under the skin. We have seen as it develops how a number of driving mechanisms pick it up and convey it to an outlet. In spite of the metamorphosis imposed on it by the colonial regime in tribal or regional conflicts, violence continues to progress, the colonized subject identifies his enemy, puts a name to all of his misfortunes, and casts all his exacerbated hatred and rage in this new direction. But how do we get from the atmosphere of violence to setting violence in motion? What blows the lid? First of all there is the fact that such a development has a certain impact on the colonist's state of bliss. The colonist who "knows" the colonial subject realizes from several pointers that something is in the process of changing. The good "natives" become scarce, silence falls when the oppressor approaches. Sometimes looks harden and attitudes and remarks are downright hostile. The nationalist parties become restless, call for more meetings, and, at the same time, security is increased and troop reinforcements are dispatched. The colonists, especially those isolated on their farms, are the first to become alarmed. They demand drastic measures.

The authorities do in fact take dramatic measures; they arrest one or two leaders, organize military parades, maneuvers and fly-overs. These demonstrations of military power, these saber-rattling exercises, this smell of gunpowder which now fills the atmosphere do not intimidate the people. These bayonets and heavy gunfire strengthen their aggressiveness. A dramatic atmosphere sets in where everyone wants to prove he is ready for anything. It is under these circumstances that the gun goes off on its own for nerves are on edge, fear has set in, and everyone is trigger-happy. A trivial incident and the machine-gunning begins: you have a Sétif in Algeria, the Central Quarries in Morocco, and Moramanga in Madagascar.

Far from breaking the momentum, repression intensifies the progress made by the national consciousness. From the moment national consciousness reaches an embryonic stage of development, it is reinforced by the bloodbath in the colonies which signifies that between oppressors and oppressed, force is the only solution. We should point out here that it is not the political parties who called for the armed insurrection or organized it. All these perpetrations of repression, all these acts committed out of fear, are not what the leaders wanted. These events catch them off guard. It is then that the colonial authorities may decide to arrest the nationalist leaders. But nowadays the governments of colonialist countries know perfectly well that it is highly danger-ous to deprive the masses of their leader. For it is then that the people hurl themselves headlong into jacqueries, mutinies and "bestial murders." The masses give free rein to their "bloodthirsty instincts" and demand the liberation of their leaders whose dif-ficult job it will be to restore law and order. The colonized who spontaneously invested their violence in the colossal task of destroying the colonial system soon find themselves chanting the passive, sterile slogan: "Free X or Y!"[4] The colonial authorities then free these men and start negotiating. The time for dancing in the streets has arrived.

In other cases, the political party apparatus may remain intact. But in the interplay of colonial repression and the spontaneous reaction by the people, the parties find themselves outmaneuvered by their militants. The violence of the masses is pitted against the occupier's military forces; the situation deteriorates and festers. The leaders still at liberty are left on the sidelines. Suddenly rendered helpless with their bureaucracy and their reason-based agenda, they can be seen attempting the supreme imposture of a rearguard action by "speaking in the name of the muzzled nation." As a general rule, the colonial authorities jump at this piece of good fortune, transform these useless characters into spokesmen, and, in next to no time, grant them independence, leaving it up to them to restore law and order.

Everybody therefore has violence on their minds and the question is not so much responding to violence with more violence but rather how to defuse the crisis.

What in fact constitutes this violence? As we have seen, the colonized masses intuitively believe that their liberation must be achieved and can only be achieved by force. What aberration of the mind drives these famished, enfeebled men lacking technology and organizational resources to think that only violence can liberate them faced with the occupier's military and economic might? How can they hope to triumph?

Since what is scandalous is that violence can be used as a party slogan and the people urged to rise up in an armed struggle. This issue of violence needs to be given careful consideration. When

---

[4] The arrested leader might very well be the authentic mouthpiece of the colonized masses. In this case, the colonial authorities will take advantage of his detention to try and establish new leaders.

German militarism decides to resolve its border problems by force, it is no surprise, but when the Angolan people, for instance, decide to take up arms, when the Algerians reject any method which does not include violence, this is proof that something has happened or is in the process of happening. The colonized peoples, these slaves of modern times, have run out of patience. They know that such madness alone can deliver them from colonial oppression. A new type of relationship is established in the world. The peoples of the Third World are in the process of shattering their chains, and what is extraordinary is that they succeed. In this age of the Sputnik we might think it ridiculous to die of hunger, but for the colonized masses the explanation is more down to earth. The truth is that no colonialist country today is capable of mounting the only form of repression which would have a chance of succeeding, i.e., a prolonged and large scale military occupation.

At home, the colonialist countries are faced with contestation and workers' demands that require the deployment of their security forces. Moreover, in the current international situation these countries need their troops to protect their own regime. Finally, the myth of the liberation movements masterminded by Moscow is all too familiar. For this panic-stricken reasoning read: "If this continues, the Communists will very likely take advantage of the unrest in order to infiltrate these regions."

In his impatience, the fact that the colonized subject brandishes the threat of violence proves that he is aware of the exceptional nature of the current situation and that he intends to make the most of it. But also on a more immediate personal level, as he sees the modern world penetrate the remotest corners of the interior, he becomes acutely aware of everything he does not possess. The masses, by a kind of (infantile) reasoning, are convinced they have been robbed. In certain developing countries, therefore, they are quick to catch on and realize two or three years after independence their hopes have been dashed: "What was the point of fighting" if nothing was really destined to change? In 1789, after the bourgeois French Revolution, the humblest French peasant gained substantially from the upheaval. But it is common knowledge that for 95 percent of the population in developing countries, independence has not brought any immediate change. Any observer with a keen eye is aware of a kind of latent discontent which like glowing embers constantly threatens to flare up again.

So they say the colonized want to move too fast. Let us never forget that it wasn't such a long time ago the colonized were accused of being too slow, lazy, and fatalistic. Obviously the violence channeled into the liberation struggle does not vanish as if by magic after hoisting the national colors. It has even less reason to disappear since nation building continues to operate within the framework of critical competition between capitalism and socialism.

This competition gives a quasi-universal dimension to the most local of disputes. Every meeting, every act of repression reverberates around the international arena. The Sharpeville massacre shook public opinion for months. In the press, over the airwaves and in private conversations, Sharpeville has become a symbol. It is through Sharpeville that men and women addressed the problem of apartheid in South Africa. And there is no reason to believe that demagoguery alone explains the sudden interest by the major powers in the petty affairs of the underdeveloped regions. Every peasant revolt, every insurrection in the Third World fits into the framework of the cold war. Two men are beaten up in Salisbury and an entire bloc goes into action, focuses on these two men and uses this beating to raise the issue of Rhodesia* — linking it to the rest of Africa and every colonized subject. But the full-scale campaign under way leads the other bloc to gauge the flaws in its sphere of influence. The colonized peoples realize

---

*Translator's Note: Present-day Zimbabwe

that neither faction is interested in disengaging itself from regional conflicts. They no longer limit their horizons to one particular region since they are swept along in this atmosphere of universal convulsion.

When every three months we learn that the sixth or seventh U.S. Fleet is heading toward some coast or other, when Khrushchev threatens to come to Castro's aid with the help of missiles, when Kennedy envisages drastic solutions for Laos, the colonized or newly independent peoples get the impression they are being forced, whether they like it or not, into a frantic march. In fact they are already marching. Let us take, for example, the case of governments of recently liberated countries. The men in power spend two thirds of their time keeping watch over their borders, averting any threat of danger, and the other third working for the country. At the same time they are looking for support. Governed by the same dialectic, the national opposition gives parliamentary channels the cold shoulder. It seeks allies who agree to support them in their ruthless endeavor at sedition. The atmosphere of violence, after having penetrated the colonial phase, continues to dominate national politics. As we have said, the Third World is not excluded. On the contrary, it is at the very center of the convulsion. This is why in their speeches the statesmen of underdeveloped countries maintain indefinitely a tone of aggressiveness and exasperation which normally should have disappeared. The often-reported impoliteness of the new leaders is understandable. What is less noticeable is the extreme courtesy these same leaders show toward their brothers and comrades. Their impolite behavior is first and foremost directed against the others, against the former colonialists who come to observe and investigate. The excolonized too often get the impression that the findings of these investigations are a foregone conclusion. The journalist is on assignment to justify them. The photos that illustrate the article provide proof that he knows what he is talking about and was actually there. The investigation sets out to prove that "everything went wrong as soon as we left." The journalists often complain they are badly treated, are forced to work under poor conditions, and come up against a wall of indifference or hostility. All this is quite normal. The nationalist leaders know that international opinion is forged solely by the Western press. When a Western journalist interviews us, however, it is seldom done to render us service. In the war in Algeria, for example, the most liberal-minded French reporters make constant use of ambiguous epithets to portray our struggle. When we reproach them for it, they reply in all sincerity they are being objective. For the colonized subject, objectivity is always directed against him. Understandable, too, is that new tone of voice which dominated international diplomacy at the United Nations General Assembly in September 1960. The representatives of the colonial countries were aggressive and violent in the extreme, but their populations found nothing exaggerated. The radicalism of the African spokespersons brought the abscess to a head and shone the spotlight on the unacceptable nature of the veto, on the collusion between the major powers, and above all on the insignificant role allotted to the Third World.

Diplomacy as initiated by the newly independent peoples is no longer a matter of nuances, innuendoes, and hypnotic passes. Their spokesmen have been assigned by their population to defend both the unity of the nation, the welfare of the masses as well as the right to freedom and self-sufficiency.

It is therefore a diplomacy in motion, in rage, which contrasts strangely with the petrified, motionless world of colonization. And when Mr. Khrushchev brandishes his shoe at the United Nations and hammers the table with it, no colonized individual, no representative of the underdeveloped countries laughs. For what Mr. Khrushchev is showing the colonized countries who are watching, is that he, the missile-wielding muzhik, is treating these wretched capitalists the way they deserve. Likewise Castro attending the UN in military uniform does not scandalize the underdeveloped countries. What Castro is demonstrating is how aware he is of the continuing regime of violence. What is surprising is that he did not enter the UN with his submachine gun; but perhaps they wouldn't have allowed that. The revolts, the acts of desperation, the factions armed with machetes or axes find their national identity in the unrelenting struggle that pits capitalism against socialism.

In 1945 the 45,000 dead at Sétif could go unnoticed; in 1947 the 90,000 dead in Madagascar were written off in a few lines in the press; in 1952 the 200,000 victims of repression in Kenya were met with relative indifference—because the international contradictions were not sufficiently clear-cut. The Korean War and the war in Indochina had already established a new phase. But it was above all Budapest and Suez which constituted the deciding moments of this confrontation.

Heartened by the unconditional support of the socialist countries the colonized hurl themselves with whatever weapons they possess against the impregnable citadel of colonialism. Although the citadel is invincible against knives and bare hands, its invincibility crumbles when we take into account the context of the cold war.

In this new context, the Americans take their role as the barons of international capitalism very seriously. At first, they advise the European countries to decolonize on gentleman's terms. In a second phase they have no hesitation first proclaiming their respect then their support for the principle: *Africa for the Africans*. Today the U.S. has no qualms officially declaring they are the defenders of the right of peoples to self-determination. The latest voyage by Mr. Mennen-Williams illustrates all too well the American consciousness that the Third World must not be sacrificed. Understandably, violence is a desperate act only if it is compared *in abstracto* to the military machine of the oppressors. On the other hand, violence in the context of international relations, we realize, represents a formidable threat to the oppressor. Persistent jacqueries and Mau-Mau agitation disrupt the economic life of a colony but pose no threat to the metropolis. A greater threat, as far as imperialism is concerned, is that socialist propaganda might infiltrate the masses and contaminate them. It is already a serious risk during the conflict's cold period; but what would happen to the colony rotted by bloody guerrilla warfare in the event of a real war?

Capitalism then realizes that its military strategy has everything to lose if national conflicts were to break out. In the framework of peaceful coexistence, therefore, every colony is destined to disappear and, taking it to the extreme, neutrality will command capitalism's respect. What must be avoided at all costs are strategic risks, the espousal by the masses of an enemy doctrine and radical hatred by tens of millions of men. The colonized peoples are perfectly aware of these imperatives which dominate international politics. This is why even those who rage against violence always plan and act on the basis of this global violence. Today the peaceful coexistence between the two blocs maintains and aggravates the violence in colonial countries. Perhaps tomorrow we shall see a shift in the violence once the colonial territories have been fully liberated. Perhaps we shall see the issue of minorities raised. Already some of them have no qualms advocating violent methods in response to their problems and it is no coincidence that, so we have learned, black radicals in the U.S. have formed armed militia groups. It is no coincidence either that in the so-called free world there are defense committees for Jewish minorities in the USSR and that General de Gaulle in one of his speeches shed a few tears for the millions of Muslims oppressed by the communist dictatorship. Imperialism and capitalism are convinced that the fight against racism and national liberation movements are purely and simply controlled and masterminded from "the outside." So they decide to deploy practical tactics such as the creation of Radio Free Europe and committees for the defense of oppressed minorities. They practice anticolonialism in the same way the French colonels in Algeria engaged in counter-terrorism with the SAS (Sections Administratives Speciales) or psychological warfare. They "used the people against the people." We know where that got them. This threatening atmosphere of violence and missiles in no way frightens or disorients the colonized. We have seen that their entire recent history has prepared them to "understand" the situation. Between colonial violence and the insidious violence in which the modern world is steeped, there is a kind of complicit correlation, a homogeneity. The colonized have adapted to this atmosphere. For once they are in tune with their time. People are sometimes surprised that, instead of buying a dress for their wife, the colonized buy a transistor radio. They shouldn't be. The colonized are convinced their fate is in the balance. They live in a doomsday atmosphere and nothing must elude them. This is why they fully understand Phouma and Phoumi, Lumumba and Tschombe, Ahidjo and Moumié, Kenyatta and those introduced from time to time to replace him. They fully understand all these men because they are able to unmask the forces behind them. The colonized, underdeveloped man is today a political creature in the most global sense of the term.

Independence has certainly brought the colonized peoples moral reparation and recognized their dignity. But they have not yet had time to elaborate a society or build and ascertain values. The glowing focal point where the citizen and individual develop and mature in a growing number of areas does not yet exist. Situated in a kind of indeterminate state they have fairly quickly convinced themselves that everything is decided elsewhere for everyone at the same time. As for the leaders, when confronted with such a situation, they hesitate and choose a policy of neutrality.

There is much to be said on the subject of neutrality. Some liken it to a kind of loathsome mercantilism which consists of taking handouts left and right. But although neutrality, a creation of the cold war, allows underdeveloped countries to receive economic aid from both sides, it does not permit either of these two sides to come to the aid of underdeveloped regions the way they should. Those literally astronomical sums invested in arms research, these engineers transformed into technicians of nuclear war could raise the living standards of the underdeveloped countries by 60 percent in fifteen years. It is therefore obvious that the underdeveloped countries have no real interest in either prolonging or intensifying this cold war. But they are never asked for their opinion. So whenever they can, they disengage. But can they really do so? For example, here is France testing its atomic bombs in Africa. Even allowing for the resolutions, the meetings and slammings of the door on diplomatic relations, it cannot be said that the African peoples had much impact on France's attitude in this particular sector.

Neutrality produces in the citizen of the Third World an attitude of mind which translates in everyday life to a brazenness and hieratic pride strangely resembling an act of defiance. This staunch refusal to compromise, this sheer determination to go it alone recall the behavior of those deprived, self-centered teenagers who are always prepared to fight to the last over a mere word. All of this disconcerts Western observers. For there is, strictly speaking, a scandalous discrepancy between what these men claim to be and what in fact they have to back them up. These countries without urban transportation, without troops, and without money cannot justify flaunting such bravado. It is without doubt an imposture. The Third World often gives the impression it revels in sensationalism and it needs its weekly dose of crises. These leaders of empty countries who talk too loud are exasperating. You'd like to shut them up. But instead they are wooed. They are given bouquets of flowers. Invitations. To be frank, everyone wants a piece of them. And that is what we call neutrality. For a population 98 percent illiterate, there is, however, an enormous amount of literature written about them. They are constantly on the move. The leaders and students of the underdeveloped countries are a gold mine for the airlines. Asian and African officials can attend a seminar on socialist planning in Moscow one week and then another on free trade in London or at Columbia University the next. As for African labor union members, they are making enormous progress. No sooner are they appointed to positions of leadership than they decide to group themselves into autonomous units. They do not have the fifty years' experience of labor unions in an industrialized country, but they already know that nonpolitical unionism is an absurdity. They have not had to deal with the bourgeois bulldozer, they have not developed a consciousness from the class struggle, but perhaps this is not required. Perhaps. We shall see that this totalizing determination which often becomes a caricature of internationalism is one of the most basic characteristics of underdeveloped countries.

But let us return to the single combat between the colonized and the colonist. It is clearly and plainly an armed struggle. Indochina, Indonesia, and, of course, North Africa are historical examples. But we should never lose sight of the fact that this struggle could have broken out anywhere, in Guinea as well as Somaliland, and even today it can break out anywhere where colonialism intends to stay, in Angola for instance. The existence of an armed struggle is indicative that the people are determined to put their faith only in violent methods. The very same people who had it constantly drummed into them that the only language they understood was that of force, now decide to express themselves with force. In fact the colonist has always shown them the path they should follow to liberation. The argument chosen by the colonized was conveyed to them by the colonist, and by an ironic twist of fate it is now the colonized who state that it is the colonizer who only understands the language of force. The colonial regime owes its legitimacy to force and at no time does it ever endeavor to cover up this nature of things. Every statue of Faidherbe or Lyautey, Bugeaud or Blandan, every one of these conquistadors ensconced on colonial soil, is a constant reminder of one and the same thing: "We are here by the force of the bayonet . . ." Everyone knows the rest of the quote. During the insurrectional stage every colonist reasons on the basis of simple arithmetic. Such a logic is no surprise to the other colonists, but it is important to point out that it is no surprise to the colonized either. And first and foremost, stating the principle "It's them or us" is not a paradox since colonialism, as we have seen, is precisely the organization of a Manichaean world, of a compartmentalized world. And when advocating an exact line of procedure the colonist asks every representative of the oppressor minority to take out 30 or 100 or 200 natives, he realizes there is no outcry of indignation and that at the most the issue boils down to whether it can be done in one step or in stages.[5]

This line of reasoning which envisages the surgical elimination of the colonized does not morally upset the colonized subject. He has always known that his dealings with the colonist would take place in a field of combat. So the colonized subject wastes no time lamenting and almost never searches for justice in the colonial context. In fact if the colonist's argument leaves the colonized subject unmoved it is because the latter poses the issue of his liberation in virtually identical terms: "Let us form groups of two or five hundred and let each group deal with a colonist." It is in this mutual frame of mind that both protagonists begin the struggle.

---

[5] It is obvious that this general clean-up destroys the thing one wants to save. This is exactly what Sartre indicates when he says: "*In short, by the very act of repeating them (i.e., racist ideas) one shows that it is impossible for everyone to unite simultaneously against the natives, that it is merely shifting recurrence, and that in any case such a unification could occur as an active grouping only so as to massacre the colonized people, which is the perpetual absurd temptation of the colonialists, and, which, if it were possible, would amount to the immediate destruction of colonization.*" Critique of Dialectical Reason. Translated by Alan Sheridan-Smith.

*   *   *

For the colonized, this violence represents the absolute praxis. The militant therefore is one who works. The questions which the organization asks the militant bear the mark of this vision of things: "Where have you worked? With whom? What have you accomplished?" The group requires each individual to have performed an irreversible act. In Algeria, for example, where almost all the men who called on the people to join the national struggle were sentenced to death or wanted by the French police, trust was proportional to the desperate nature of each case. A new militant could be trusted only when he could no longer return to the colonial system. Such a mechanism apparently existed in Kenya with the Mau-Mau, who required every member of the group to strike the victim. Everyone was therefore personally responsible for the death of the victim. To work means to work towards the death of the colonist. Claiming responsibility for the violence also allows those members of the group who have strayed or have been outlawed to come back, to retake their place and be reintegrated. Violence can thus be understood to be the perfect mediation. The colonized man liberates himself in and through violence. This praxis enlightens the militant because it shows him the means and the end. Césaire's poetry takes on a prophetic significance in this very prospect of violence. Let us recall one of the most decisive pages of his tragedy where the Rebel (what a coincidence!) proclaims:

REBEL (*toughly*)
My family name: offended; my given name: humiliated; my profession: rebel; my age: the stone age.
MOTHER
My race: the human race. My religion: brotherhood . . .
REBEL
My race: the fallen race. My religion . . .
but it is not you who will prepare it with your disarmament;
it is I with my revolt and my poor clenched fists and my bushy head.
(*Very calmly*)

I recall a November day; he was not six months old and the master came into the shack murky as an April moon, and he was probing the child's small muscled limbs, he was a very good master, he ran his fat fingers caressingly across his little dimpled face. His blue eyes were laughing and his mouth was teasing him with sugary things: this one will make a good one, the master said looking at me, and he was saying other friendly things, the master was, that you had to start very early, that twenty years were not too much to make a good Christian and a good slave, a good subject, utterly devoted, a good slavedriver for an overseer, with a sharp eye and a strong arm. And this man was speculating over my son's cradle, a slavedriver's cradle.

MOTHER

Alas you will die.

REBEL

Killed . . . I killed him with my own hands. . . .

Yes: a fecund and copious death. . . .

It was night. We crawled through the sugarcane.

The cutlasses were chortling at the stars, but we didn't care about the stars.

The cane slashed our faces with streams of green blades.

MOTHER

I had dreamed of a son who would close his mother's eyes.

REBEL

I chose to open my child's eyes to another sun.

MOTHER

. . . O my son . . . an evil and pernicious death.

REBEL

Mother, a verdant and sumptuous death.

MOTHER

From too much hate.

REBEL

From too much love.

MOTHER

Spare me, I'm choking from your shackles, bleeding from your wounds.

REBEL

And the world does not spare me. . . . There is not in the world one single poor lynched bastard, one poor tortured man, in whom I am not also murdered and humiliated.

MOTHER

God in Heaven, deliver him!

REBEL

My heart, you will not deliver me of my memories. . . .
It was a November night. . . .
And suddenly clamors lit up the silence,
we had leapt, we the slaves, we the manure, we beasts with patient hooves.
We were running like lunatics; fiery shots broke out. . . . We were striking. Sweat and blood cooled us off. We were striking amidst the screams and the screams became more strident and a great clamor rose toward the east, the outbuildings were burning and the flames sweetly splashed our cheeks.
Then came the attack on the master's house.
They were shooting from the windows.
We forced the doors.
The master's bedroom was wide open. The master's bedroom was brilliantly lit, and the master was there, very calm. . . . and all of us stopped . . . he was the master. . . . I entered. It's you, he said, very calmly. . . . It was me, it was indeed me, I told him, the good slave, the faithful slave, the slave slave, and suddenly my eyes were two cockroaches frightened on a rainy day. . . . I struck, the blood spurted: it is the only baptism that today I remember.[6]

It is understandable how in such an atmosphere everyday life becomes impossible. Being a fellow, a pimp, or an alcoholic is no longer an option. The violence of the colonial regime and the counterviolence of the colonized balance each other and respond to each other in an extraordinary reciprocal homogeneity. The greater the number of metropolitan settlers, the more terrible the violence will be. Violence among the colonized will spread in proportion to the violence exerted by the colonial

---

[6] Aimé Césaire, "And the dogs were silent" in *Lyric and Dramatic Poetry—1946–82*, trans. Clayton Eshleman and Annette Smith (Charlottesville: The University Press of Virginia, 1990).

regime. In the initial phase of this insurrectional period the metropolitan governments are slaves of the colonists. These colonists are a threat to both the colonized and their own governments. They will use the same methods indiscriminately. The assassination of the mayor of Evian can be likened to the assassination of Ali Boumendjel in its method and motivation. For the colonists the alternative is not between an Algerian Algeria and a French Algeria, but between an independent Algeria and a colonial Algeria. Anything else is hot air or an act of treason. The colonist's logic is unrelenting and one is only baffled by the counterlogic of the colonized's behavior if one has remained out of touch with the colonists' way of thinking. Once the colonized have opted for counterviolence, police reprisals automatically call for reprisals by the nationalist forces. The outcome, however, is profoundly unequal, for machine-gunning by planes or bombardments from naval vessels outweigh in horror and scope the response from the colonized. The most alienated of the colonized are once and for all demystified by this pendulum motion of terror and counterterror. They see for themselves that any number of speeches on human equality cannot mask the absurdity whereby seven Frenchmen killed or wounded in an ambush at the Sakamody pass sparks the indignation of civilized consciences, whereas the sacking of the Guergour *douars*, the Djerah *dechra*, and the massacre of the population behind the ambush count for nothing. Terror, counterterror, violence, counterviolence. This is what observers bitterly report when describing the circle of hatred which is so manifest and so tenacious in Algeria.

In the armed struggle there is what we could call the point of no return. It is almost always attributable to the sweeping repression which encompasses every sector of the colonized population. This point was reached in Algeria in 1955 with the 12,000 victims of Philippeville and in 1956 by Lacoste's creation of rural and urban militias.[7] It then becomes evident for everyone and even for the colonists that "things cannot go on as they are and

---

[7] In order to gauge the importance of this decision by the French government in Algeria we need to return to this period. In issue no. 4 of *Résistance Algérienne* dated March 28, 1957, we read:

"In response to the wishes of the United Nations General Assembly, the French government has recently decided to create urban militias. Enough bloodshed, said the UN. Let us form militias, replies Lacoste. Cease fire, advised the UN. Let us arm the civilians, screams Lacoste. The two parties involved are requested to make initial contacts in order to agree on a democratic and peaceful solution, the UN recommended. Lacoste decrees that henceforth every European shall be armed and should fire on anybody appearing suspect. The savage, iniquitous repression bordering on genocide must above all things be combated by the authorities, was then the general opinion. Lacoste retorts: Let us systematize the repression, let us organize a manhunt of Algerians. And symbolically he hands over civilian power to the military and military power to the civilians. The circle is sealed. In the middle, the Algerian, disarmed, starved, hounded, jostled, struck, lynched and soon to be shot because he is a suspect. Today in Algeria there is not a single Frenchman who is not authorized or welcome to make use of his arms. Not a single Frenchman in Algeria one month after the UN's appeal for calm who does not have permission or the obligation to unearth, fabricate and hunt down suspects.

One month after the UN General Assembly's resolution there is not a single European in Algeria who is not party to the most appalling act of extermination in modern times. Democratic solution? Okay, concedes Lacoste, let's start by eliminating the Algerians. In order to do so let's arm the civilians and let them do the job. The majority of the Parisian press cautiously reported the creation of these armed gangs. Fascist militia, they said. Yes. But at the level of the individual and human rights what is fascism but colonialism at the very heart of traditionally colonialist countries? Systematically authorized and condoned assassination they suggested. But for one hundred and thirty years hasn't Algerian flesh borne the marks of ever gaping, ever growing, ever deeper wounds? We should be careful, advises Monsieur Kenne-Vignes, parliamentary member for the M.R.P. party, not to widen the abyss between the two communities in Algeria by creating these militias. Yes. But isn't the colonial status the organized enslavement of an entire people? The Algerian Revolution is precisely the living challenge to this enslavement and this abyss. The Algerian Revolution addresses the occupying nation as follows: 'Remove your fangs from Algeria's bruised and wounded flesh! Let the Algerian people speak!'

The creation of these militias, they say, will alleviate the army. They will free units whose mission is to protect the borders with Tunisia and Morocco.

have to change." The colonized, however, do not keep accounts. They register the enormous gaps left in their ranks as a kind of necessary evil. Since they have decided to respond with violence, they admit the consequences. Their one demand is that they are not asked to keep accounts for others as well. To the expression: "All natives are the same," the colonized reply: "All colonists are the same."[8] When the colonized subject is tortured, when his

---

A six hundred thousand strong army. Almost the entire navy and airforce. A vast police network, operating expeditiously, with a staggering record since it recruited the ex-torturers of the Moroccan and Tunisian peoples. Territorial units one hundred thousand men strong. The job of the army must be alleviated. Let's create urban militias. So impressive is Lacoste's criminal and hysterical frenzy it convinces even clear-sighted Frenchmen. The truth is that the justification for creating such militias is contradictory in itself. The French army's job is infinite. From the moment its mission is to gag the mouths of the Algerians the door to the future is closed for ever. Above all there is a refusal to analyze, to understand and to gauge the depth and the density of the Algerian Revolution: every district, every section, every street, every housing block, every floor has its community leader. . . . Coverage on the ground is now backed up by coverage floor by floor.

In 48 hours two thousand candidates were enrolled. The Europeans of Algeria immediately responded to Lacoste's call for murder. From now on every European will have to make a list of the surviving Algerians in his sector. Gathering intelligence, 'rapid response' to terrorism, identifying suspects, elimination of runaways and police reinforcements. Yes the army must be alleviated of such jobs. Combing the ground is now backed up by combing floor by floor. Haphazard killings are now backed up by premeditated murder. Stop the bloodshed, urged the UN. The best way of doing so, retorts Lacoste, is to have no more blood to shed. After having been delivered up to Massu's hordes the Algerian people are now entrusted to the care of the urban militias. Lacoste's decision to create these militias clearly means hands off HIS war. It is proof there are no limits once the rot has set in. Of course now he is a prisoner, but what a delight to drag down everyone with him.

After every one of these decisions the Algerian people increase their muscular tension and intensify their struggle. After every one of these organized, requisitioned killings the Algerian people better structure their consciousness and strengthen their resistance. Yes. The tasks for the French army are infinite because the unity of the Algerian people is infinite, O so infinite!"

[8] This is the reason why at the outbreak of hostilities, no prisoners are taken. It is only through politicizing the *cadres* that the leaders manage to get the masses to accept (1) that the recruits dispatched from the *métropole* are not

wife is killed or raped, he complains to no one. The authorities of oppression can appoint as many commissions of inquiry and investigation as they like. In the eyes of the colonized, these commissions do not exist. And in fact, soon it will be seven years of crimes committed in Algeria and not a single Frenchman has been brought before a French court of justice for the murder of an Algerian. In Indochina, Madagascar, and the colonies, the "native" has always known he can expect nothing from the other side. The work of the colonist is to make even dreams of liberty impossible for the colonized. The work of the colonized is to imagine every possible method for annihilating the colonist. On the logical plane, the Manichaeanism of the colonist produces a Manichaeanism of the colonized. The theory of the "absolute evil of the colonist" is in response to the theory of the "absolute evil of the native."

The arrival of the colonist signified syncretically the death of indigenous society, cultural lethargy, and petrifaction of the individual. For the colonized, life can only materialize from the rotting cadaver of the colonist. Such then is the term-for-term correspondence between the two arguments.

But it so happens that for the colonized this violence is invested with positive, formative features because it constitutes their only work. This violent praxis is totalizing since each individual represents a violent link in the great chain, in the almighty body of violence rearing up in reaction to the primary violence of the colonizer. Factions recognize each other and the future nation is already indivisible. The armed struggle mobilizes the people, i.e., it pitches them in a single direction, from which there is no turning back.

---

always sent of their own free will and in some cases even are sickened by this war; (2) that it is in the current interest of the movement to wage a struggle abiding by certain international conventions; (3) that an army which takes prisoners is an army, and ceases to be considered a gang of outlaws; (4) in any case, the possession of prisoners constitutes a significant means of applying pressure for protecting our militants held by the enemy.

When it is achieved during a war of liberation the mobilization of the masses introduces the notion of common cause, national destiny, and collective history into every consciousness. Consequently, the second phase, i.e., nation building, is facilitated by the existence of this mortar kneaded with blood and rage. This then gives us a better understanding of the originality of the vocabulary used in underdeveloped countries. During the colonial period the people were called upon to fight against oppression. Following national liberation they are urged to fight against poverty, illiteracy, and underdevelopment. The struggle, they say, goes on. The people realize that life is an unending struggle.

The violence of the colonized, we have said, unifies the people. By its very structure colonialism is separatist and regionalist. Colonialism is not merely content to note the existence of tribes, it reinforces and differentiates them. The colonial system nurtures the chieftainships and revives the old *marabout* confraternities. Violence in its practice is totalizing and national. As a result, it harbors in its depths the elimination of regionalism and tribalism. The nationalist parties, therefore, show no pity at all toward the *kaids* and the traditional chiefs. The elimination of the *kaids* and the chiefs is a prerequisite to the unification of the people.

At the individual level, violence is a cleansing force. It rids the colonized of their inferiority complex, of their passive and despairing attitude. It emboldens them, and restores their self-confidence. Even if the armed struggle has been symbolic, and even if they have been demobilized by rapid decolonization, the people have time to realize that liberation was the achievement of each and every one and no special merit should go to the leader. Violence hoists the people up to the level of the leader. Hence their aggressive tendency to distrust the system of protocol that young governments are quick to establish. When they have used violence to achieve national liberation, the masses allow nobody to come forward as "liberator." They prove themselves to be jealous of their achievements and take care not to place their future, their destiny, and the fate of their homeland into the hands of a living god. Totally irresponsible yesterday, today they are bent on understanding everything and determining everything. Enlightened by violence, the people's consciousness rebels against any pacification. The demagogues, the opportunists and the magicians now have a difficult task. The praxis which pitched them into a desperate man-to-man struggle has given the masses a ravenous taste for the tangible. Any attempt at mystification in the long term becomes virtually impossible.

ON VIOLENCE IN THE INTERNATIONAL CONTEXT

We have many times indicated in the preceding pages that in underdeveloped countries the political leader is constantly calling on the people to fight. To fight against colonialism, to fight against poverty and underdevelopment, to fight against debilitating traditions. The vocabulary he uses is that of a chief of staff: "Mobilization of the masses," "the agricultural front," "the illiteracy front," "defeats suffered," "victories won." During its early years the young independent nation evolves in the atmosphere of a battleground. This is because the political leader of an underdeveloped country is terror-stricken at the prospect of the long road that lies ahead. He appeals to the people and tells them: "Let us roll up our sleeves and get to work." Gripped in a kind of creative frenzy the nation plunges into action of a hugely disproportionate nature. The agenda is not only to pull through but to catch up with the other nations as best one can. There is a widespread belief that the European nations have reached their present stage of development as a result of their labors. Let us prove therefore to the world and ourselves that we are capable of the same achievements. Posing the problem of development of underdeveloped countries in this way seems to us to be neither right nor reasonable.

The European nations achieved their national unity at a time when the national bourgeoisies had concentrated most of the wealth in their own hands. Shopkeepers and merchants, clerks and bankers monopolized finance, commerce, and science within the national framework. The bourgeoisie represented the most dynamic and prosperous class. Its rise to power enabled it to launch into operations of a crucial nature such as industrialization, the development of communications, and, eventually, the quest for overseas outlets.

In Europe, barring a few exceptions (England, for instance, had taken a slight lead), states achieving national unity were in roughly the same economic situation. Because of the nature of their development and progress, no nation really *insulted* the others.

Today, national independence and nation building in the underdeveloped regions take on an entirely new aspect. In these regions, except for some remarkable achievements, every country suffers from the same lack of infrastructure. The masses battle with the same poverty, wrestle with the same age-old gestures, and delineate what we could call the geography of hunger with their shrunken bellies. A world of underdevelopment, a world of poverty and inhumanity. But also a world without doctors, without engineers, without administrators. Facing this world, the European nations wallow in the most ostentatious opulence. This European opulence is literally a scandal for it was built on the backs of slaves, it fed on the blood of slaves, and owes its very existence to the soil and subsoil of the underdeveloped world. Europe's well-being and progress were built with the sweat and corpses of blacks, Arabs, Indians, and Asians. This we are determined never to forget. When a colonialist country, embarrassed by a colony's demand for independence, proclaims with the nationalist leaders in mind: "If you want independence, take it and return to the Dark Ages," the newly independent people nod their approval and take up the challenge. And what we actually see is the colonizer withdrawing his capital and technicians and encircling the young nation with an apparatus of economic pressure.[9] The apotheosis of independence becomes the curse of independence. The sweeping powers of coercion of the colonial authorities condemn the young nation to regression. In other words, the colonial power says: "If you want independence, take it and suffer the consequences." The nationalist leaders then are left with no other choice but to turn to their people and ask them to make a gigantic effort. These famished individuals are required to undergo a regime of austerity, these atrophied muscles are required to work out of all proportion. An autarkic regime is established and each state, with the pitiful resources at its disposal, endeavors to address the mounting national hunger and the growing national poverty. We are witness to the mobilization of a

---

[9] In the current international context capitalism does not impose an economic blockade solely upon the colonies in Africa and Asia. The U.S. with its anti-Castro policy has inaugurated in the Western Hemisphere a new chapter in the history of man's laborious fight for freedom. Latin America composed of independent countries sitting at the UN with their own national currency should be a lesson for Africa. Since their liberation these former colonies live in terror and destitution under Western capitalism's stranglehold.
The liberation of Africa and the development of man's consciousness have enabled the peoples of Latin America to break the spiral of dictatorships where one regime looked very much like the next. Castro takes power in Cuba and hands it to the people. The Yankees feel this heresy to be a national scourge and the U.S. organizes counter-revolutionary brigades, fabricates a provisional government, burns the sugar cane harvests, and finally decides to place an implacable stranglehold on the Cuban people. It won't be easy, however. The Cuban people will suffer, but they will win in the end. Janos Quadros, the president of Brazil, recently declared in a declaration of historical importance that his country will defend the Cuban Revolution by every means possible. Perhaps the U.S. too will bow to the will of the people. That will be a day for rejoicing since it will be a crucial moment for men and women throughout the world. The almighty power of the dollar, whose security after all is only guaranteed by the slaves of this world, toiling in the oil wells of the Middle East, the mines of Peru and the Congo, and the United Fruit or Firestone plantations, will then cease to dominate these slaves who created it and who continue to drain their heads and bellies of all their substance to feed it.

people who now have to work themselves to exhaustion while a contemptuous and bloated Europe looks on.

Other Third World countries refuse to accept such an ordeal and agree to give in to the terms of the former colonial power. Taking advantage of their strategic position in the cold war struggle, these countries sign agreements and commit themselves. The formerly colonized territory is now turned into an economically dependent country. The former colonizer, which has kept intact and, in some cases, reinforced its colonial marketing channels, agrees to inject small doses into the independent nation's budget in order to sustain it. Now that the colonial countries have achieved their independence the world is faced with the bare facts that makes the actual state of the liberated countries even more intolerable. The basic confrontation which seemed to be colonialism versus anticolonialism, indeed capitalism versus socialism, is already losing its importance. What matters today, the issue which blocks the horizon, is the need for a redistribution of wealth. Humanity will have to address this question, no matter how devastating the consequences may be.

It was commonly thought that the time had come for the world, and particularly for the Third World, to choose between the capitalist system and the socialist system. The underdeveloped countries, which made use of the savage competition between the two systems in order to win their national liberation, must, however, refuse to get involved in such rivalry. The Third World must not be content to define itself in relation to values which preceded it. On the contrary, the underdeveloped countries must endeavor to focus on their very own values as well as methods and style specific to them. The basic issue with which we are faced is not the unequivocal choice between socialism and capitalism such as they have been defined by men from different continents and different periods of time. We know, of course, that the capitalist way of life is incapable of allowing us to achieve our national and universal project. Capitalist exploitation, the cartels and monopolies, are the enemies of the underdeveloped countries. On the other hand, the choice of a socialist regime, of a regime entirely devoted to the people, based on the principle that man is the most precious asset, will allow us to progress faster in greater harmony, consequently ruling out the possibility of a caricature of society where a privileged few hold the reins of political and economic power without a thought for the nation as a whole.

But in order for this regime to function feasibly and for us to constantly abide by the principles which have been our inspiration, we need something other than human investment. Certain underdeveloped countries expend a huge amount of energy along these lines. Men and women, young and old, enthusiastically commit themselves to what amounts to forced labor and proclaim themselves slaves of the nation. This spirit of self-sacrifice and devotion to the common interest fosters a reassuring national morale which restores man's confidence in the destiny of the world and disarms the most reticent of observers. We believe, however, that such an effort cannot be sustained for long at such an infernal pace. These young nations accepted to take up the challenge after the unconditional withdrawal of the colonizer. The country finds itself under new management, but in actual fact everything has to be started over from scratch, everything has to be rethought. The colonial system, in fact, was only interested in certain riches, certain natural resources, to be exact those that fueled its industries. Up till now no reliable survey has been made of the soil or subsoil. As a result the young independent nation is obliged to keep the economic channels established by the colonial regime. It can, of course, export to other countries and other currency zones, but the basis of its exports remains basically unchanged. The colonial regime has hammered its channels into place and the risk of not maintaining them would be catastrophic. Perhaps everything needs to be started over again: The type of exports needs to be changed, not just their destination; the soil needs researching as well as the subsoil, the rivers and why not the sun. In order to do this, however, something other than human investment is needed. It requires capital, technicians, engineers and mechanics, etc. Let us confess, we believe that the huge effort demanded of the people of the underdeveloped nations by their leaders will not produce the results expected. If working conditions are not modified it will take centuries to humanize this world which the imperialist forces have reduced to the animal level.[10]

The truth is we must not accept such conditions. We must refuse outright the situation to which the West wants to condemn us. Colonialism and imperialism have not settled their debt to us once they have withdrawn their flag and their police force from our territories. For centuries the capitalists have behaved like real war criminals in the underdeveloped world. Deportation, massacres, forced labor, and slavery were the primary methods used by capitalism to increase its gold and diamond reserves, and establish its wealth and power. Not so long ago, Nazism transformed the whole of Europe into a genuine colony. The governments of various European nations demanded reparations and the restitution in money and kind for their stolen treasures. As a result, cultural artifacts, paintings, sculptures, and stained-glass windows were returned to their owners. In the aftermath of the war the Europeans were adamant about one thing: "Germany will pay." At the opening of the Eichmann trial Mr. Adenauer, on behalf of the German people, once again asked forgiveness from the Jewish people. Mr. Adenauer renewed his country's

---

[10] Some countries which have benefited from a large European settlement acquire walls and avenues with their independence and tend to forget the poverty and starvation in the back-country. In a kind of complicity of silence, by an irony of fate, they act as if their towns were contemporary with independence.

commitment to continue paying enormous sums to the state of
Israel to compensate for Nazi crimes.[11]

At the same time we are of the opinion that the imperialist
states would be making a serious mistake and committing an
unspeakable injustice if they were content to withdraw from our
soil the military cohorts and the administrative and financial
services whose job it was to prospect for, extract and ship our
wealth to the metropolis. Moral reparation for national independence does not fool us and it doesn't feed us. The wealth of the
imperialist nations is also our wealth. At a universal level, such
a statement in no way means we feel implicated in the technical
feats or artistic creations of the West. In concrete terms Europe
has been bloated out of all proportions by the gold and raw materials from such colonial countries as Latin America, China, and
Africa. Today Europe's tower of opulence faces these continents,
for centuries the point of departure of their shipments of diamonds, oil, silk and cotton, timber, and exotic produce to this
very same Europe. Europe is literally the creation of the Third
World. The riches which are choking it are those plundered from
the underdeveloped peoples. The ports of Holland, the docks in
Bordeaux and Liverpool owe their importance to the trade and

---

[11] And it is true that Germany has not paid in full the reparations for its
war crimes. The compensation imposed on the conquered nation has not been
claimed in full because the injured parties included Germany in their anti-
Communist defense system. The colonialist countries are motivated by the
same concerns when they try to obtain military bases and enclaves from their
former colonies, failing their integration into the system of the West. They
have decided by common agreement to waive their claims in the name of
NATO's strategy, in the name of the free world. And we have seen Germany
receive wave after wave of dollars and equipment. A strong and powerful
Germany back on its feet was a necessity for the Western camp. It was clearly
in the interests of a so-called free Europe to have a prosperous, reconstructed
Germany capable of serving as a bastion against the threatened Red hordes.
Germany has manipulated the European crisis. Consequently, the U.S. and
the other European states feel legitimately bitter toward this Germany, once
brought to its knees and now one of their most ruthless competitors on the
market.

deportation of millions of slaves. And when we hear the head of a European nation declare with hand on heart that he must come to the aid of the unfortunate peoples of the underdeveloped world, we do not tremble with gratitude. On the contrary, we say among ourselves, "it is a just reparation we are getting." So we will not accept aid for the underdeveloped countries as "charity." Such aid must be considered the final stage of a dual consciousness—the consciousness of the colonized that *it is their due* and the consciousness of the capitalist powers that effectively *they must pay up.*[12] If through lack of intelligence—not to mention ingratitude—the capitalist countries refused to pay up, then the unrelenting dialectic of their own system would see to it that they are asphyxiated. It is a fact that the young nations attract little private capital. A number of reasons justify and explain these reservations on the part of the monopolies. As soon as the capitalists know, and they are obviously the first to know, that their government is preparing to decolonize, they hasten to withdraw all their capital from the colony. This spectacular flight of capital is one of the most constant phenomena of decolonization.

In order to invest in the independent countries, private companies demand terms which from experience prove unacceptable or unfeasible. True to their principle of immediate returns as soon as they invest "overseas," capitalists are reluctant to invest in the long term. They are recalcitrant and often openly hostile to the so-called economic planning programs of the young regimes. At the most they are willing to lend capital to the young

---

[12] "To make a radical distinction between the construction of socialism in Europe and 'relations with the Third World' (as if our only relations with it were external) is, knowingly or unknowingly, giving priority to restructuring the colonial heritage over the liberation of the underdeveloped countries, in other words constructing a de luxe type of socialism on the fruits of imperial plunder—as if a gang were to share out the loot more or less equitably even if it means giving a little to the poor by way of charity and forgetting they are giving back to the people they stole from." Marcel Péju, "Mourir pour de Gaulle?" in *Temps Modernes* No. 175–176, October–November 1960.

nations on condition it is used to buy manufactured goods and machinery, and therefore keep the factories in the metropolis running.

In fact the Western financiers are wary of any form of risk taking. Their demands, therefore, are for political stability and a peaceful social climate which are impossible to achieve given the appalling situation of the population as a whole in the aftermath of independence. In their search, then, for a guarantee which the former colony cannot vouch for, they demand that certain military bases be kept on and the young nation enter into military and economic agreements. The private companies put pressure on their own government to ensure that the troops stationed in these countries are assigned to protecting their interests. As a last resort these companies require their government to guarantee their investments in such and such an underdeveloped region.

As a result few countries meet the conditions required by the cartels and monopolies. So the capital, deprived of reliable outlets, remains blocked in Europe and frozen. Especially as the capitalists refuse to invest in their own country. Returns in this case are in fact minimal and the fiscal pressure disheartens the boldest.

The situation in the long-term is catastrophic. Capital no longer circulates or else is considerably reduced. The Swiss banks refuse funding and Europe suffocates. Despite the enormous sums swallowed up by military expenditures, international capitalism is in desperate straits.

But another danger looms on the horizon. Since the Third World is abandoned and condemned to regression, in any case stagnation, through the selfishness and immorality of the West, the underdeveloped peoples decide to establish a collective autarchy. The industries of the West are rapidly deprived of their overseas outlets. Capital goods pile up in the warehouses and the European market witnesses the inexorable rivalry between financiers and cartels. Factory closures, layoffs, and unemployment force the European proletariat to engage in an open struggle with the capitalist regime. The monopolies then realize that their true interests lie in aiding, and massively aiding without too many conditions, the underdeveloped countries. It is clear therefore that the young nations of the Third World are wrong to grovel at the feet of the capitalist countries. We are powerful in our own right and the justness of our position. It is our duty, however, to tell and explain to the capitalist countries that they are wrong to think the fundamental issue of our time is the war between the socialist regime and them. An end must be put to this cold war that gets us nowhere, the nuclear arms race must be stopped and the underdeveloped regions must receive generous investments and technical aid. The fate of the world depends on the response given to this question.

And it is pointless for the capitalist regimes to try and implicate the socialist regimes in the "fate of Europe" confronted by the starving multitudes of colored peoples. Colonel Gagarin's exploit, whatever General de Gaulle thinks, is not a feat which "does credit to Europe." For some time now the leaders of the capitalist regimes and their intellectuals have had an ambivalent attitude towards the Soviet Union. After having joined forces to eliminate the socialist regime they now realize they have to come to terms with it. So they switch on the smiles, multiply the overtures and make constant reminders to the Soviet people that they "are part of Europe."

Brandishing the Third World as a flood which threatens to engulf the whole of Europe will not divide the progressive forces whose intentions are to lead humanity in the pursuit of happiness. The Third World has no intention of organizing a vast hunger crusade against Europe. What it does expect from those who have kept it in slavery for centuries is to help it rehabilitate man, and ensure his triumph everywhere, once and for all.

But it is obvious we are not so naive as to think this will be achieved with the cooperation and goodwill of the European governments. This colossal task, which consists of reintroducing man into the world, man in his totality, will be achieved with the crucial help of the European masses who would do well to confess that they have often rallied behind the position of our common masters on colonial issues. In order to do this, the European masses must first of all decide to wake up, put on their thinking caps and stop playing the irresponsible game of Sleeping Beauty.

Grandeur and Weakness
of Spontaneity

These reflections on violence have made us realize the frequent discrepancy between the cadres of the nationalist party and the masses, and the way they are out of step with each other. In any union or political organization there is a traditional gap between the masses who demand an immediate, unconditional improvement of their situation, and the cadres who, gauging the difficulties likely to be created by employers, put a restraint on their demands. Hence the oft-remarked tenacious discontent of the masses with regard to the cadres. After a day of demonstrations, while the cadres are celebrating victory, the masses well and truly get the feeling they have been betrayed. It is the repeated demonstrations for their rights and the repeated labor disputes that politicize the masses. A politically informed union official is someone who knows that a local dispute is not a crucial confrontation between him and management. The colonized intellectuals, who in their respective metropolises have studied the mechanism of political parties, establish similar organizations so as to mobilize the masses and put pressure on the colonial administration. The formation of nationalist parties in the colonized countries is contemporary with the birth of an intellectual and business elite. These elite attach primordial importance to the organization as such, and blind devotion to the organization often takes priority over a rational study of colonial society. The notion of party is a notion imported from the metropolis. This instrument of modern resistance is grafted onto a protean, unbalanced reality where slavery, bondage, barter, cottage industries, and stock transactions exist side by side.

The weakness of political parties lies not only in their mechanical imitation of an organization which is used to handling the struggle of the proletariat within a highly industrialized capitalist society. Innovations and adaptations should have been made as to the type of organization at a local level. The great mistake, the inherent flaw of most of the political parties in the underdeveloped regions has been traditionally to address first and foremost the most politically conscious elements: the urban proletariat, the small tradesmen and the civil servants, i.e., a tiny section of the population which represents barely more than one percent.

However, although this proletariat understood the party propaganda and read its publications, it was much less prepared to respond to any slogans taking up the unrelenting struggle for national liberation. It has been said many times that in colonial territories the proletariat is the kernel of the colonized people most pampered by the colonial regime. The embryonic urban proletariat is relatively privileged. In the capitalist countries, the proletariat has nothing to lose and possibly everything to gain. In the colonized countries, the proletariat has everything to lose. It represents in fact that fraction of the colonized who are indispensable for running the colonial machine: tram drivers, taxi drivers, miners, dockers, interpreters, and nurses, etc. These elements make up the most loyal clientele of the nationalist parties and by the privileged position they occupy in the colonial system represent the "bourgeois" fraction of the colonized population.

So it is understandable that the clientele of the nationalist parties is above all urban: technicians, manual workers, intellectuals, and tradespeople living mainly in the towns. Their way of thinking in many ways already bears the mark of the technically advanced and relatively comfortable environment in which they live. Here "modernism" is king. These are the very same circles which will oppose obscurantist traditions and propose innovations, thereby entering into open conflict with the old granite foundation that is the national heritage.

The large majority of the nationalist parties regard the rural masses with great mistrust. These masses give them the impression of being mired in inertia and sterility. Fairly quickly the nationalist party members (the urban workers and intellectuals) end up passing the same pejorative judgment on the peasantry as the colonists. In our endeavor to understand the reasons for this distrust of the rural masses by the political parties we should not forget that colonialism has often strengthened or established its domination by an organized petrification of the peasantry. Regimented by *marabouts*, witch doctors and traditional chiefs, the rural masses still live in a feudal state whose overbearingly medieval structure is nurtured by the colonial administrators and army.

The young national bourgeoisie, especially the business sector, now competes with these feudal rulers in a number of areas: *Marabouts* and witch doctors prevent the sick from consulting a physician; the rulings of the *djemaas* make lawyers redundant; the *kaids* use their political and administrative powers to launch a trucking business or establish a commerce; the local chiefs oppose the introduction of trade and new products in the name of religion and tradition.

The young class of colonized businessmen and traders needs to eliminate these prohibitions and barriers in order to grow. The indigenous clientele which represents the exclusive preserve of the feudal overlords and sees itself more or less banned from purchasing new products, constitutes therefore a market which both parties are fighting over.

The feudal agents form a barrier between the young Westernized nationalists and the masses. Every time the elite makes a gesture toward the rural masses, the tribal chiefs, the religious rulers, and the traditional authorities issue repeated warnings, threats, and excommunications. These traditional authorities, sanctioned by the occupying power, feel threatened by the growing endeavors of the elite to infiltrate the rural masses. They know too well that the ideas imported by these urban elements are likely to threaten the very existence of their feudal authority. As a result, their enemy is not the occupying power with whom, in fact, they get along very well, but these modernists who are bent on dislocating the indigenous society and in doing so, take the bread out of their mouths.

The Westernized elements' feelings toward the peasant masses recall those found among the proletariat in the industrialized nations. The history of bourgeois revolutions and the history of proletarian revolutions have demonstrated that the peasant masses often represent a curb on revolution. In the industrialized countries the peasant masses are generally the least politically conscious, the least organized as well as the most anarchistic elements. They are characterized by a series of features—individualism, lack of discipline, the love of money, fits of rage, and deep depression—defining an objectively reactionary behavior.

We have seen that the nationalist parties base their methods and doctrines on the Western parties and therefore in the majority of cases do not direct their propaganda at the rural masses. In fact, a rational analysis of colonial society would have shown them that the colonized peasants live in a traditional environment whose structures have remained intact, whereas in the industrialized countries it is these traditional circles which have been splintered by the progress of industrialization. It is within the burgeoning proletariat that we find individualistic behavior in the colonies. Abandoning the countryside and its insoluble problems of demography, the landless peasants, now a lumpenproletariat, are driven into the towns, crammed into shanty towns and endeavor to infiltrate the ports and cities, the creations of colonial domination. As for the mass of the peasantry, they continue to live in a petrified context, and those who cannot scrape a living in the countryside have no other choice but to emigrate to the cities. The peasant who stays put is a staunch defender of tradition, and in a colonial society represents the element of discipline whose social structure remains community-minded. Such a static society, clinging to a rigid context, can of course sporadically generate episodes of religious fanaticism and tribal warfare. But in their spontaneity the rural masses remain disciplined and altruistic. The individual steps aside in favor of the community.

The peasants distrust the town dweller. Dressed like a European, speaking his language, working alongside him, sometimes living in his neighborhood, he is considered by the peasant to be a renegade who has given up everything which constitutes the national heritage. The town dweller is a "traitor, a mercenary" who apparently gets along very well with the occupier and strives to succeed in the context of the colonial system. Hence the reason why we often hear the peasant say that the town dwellers have no moral standards. This is not the traditional opposition between town and country. It is the opposition between the colonized excluded from the benefits of colonialism and their counterparts who manage to turn the colonial system to their advantage.

The colonialists, moreover, use this antagonism in their opposition to the nationalist parties. They mobilize the population in the mountains and the interior against the urban population. They set the back country against the coast, they revive tribal identities, and it should come as no surprise to see Kalondji crowned king of Kasai or some years back, the Assembly of Chiefs in Ghana hold its ground against N'Krumah.

The political parties are unable to establish roots in the countryside. Instead of adapting the existing structures in order to invest them with nationalist or progressive elements, they are intent on disrupting traditional existence within the context of the colonial system. They imagine they can jump-start the nation whereas the mesh of the colonial system is still tightly interlocked. They make no effort to reach out to the masses. They do not place their theoretical knowledge at the service of the people, but instead try to regiment the masses according to a pre-determined schema. Consequently, they parachute into the villages inexperienced or unknown leaders from the capital who, empowered by the central authorities, endeavor to manage the *douar* or the village like a company committee. The traditional chiefs are ignored, sometimes taken down a peg. Instead of integrating the history of the village and conflicts between tribes and clans into the people's struggle, the history of the future nation has a singular disregard for minor local histories and tramples on the only thing relevant to the nation's actuality. The elders, held in respect in traditional societies and generally invested with an undeniable moral authority, are publicly ridiculed. The occupier's services have no scruples making use of the ensuing resentment and are kept informed of the slightest decision adopted by this caricature of authority. A well-informed police repression, based on factual intelligence gathering, is quick to follow. The leaders parachuted in from the outside and the main members of the new assembly are arrested.

These setbacks confirm "the theoretical analysis" of the nationalist parties. The disastrous attempts at regimenting the rural masses reinforce the parties' distrust and crystallize their aggressiveness toward this section of the population. After the victorious struggle for national liberation, the same mistakes are repeated fostering the trend to decentralize and self-govern. The tribalism of the colonial phase is replaced by regionalism in the national phase expressed institutionally as federalism.

But it so happens that the rural masses, in spite of the little control the parties have over them, play a crucial role either in the gestation of the national consciousness or in relaying the initiatives of the nationalist parties, and in some rare cases taking over purely and simply from the parties' sterility.

The nationalist parties' propaganda always finds a response among the peasantry. The memory of the precolonial period is still very much alive in the villages. Mothers still hum to their children the songs which accompanied the warriors as they set off to fight the colonizer. At the age of twelve or thirteen the young villagers know by heart the names of the elders who took part in the last revolt, and the dreams in the *douars* and villages are not those of the children in the cities dreaming of luxury goods or passing their exams but dreams of identification with such and such a hero whose heroic death still brings tears to their eyes.

At a time when the nationalist parties are endeavoring to organize the embryonic working class in the towns, we are witnessing apparently inexplicable social unrest in the interior. We can take as an example the infamous 1947 insurrection in Madagascar. The colonial services stated categorically that it was a peasant revolt. In fact we now know that things, as always, were much more complex. During the Second World War the major colonial companies extended their influence and grabbed any remaining land. There was also talk at the same period of the possible settlement on the island of Jewish, Kabyle, and West Indian refugees. The rumor also spread of an imminent invasion of the island by the whites from South Africa abetted by the colonists. After the war, therefore, the candidates on the nationalist ticket were triumphantly elected. Immediately afterwards, factions of the MDRM party (Mouvement Démocratique de la Rénovation Malgache) underwent repression. In order to achieve their ends the colonial authorities employed the usual methods: mass arrests; intertribal, racist propaganda; and the creation of a party with the unorganized factions of the lumpenproletariat. This party, called the Disinherited of Madagascar (PADESM), and its decidedly provocative actions, was to provide the colonial authorities with the legal pretext it needed to maintain law and order. Such a premeditated, commonplace operation as eliminating a political party, however, here took on gigantic proportions. On the defensive for three or four years the rural masses suddenly felt themselves in mortal danger and decided to violently resist the colonialist forces. Armed with spears, and more often with sticks and stones, the population rose up in a widespread revolt with the aim of national liberation. We know how it ended.

Such armed revolts constitute but one of the methods used by the rural masses to join in the national struggle. In some cases the peasants act as a relay following the unrest in the towns where the nationalist party is the object of police repression. The news reaches the interior exaggerated out of all proportion: leaders arrested, others gunned down, the city running red with the blood of blacks, the poor white settlers swimming in Arab blood. All the pent-up hatred, all the exacerbated hatred then explodes. The local police station is taken over, the officers hacked to pieces, the elementary school teacher murdered, the doctor gets away with his life only because he is absent, etc., etc. Pacifying troops are dispatched to the field, the air force drops bombs. The banner of revolt is then unfurled, the old warrior traditions resurface, the women cheer on the men who band together and take up their positions in the mountains, and guerrilla warfare begins. Spontaneously the peasants create a widespread sense of insecurity; colonialism takes fright, settles into a state of war, or else negotiates.

How do the nationalist parties react to this decisive irruption by the peasant masses into the national struggle? We have seen that the majority of the nationalist parties have not written the need for armed intervention into their propaganda. They are not opposed to a sustained revolt, but they leave it up to the spontaneity of the rural masses. In other words, their attitude towards these new developments is as if they were heaven-sent, praying they continue. They exploit this godsend, but make no attempt to organize the rebellion. They do not dispatch agents to the interior to politicize the masses, to enlighten their consciousness or raise the struggle to a higher level. They hope that swept along by its own momentum the action of the masses will not flag. There is no contamination of the rural movement by the urban movement. Each side evolves according to its own dialectic.

At a time when the rural masses are totally receptive, the nationalist parties make no attempt to introduce them to an agenda. They have no objective to offer and simply hope that the movement will continue indefinitely and that the bombardments will not win the day. We thus see that the nationalist parties do not make use of even this opportunity to integrate the rural masses and raise their political awareness as well as their struggle to a higher level. They stubbornly maintain their criminal position of distrust with regard to the interior.

The political cadres hole up in the towns and make it clear to the colonial authorities they have no connections with the rebels, or else leave the country. Seldom do they join forces with the people in the mountains. In Kenya, for example, during the Mau-Mau insurrection no known nationalist claimed he was a member of the movement or attempted to defend it.

There are no constructive talks, no confrontation between the different social strata of the nation. Once independence has been achieved after repression of the rural masses and collusion between the colonial authorities and the nationalist parties, we find this mutual incomprehension exacerbated. The peasantry balk at the structural reforms proposed by the government as well as the even objectively progressive social innovations, precisely because the current leaders of the regime did not explain to the people during the colonial period the party objectives, national policy, and international issues, etc.

The mistrust felt by the rural population and the traditional leaders toward the nationalist parties during the colonial period is matched by equal hostility during the national period. The

colonialist secret service, which is still at work after independence, foments discontent and still manages to create serious
difficulties for the young governments. When all is said and done,
the government is merely paying for its idleness during the liberation period and its enduring contempt for the peasantry. The
nation may well have a rational, even progressive head, but its
huge body remains retarded, rebellious and recalcitrant.

The temptation is great therefore to crush this body by centralizing the administration and keeping a firm control over
the people. This is one of the reasons why we often hear that the
underdeveloped countries need a dose of dictatorship. The leaders distrust the rural masses. This distrust, moreover, can take
on serious proportions. Such is the case for certain governments
that, long after national independence, consider the interior
as an unpacified region where the head of state and his minsters
only venture during army maneuvers. The interior is considered
a virtual terra incognita. Paradoxically, the national government's
attitude toward the rural masses is reminiscent in some ways
of the colonial power. "We are not too sure how the masses will
react"; "We need to use the lash if we want to take this country
out of the Dark Ages," the young leaders are not afraid to say.
But, as we have seen, the political parties' disregard for the rural
masses during the colonial period can only be prejudicial to
national unity and to setting rapidly the nation in motion.

Sometimes colonialism endeavors to diversify and dislocate the
nationalist upsurge. Instead of stirring up the sheiks and the chiefs
against the "revolutionaries" in the towns, the Native Bureaus
organize the tribes and religious brotherhoods into parties. Confronted with an urban party which is beginning to "embody the
will of the nation" and constitute a threat to the colonial regime,
factions are born, and sympathies and parties based on tribe and
region emerge. The entire tribe is transformed into a political party
in close consultation with the colonialists. Roundtable discussions

can now begin. The party of national unity is swamped by the very number of political factions. The tribal parties oppose centralization and unity and denounce the one party dictatorship.

Later on the same tactics will be used by the national opposition. The occupier has already made his choice from the two or three nationalist parties who led the liberation struggle. The method of choice is typical: Once a party has achieved national unanimity and has emerged as the sole negotiator, the occupier begins his maneuvering and delays negotiations as long as possible. The delay is used to whittle away the party's demands and obtain concessions from the leadership to remove certain "extremist" elements.

If, however, no single party emerges, the occupier is content to favor the one which seems to him to be the most "reasonable." The nationalist parties, which were excluded from the negotiations, then loudly denounce the agreement concluded between the other party and the occupier. The party which takes over power from the occupier, conscious of the danger of the rival party's vague, strictly demagogic positions, endeavors to dismantle and outlaw it. The persecuted party has no other alternative but to take refuge on the periphery of the towns and in the interior. It attempts to stir up the rural masses against the "mercenaries of the coast and the corrupt elements in the capital." Any excuse is good enough—from religious arguments to the tradition-breaking innovations introduced by the new national authority. It exploits the obscurantist tendencies of the rural masses. Its so-called revolutionary doctrine is in fact based on the reactionary, heated, and spontaneous nature of the peasantry. It spreads the rumor here and there that the mountainous regions of the interior are on the move, that there is discontent among the peasants. It claims that in one region the police have opened fire on the peasants, reinforcements have been dispatched, and the government is about to collapse. With no clear program and no other objective but to take over from the team in power, the opposition parties put their fate in the hands of the spontaneous and obscure mass of the peasantry.

Conversely, in some cases the opposition no longer seeks support from the rural masses but from the progressive elements of the young nation's labor unions. In this case the government calls upon the masses to resist the workers' demands, calling them rash, antitraditionalist maneuvers. The observations we have noted concerning the political parties can now be applied to the labor unions, mutatis mutandis. The first labor unions in the colonial territories are usually local branches of their metropolitan counterparts and their slogans echo those of the metropolis.

Once the crucial phase of the liberation struggle begins to take shape, a group of indigenous union leaders decides to create a national labor movement. The locals desert en masse the previous organization imported from the metropolis. The formation of this union is another way for the urban population to exert pressure on the colonial authorities. We have already said that the proletariat in the colonies is embryonic and represents the most privileged fraction of the population. The national labor unions born out of the liberation struggle are urban organizations and their program is above all political and nationalist. But this national union born during the decisive phase of the fight for independence is in fact the legal enlistment of dynamic, politically conscious nationalist elements.

The rural masses, despised by the political parties, continue to be kept on the sidelines. There is, of course, an agricultural workers' union but such a formation is content to satisfy the formal need for "a united front against colonialism." The union leaders who began their careers in the context of the metropolitan unions are at a loss when it comes to organizing the rural masses. They have lost touch with the peasantry and are mainly concerned with enlisting steelworkers, dockers and civil servants in the utilities sector, etc.

During the colonial phase the nationalist labor unions represent a spectacular strike force. In the towns these unions can paralyze or at least disrupt at any moment the colonialist economy. Since the European settlements are mostly confined to the towns, the psychological repercussions are considerable: no gas, no electricity, no garbage pickup, and produce lies rotting on the wharfs. These metropolitan enclaves, which the towns represent in the colonial context, are profoundly affected by this labor unrest. The stronghold of colonialism, the capital, has difficulty withstanding such a battering. But the rural masses of the interior remain unaffected by this confrontation.

There is, therefore, a clear disproportion from the national point of view between the importance of the labor unions and the rest of the nation. After independence the workers enlisted in the unions have the impression of running on empty. Once the limited objectives they set themselves have been achieved, they prove to be extremely precarious given the huge task of nation building. Faced with a national bourgeoisie whose relations with the government are often very close, the union leaders discover they can no longer confine themselves to labor disputes. Congenitally isolated from the rural masses, incapable of extending their influence beyond the urban periphery, the unions adopt an increasingly political stance. In fact they become political candidates. They endeavor by every means possible to drive the bourgeoisie into a corner: protests are made against keeping foreign bases on national soil, commercial deals are exposed, and criticism is voiced against the national government's foreign policy. The workers, now "independent," are getting nowhere. The unions realize in the aftermath of independence that if their social demands were to be expressed they would scandalize the rest of the nation. The workers are in fact pampered by the regime. They represent the most well-to-do fraction of the people. Any unrest aimed at winning improved living standards for the laborers and dock workers would not only be unpopular but might very well stir up the hostility of the disinherited rural population. The unions, banned from union activities, make no headway.

This malaise conveys the objective need for a social program which, at long last, concerns the entire nation. The unions suddenly discover that the interior must also be enlightened and organized. But since they never bothered to establish working links between their organization and the peasantry, who represent the only spontaneously revolutionary force in the country, the unions prove to be ineffective and realize the anachronistic nature of their program.

The union leaders, immersed in worker-control politics, inevitably reach the preparatory stage for a coup d'état. But here again the interior is excluded. It is a showdown restricted to the national bourgeoisie and the unionized workers movement. The national bourgeoisie, appropriating the old traditions of colonialism, flexes its military and police muscle, whereas the unions organize meetings and mobilize tens of thousands of their members. The peasants shrug their shoulders as they muse over this national bourgeoisie and these workers who after all have enough to eat. The peasants shrug their shoulders for they realize that both parties treat them as a makeshift force. The unions, the parties and the government, in a kind of immoral Machiavellianism, use the peasant masses as a blind, inert force of intervention. As a kind of brute force.

In certain circumstances, however, the peasant masses make a crucial contribution to the struggle for national liberation as well as to the course of action opted for by the future nation. For the underdeveloped countries this phenomenon is of fundamental importance, and this is the reason why we propose to study it in detail.

We have seen that the nationalist parties' will to smash colonialism works hand in hand with the will to remain on good terms with the colonial authorities. Within these parties two lines of action can emerge. First of all, some of the intellectual elements, who have made a thorough analysis of the colonial reality and the international situation, begin to criticize the ideological vacuum of the national party and its dearth of strategy and tactics. They never tire of asking the leaders the crucial questions "What is nationalism? What does it mean to you? What does the term signify? What is the point of independence? And first how do you intend to achieve it?" while at the same time demanding that methodological issues be vigorously addressed. To electioneering methods they suggest adding "any other means." At the first signs of a skirmish, the leaders are quick to call them juvenile hotheads. But because these demands are neither juvenile nor hotheaded, the revolutionary elements articulating them are rapidly isolated and removed. The leaders cloaked in their experience ruthlessly reject "these upstarts, these anarchists."

The party machine tends to resist any innovation. The revolutionary minority finds itself isolated, confronted by a leadership, frightened and anguished at the idea it could be swept away in a whirlwind whose nature, strength and direction are beyond its imagining.

The second line of action involves the senior or junior cadres whose activities have been the object of colonialist police persecution. It is worth noting that these men attained the leadership of the party through sheer hard work, self-sacrifice, and an exemplary patriotism. These men from the rank and file are often laborers, seasonal workers and sometimes even genuinely unemployed. For them, being activists in a national party is not a question of politics but the only way of casting off their animal status for a human one. These men, uncomfortable with the party's exacerbated legalism, demonstrate, within the limits of their assigned activities, a spirit of initiative, courage, and a sense of purpose which almost systematically make them targets for the forces of colonialist repression. Arrested, convicted, tortured, and amnestied, they use their period of detention to compare ideas and harden their determination. Strengthened by the ordeal of hunger strikes and the brutal solidarity of the prisons that are little better than communal graveyards, they live out their liberation as a godsent opportunity to launch the armed struggle. Meanwhile outside, the colonial authorities, besieged now from all sides, are making overtures to the nationalist moderates.

What we see therefore is a splintering close to breaking point between the official and the unofficial party factions. The unofficial elements are made to feel undesirable, and are shunned. The legal factions come to their aid, but taking so many precautions that the unofficial factions already feel themselves to be outsiders. These men then make contact with the intellectual elements whose position they admired a few years previously. The encounter leads to the formation of an underground party, parallel to the official party. But the repression of these irredeemable elements intensifies as the official party draws closer to colonialism and attempts to change it "from the inside." The unofficial faction then finds itself in an historical dead end.

Driven from the towns, these men first of all take refuge in the urban periphery. But the police network smokes them out and forces them to leave the towns for good and abandon the arena of political struggle. They retreat to the interior, the mountains, and deep into the rural masses. Initially, the masses close in around them, protecting them from the manhunt. The nationalist militant who decides to put his fate in the hands of the peasant masses, instead of playing hide-and-seek with the police in the urban centers, will never regret it. The peasant cloak wraps him in a mantle of unimagined tenderness and vitality. Veritable exiles in their own country and severed from the urban milieu where they drew up the concepts of nation and political struggle, they take to the *maquis*. Constantly forced to remain on the move to elude the police, walking by night so as not to attract attention, they are able to travel the length and breadth of their country and get to know it. Gone are the cafés, the discussions about the coming elections or the cruelty of such-and-such a police officer.

Their ears hear the true voice of the country and their eyes see the great and infinite misery of the people. They realize that precious time has been wasted on futile discussion about the colonial regime. They realize at last that change does not mean reform, that change does not mean improvement. Now possessed with a kind of vertigo they realize that the political unrest in the towns will always be powerless to change and overthrow the colonial regime.

Discussions with the peasants now become a ritual for them. They discover that the rural masses have never ceased to pose the problem of their liberation in terms of violence, of taking back the land from the foreigners, in terms of *national struggle* and armed revolt. Everything is simple. These men discover a coherent people who survive in a kind of petrified state, but keep intact their moral values and their attachment to the nation. They discover a generous people, prepared to make sacrifices, willing to give all they have, impatient, with an indestructible pride. Understandably, the encounter between these militants, hounded by the police, and these restless, instinctively rebellious masses can produce an explosive mixture of unexpected power. The men from the towns let themselves be guided by the people and at the same time give them military and political training. The people sharpen their weapons. In fact the training proves short-lived, for the masses, realizing the strength of their own muscles, force the leaders to accelerate events. The armed struggle is triggered.

Insurrection disorients the political parties. Their doctrine has always claimed the ineffectiveness of any confrontation and their very existence serves to condemn any idea of revolt. Certain political parties secretly share the optimism of the colonists and are glad to be no party to this madness which, it is said, can only end in bloodshed. But the flames have been lit and like an epidemic, spread like wildfire throughout the country. The tanks and planes do not achieve the success they counted on. Faced with the extent of the damage, colonialism begins to have second thoughts. Voices are raised within the oppressor nation that draw attention to the gravity of the situation.

As for the people living in their huts and their dreams, their hearts begin to beat to the new national rhythm and they softly sing unending hymns to the glory of the fighters. The insurrection has already spread throughout the nation. It is now the turn of the parties to be isolated.

Sooner or later, however, the leaders of the insurrection realize the need to extend the insurrection to the towns. Such a realization is not fortuitous. It completes the dialectic which governs the development of an armed struggle for national liberation. Although the rural areas represent endless reserves of popular energy and its groups of armed men maintain a reign of insecurity, colonialism never really doubts the strength of its system. It does not feel in actual danger. The leaders of the insurrection therefore decide to move the war into enemy territory, i.e., into the serenity and grandiloquence of the cities.

It is no easy matter for the leadership to foment an insurrection in the cities. We have seen that most of the leaders, born or raised in the towns, were so hounded by the colonialist police and so generally misunderstood by the rationally minded, overcautious cadres of the political parties, that they fled their home environment. Their retreat to the interior was both an escape from repression and a distrust of the old political formations. The natural urban relays for these leaders are the nationalists who have made a name for themselves in the political parties. But we have seen that their recent history has little in common with these timorous leaders who spend their time mired in endless discussions on the evils of colonialism.

Moreover, the first overtures made by the men from the *maquis* in the direction of their former friends, those they consider to be farthest to the left, confirm their fears and eradicate any desire to renew their acquaintance with them again. In fact the insurrection, which starts in the rural areas, is introduced into the towns by that fraction of the peasantry blocked at the urban periphery, those who still have not found a single bone to gnaw in the colonial system. These men, forced off the family land by the growing population in the countryside and by colonial expropriation, circle the towns tirelessly, hoping that one day or another they will be let in. It is among these masses, in the people of the shanty towns and in the lumpenproletariat that the insurrection will find its urban spearhead. The lumpenproletariat, this cohort of starving men, divorced from tribe and clan, constitutes one of the most spontaneously and radically revolutionary forces of a colonized people.

In Kenya, during the years preceding the Mau-Mau revolt, the British colonial authorities increased their intimidation tactics against the lumpenproletariat. The police and missionaries coordinated their efforts in the years 1950–51 to respond appropriately to the enormous influx of young Kenyans from the countryside and the forest who, unable to find jobs, took to stealing, debauchery and alcoholism, etc. Juvenile delinquency in the colonized countries stems directly from this lumpenproletariat. Similarly, drastic measures were taken in the Congo from 1957 onwards to send back to the interior the "young hooligans" who were disturbing the peace. Relocation camps were opened and assigned to the evangelical missions under the protection, of course, of the Belgian army.

The formation of a lumpenproletariat is a phenomenon which is governed by its own logic, and neither the overzealousness of the missionaries nor decrees from the central authorities can check its growth. However hard it is kicked or stoned it continues to gnaw at the roots of the tree like a pack of rats.

The shanty town is the consecration of the colonized's biological decision to invade the enemy citadel at all costs, and if need be, by the most underground channels. The lumpenproletariat constitutes a serious threat to the "security" of the town and signifies the irreversible rot and the gangrene eating into the heart of colonial domination. So the pimps, the hooligans, the unemployed, and the petty criminals, when approached, give the liberation struggle all they have got, devoting themselves to the cause like valiant workers. These vagrants, these second-class citizens, find their way back to the nation thanks to their decisive, militant action. Unchanged in the eyes of colonial society or vis-à-vis the moral standards of the colonizer, they believe the power of the gun or the hand grenade is the only way to enter the cities. These jobless, these species of subhumans, redeem themselves in their own eyes and before history. The prostitutes too, the domestics at two thousand francs a month, the hopeless cases, all those men and women who fluctuate between madness and suicide, are restored to sanity, return to action and take their vital place in the great march of a nation on the move.

The nationalist parties are unable to grasp this new phenomenon that precipitates their disintegration. The outbreak of the insurrection in the towns modifies the nature of the struggle. Whereas the mass of the colonialist troops were aimed at the interior, they now surge back to the towns in order to safeguard people and property. The forces of repression are dispersed, danger lurks in every quarter. It is the national territory, the entire colony which enters into a trance. Armed groups of peasants watch as the military loosens its grip. The insurrection in the towns is an unexpected lifesaver.

The leaders of the insurrection, observing the ardor and enthusiasm of the people as they deal decisive blows to the colonialist machine, become increasingly distrustful of traditional politics. Every victory justifies their hostility towards what they now call hot air, verbiage, bantering, and futile agitation. They feel a hatred for "politics" and demagoguery. Hence in the initial phase the cult of spontaneity is triumphant.

The rash of revolts which break out in the interior testify to the nation's substantial presence in every quarter. Every colonized subject in arms represents a piece of the nation on the move. These revolts jeopardize the colonial regime, force it to mobilize its troops by dispersing them, and threaten to suffocate them at any moment. They are governed by a simple doctrine: The nation must be made to exist. There is no program, no discourse, there are no resolutions, no factions. The problem is clear-cut: The foreigners must leave. Let us build a common front against the oppressor and let us reinforce it with armed struggle.

As long as colonialism remains in a state of anxiety, the national cause advances and becomes the cause of each and everyone. The struggle for liberation takes shape and already involves the entire country. During this period, spontaneity rules. Initiative rests with local areas. On every hilltop a government in miniature is formed and assumes power. In the valleys and in the forests, in the jungle and in the villages, everywhere, one encounters a national authority. The action of each and everyone substantiates the nation and undertakes to ensure its triumph locally. We are dealing with a strategy of immediacy which is both all-embracing and radical. The objective, the program of every spontaneously formed group is liberation at a local level. If the nation is present everywhere, it must then be here. One step further and it is present only here. Tactics and strategy merge. The art of politics is quite simply transformed into the art of war. The militant becomes the fighter. To wage war and to engage in politics are one and the same thing.

This dispossessed population, used to living in a narrow cycle of conflict and rivalry, solemnly sets about cleansing and purifying the local face of the nation. In a state of genuine collective ecstasy rival families decide to wipe the slate clean and forget the past. Reconciliations abound. Deep-buried, traditional hatreds are dug up, the better to root them out. Faith in the nation furthers political consciousness. National unity begins with the unity of the group, the settling of old scores, and the elimination once and for all of any resentment. Those indigenous elements who have dishonored the country by their activities and their complicity with the occupier are also included in the cleansing process. Traitors and mercenaries, however, are judged and punished. On their continuing road to self-discovery the people legislate and claim their sovereignty. Every component roused from its colonial slumber lives at boiling point. The villages witness a permanent display of spectacular generosity and disarming kindness, and an unquestioned determination to die for the "cause." All of this is reminiscent of a religious brotherhood, a church, or a mystical doctrine. No part of the indigenous population can remain indifferent to this new rhythm which drives the nation. Emissaries are dispatched to the neighboring tribes. They represent the insurrection's first liaison system and introduce the rhythm and movement of the revolution to the regions still mired in immobility. Tribes well-known for their stubborn rivalry disarm amid rejoicing and tears, and pledge their help and support. In this atmosphere of brotherly solidarity and armed struggle, men link arms with their former enemies. The national circle widens and every new ambush signals the entry of new tribes. Every village becomes a free agent and a relay point. Solidarity among tribes, among villages and at the national level is first discernible in the growing number of blows dealt to the enemy. Every new group, every new volley of cannon fire signals that everybody is hunting the enemy, everybody is taking a stand.

This solidarity grows much stronger during the second period when the enemy offensive is launched. Once the uprising has begun the colonial forces regroup, reorganize and adapt their fighting tactics to the type of insurrection. This offensive throws the euphoria and idyll of the first phase into question. The enemy launches an attack and concentrates large numbers of troops at precise locations. Local groups are swiftly overwhelmed, and all the more so because they first tend to tackle the fighting head on. The optimism of the initial phase had made them intrepid, even rash. The group, who was persuaded their own mountain peak was the nation, refuses to pull back, and to beat a retreat is out of the question. Losses are considerable and the survivors are wracked by doubt. The local community endures the attack as a crucial test. It behaves literally as if the fate of the country were at stake at that very place and at that very moment.

But it soon becomes clear that this impetuous spontaneity, which is intent on rapidly settling its score with the colonial system, is destined to fail as a doctrine. A deeply pragmatic realism replaces yesterday's jubilation and the illusion of eternity. The lesson of hard facts and the bodies mowed down by machine guns result in a radical rethinking of events. The basic instinct of survival calls for a more flexible, more agile response. This adjustment in fighting technique was typical of the first months of the war of liberation by the Angolan people. On March 15, 1961, we recall, the Angolan peasants in groups of two or three thousand attacked the Portuguese positions. Men, women, and children, armed and unarmed, courageously and enthusiastically hurled themselves en masse in wave after wave against the regions dominated by the colonists, the military, and the Portuguese flag. Villages and airports were surrounded and suffered numerous attacks, but thousands of Angolans were mowed down by colonialist machine gun fire. The leaders of the Angolan uprising soon realized that they would have to adopt different tactics if they really wanted to liberate their country. The Angolan leader, Roberto Holden, therefore, has recently reorganized the Angolan National Army using the model of other liberation wars and guerrilla warfare techniques.

In guerrilla warfare, in fact, you no longer fight on the spot but on the march. Every fighter carries the soil of the homeland to war between his bare toes. The national liberation army is not an army grappling with the enemy in a single, decisive battle, but travels from village to village, retreating into the forest and jumping for joy when the cloud of dust raised by the enemy's troops is seen in the valley. The tribes begin to mobilize, the units move their positions, changing terrain. The people from the north march toward the west, those on the plains struggle up to the mountains. No strategic position is given preference. The enemy thinks he is in pursuit but we always manage to come up behind him, attacking him at the very moment when he least expects it. Now it is we who are in pursuit. Despite all his technology and firepower the enemy gives the impression he is floundering and losing ground. We never stop singing.

In the meantime, however, the leaders of the insurrection realize that their units need enlightening, instruction, and indoctrination; an army needs to be created, a central authority established. The picture of the nation in arms, divided into splinter groups, calls for rethinking and a new vision. The leaders who had fled the futile atmosphere of urban politics rediscover politics, no longer as a sleep-inducing technique or a means of mystification, but as the sole means of fueling the struggle and preparing the people for clear-sighted national leadership. The leaders of the insurrection realize that any peasant revolt, even on a grand scale, needs control and guidance. They, therefore, must transform the movement from a peasant revolt into a revolutionary war. They discover that in order to succeed the struggle must be based on a clear set of objectives, a well-defined methodology and above all, the recognition by the masses of an urgent timetable. One can hold out for three days, three months at the most, using the masses' pent-up resentment, but one does not win a national war, one does not rout the formidable machine of the enemy or transform the individual if one neglects to raise the consciousness of the men in combat. Neither the heroic fight to the finish nor the beauty of the battle cry is enough.

The expansion of the liberation war can anyway be relied on to deal a crucial blow to the leaders' convictions. The enemy now modifies its tactics. To its brutal policy of repression it adds a judicious and spectacular combination of detente, divisive maneuvers and psychological warfare. Here and there it successfully endeavors to revive tribal conflicts, using agents provocateurs engaged in what is known as countersubversion. Colonialism uses two types of indigenous collaborators to achieve its ends. First of all, there are the usual suspects: chiefs, *kaids*, and witch doctors. As we have seen, the peasant masses, steeped in a never-changing routine, continue to revere their religious leaders, descendants of illustrious families. The tribe, with one voice, embarks on the path designated by the traditional chief. Colonialism secures the services of these loyal servants by paying them a small fortune.

Colonialism also finds ample material in the lumpenproletariat for its machinations. In fact, any national liberation movement should give this lumpenproletariat maximum attention. It will always respond to the call to revolt, but if the insurrection thinks it can afford to ignore it, then this famished underclass will pitch itself into the armed struggle and take part in the conflict, this time on the side of the oppressor. The oppressor, who never misses an opportunity to let the blacks tear at each other's throats, is only too willing to exploit those characteristic flaws of the lumpenproletariat, namely its lack of political consciousness and ignorance. If this readily available human reserve is not immediately organized by the insurrection, it will join the colonialist troops as mercenaries. In Algeria it was the Harkis and the Messalists who were drawn from the lumpenproletariat; in Angola, it supplied the road gangs who opened the way for the Portuguese troops; in the Congo, it can be found in the regionalist demonstrations in the provinces of Kasai and Katanga, while in Léopoldville it was used by the enemies of the Congo to organize "spontaneous" meetings against Lumumba.

The enemy who analyzes the forces of the insurrection, who delves deeper and deeper into the study of that global adversary, the colonized subject, identifies the ideological weakness and spiritual instability of certain segments of the population. The enemy discovers, alongside a well-organized and disciplined insurrectionary front line, a human mass whose commitment is constantly threatened by the addictive cycle of physiological poverty, humiliation, and irresponsibility. The enemy will use this mass even if it costs a fortune. He will create spontaneity by the force of the bayonet or exemplary punishment. Dollars and Belgian francs are poured into the Congo while in Madagascar anti-Hova atrocities are on the increase, and in Algeria, recruits, veritable hostages, are enrolled in the French army. The leader of the insurrection watches as the nation literally keels over. Whole tribes are transformed into Harkis and, armed with the latest weapons, set off on the warpath to invade the rival tribe, labeled nationalist for the occasion. Unanimity in combat, so rich and so grandiose during the initial hours of the insurrection, is undermined. National unity crumbles, the insurrection is at a crucial turning point. The political education of the masses is now recognized as an historical necessity.

This spectacular voluntarism which was to lead the colonized people in a single move to absolute sovereignty, the certainty one had that all the pieces of the nation could be gathered up in one fell swoop and from the same, shared perspective, and the strength grounded in this hope, have proved in the light of experience to be a very great weakness. As long as he imagined he could switch straight from colonized subject to sovereign citizen of an independent nation, as long as he believed in the mirage sustained by his unmediated physical strength, the colonized achieved no real progress along the road to knowledge. His consciousness remained rudimentary. We have seen that the colonized subject fervently engages in the struggle, especially if it is armed. The peasants were especially eager to join the rebellion because they had constantly clung to a virtually anticolonial way of life. From time immemorial the peasants had more or less safeguarded their subjectivity from colonial imposition thanks to stratagems and balancing acts worthy of a magician. They even managed to believe that colonialism was not really victorious. The pride of the peasant, his reluctance to go down into the towns and rub shoulders with the world built by the foreigner, and the way he constantly shrunk back every time an agent of the colonial regime approached, served as a permanent reminder that he was pitting his own dichotomy against that of the colonist.

Antiracist racism and the determination to defend one's skin, which is characteristic of the colonized's response to colonial oppression, clearly represent sufficient reasons to join the struggle. But one does not sustain a war, one does not endure massive repression or witness the disappearance of one's entire family in order for hatred or racism to triumph. Racism, hatred, resentment, and "the legitimate desire for revenge" alone cannot nurture a war of liberation. These flashes of consciousness which fling the body into a zone of turbulence, which plunge it into a virtually pathological dreamlike state where the sight of the other induces vertigo, where my blood calls for the blood of the other, where my death through mere inertia calls for the death of the other, this passionate outburst in the opening phase, disintegrates if it is left to feed on itself. Of course the countless abuses perpetrated by the colonialist forces reintroduce emotional factors into the struggle, give the militant further cause to hate and new reasons to set off in search of a "colonist to kill." But, day by day, leaders will come to realize that hatred is not an agenda. It would be perverse to count on the enemy who always manages to commit as many crimes as possible and can be relied upon to widen "the rift," thus driving the population as a whole to revolt. Whatever the case, we have already indicated that the enemy endeavors to win over certain segments of the population, certain regions and chiefs. During the struggle the colonists and the police force are instructed to modify their behavior and "to become more human." They even go so far as to introduce the terms "Sir" or "Ma'am" in their relations with the colonized. There is no end to the politeness and consideration. In fact the colonized get the feeling that things are changing.

The colonized, who took up arms not only because they were dying of hunger and witnessing the disintegration of their society but also because the colonist treated them like animals and considered them brutes, respond very favorably to such measures. These psychological devices defuse their hatred. Experts and sociologists are a guiding force behind these colonialist maneuvers and conduct numerous studies on the subject of complexes—the complex of frustration, the complex of aggressiveness, and the complex of colonizability. The colonized subject is upgraded, and attempts are made to disarm him psychologically and, naturally, with a few coins. These paltry measures and clever window dressing manage to achieve some success. The colonized subject is so starved of anything that humanizes him, even if it is third rate, that these trivial handouts in some cases manage to impress him. His consciousness is so vulnerable and so inscrutable that it is ignited by the slightest spark. The great undiscriminating thirst for enlightenment of the early days is threatened at every moment by a dose of mystification. The violent, unanimous demands of the revolution, which once lit up the sky, now shrink to more modest proportions. The raging wolf, rabid with hunger, and the whirlwind, blowing in a genuine wind of revolt, may be rendered completely unrecognizable if the struggle continues, and it does continue. The colonized subject is at constant risk of being disarmed by any sort of concession.

The leaders of the insurrection discover this instability of the colonized with horror. At first disconcerted, they then realize the need to explain and ensure that the colonized's consciousness does not get bogged down. In the meantime the war goes on, the enemy organizes itself, gathers strength and preempts the strategy of the colonized. The struggle for national liberation is not a question of bridging the gap in one giant stride. The epic is played out on a difficult, day-to-day basis and the suffering endured far exceeds that of the colonial period. Down in the towns the colonists have apparently changed. Our people are happier. *They are respected.* A daily routine sets in, and the colonized engaged in the struggle, the people who must continue to give it their support, cannot afford to give in. They must not think the objective has already been achieved. When the actual objectives of the struggle are described, they must not think they are impossible. Once again, clarification is needed and the people have to realize where they are going and how to get there. The war is not one battle but a succession of local struggles, none of which, in fact, is decisive.

There is therefore a need to save one's strength and not waste it by throwing everything into the balance. The reserves of colonialism are far richer and more substantial than those of the colonized. And the war goes on. The enemy digs in. The great showdown is not for today or for tomorrow. In fact it began on the very first day, and will not end with the demise of the enemy but quite simply when the latter has come to realize, for a number of reasons, that it is in his interest to terminate the struggle and acknowledge the sovereignty of the colonized people. The objectives of the struggle must not remain as loosely defined as they were in the early days. If we are not careful there is the constant risk that the people will ask why continue the war, every time the enemy makes the slightest concession. We have become so used to the occupier's contempt and his determination to maintain his stranglehold, whatever the cost, that any semblance of generosity or any sign of goodwill is greeted with surprise and jubilation. The colonized then tend to break into song. The militant must be supplied with further, more searching explanations so that the enemy's concessions do not pull the wool over his eyes. These concessions, which are nothing but concessions, do not address the essence of the problem, and from the colonized's perspective, it is clear that a concession does not truly address the problem until it strikes the heart of the colonial regime.

To be more exact, the occupier can easily phase out the violent aspects of his presence. In fact, this dramatic phasing out not only spares the occupier much expense but also has the further benefit of allowing him to better concentrate his powers. But there is a heavy price to pay: to be exact, the price of a more coercive control over the country's future. Historical examples have demonstrated that the masquerade of concessions and the heavy price paid by certain countries have ended in a servitude that is not only more discreet, but also more complete. The people and every militant should be conscious of the historical law which stipulates that certain concessions are in fact shackles. If there is no attempt at clarifying this it is surprising how easy it is for the leaders of certain political parties to engage in nameless compromise with the former colonizer. The colonized must be made to see that colonialism never gives away anything for nothing. Whatever gains the colonized make through armed or political struggle, they are not the result of the colonizer's good will or goodness of heart but to the fact that he can no longer postpone such concessions. Moreover, the colonized subject must be aware that it is not colonialism which makes the concessions but him. When the British government decides to grant the African population a few more seats in the Kenyan Assembly it would be impudent or foolish to think that the British government has made any concessions. Isn't it obvious that it is the Kenyan population who has won the concessions? The colonized people, and those who have been stripped of their possessions, must lose the mentality they have had up till now. The colonized, at the most, can accept a concession from the colonial authorities, but never a compromise.

All this clarification, this subsequent raising of awareness and the advances along the road to understanding the history of societies can only be achieved if the people are organized and guided. This organization is established by the revolutionary elements arriving from the towns at the beginning of the insurrection and those who make their way to the interior as the struggle intensifies. It is this core which constitutes the embryonic political body of the insurrection. As for the peasants, they improve their knowledge through practical experience and prove apt to lead the people's struggle. A wave of awareness and mutual enrichment flows between the nation on a war footing, and its leaders. Traditional institutions are reinforced, expanded and sometimes literally transformed. The tribunal for local conflicts, the *djemaas*, and the village assemblies are transformed into revolutionary tribunals and politico-military committees. In every combat unit and in every village, legions of political commissioners are at work enlightening the people on issues which have become stumbling blocks of incomprehension. If it were not for these commissioners, who are not afraid to address certain issues, the people would find themselves disoriented. For example, the militant in arms often becomes irritated at the sight of much of the local population going about their business in the towns as if they were oblivious to what is going on in the mountains, as if they did not know that the crucial operations have begun. The silence of the towns and the continuation of the daily routine give the peasant the bitter impression that an entire sector of the nation is content to sit back and watch. Such observations disgust the peasants and reinforce their tendency to despise and generally condemn the townsfolk. The task of the political commissioner is to nuance their position and make them aware that certain segments of the population have their own specific interests which do not always coincide with the national interest. The people then realize that national independence brings to light multiple realities which in some cases are divergent and conflicting. At this exact moment in the struggle clarification is crucial as it leads the people to replace an overall undifferentiated nationalism with a social and economic consciousness. The people who in the early days of the struggle had adopted the primitive Manichaeanism of the colonizer—Black versus White, Arab versus Infidel—realize en route that some blacks can be whiter than the whites, and that the prospect of a national flag or independence does not automatically result in certain segments of the population giving up their privileges and their interests. The people realize that there are indigenous elements in their midst who, far from being at loose ends, seem to take advantage of the war to better their material situation and reinforce their burgeoning power. These profiteering elements realize considerable gains from the war at the expense of the people who, as always, are prepared to sacrifice everything and soak the national soil with their blood. The militant who confronts the colonialist war machine with his rudimentary resources realizes that while he is demolishing colonial oppression he is indirectly building another system of exploitation. Such a discovery is galling, painful, and sickening. It was once all so simple with the bad on one side and the good on the other. The idyllic, unreal clarity of the early days is replaced by a penumbra which dislocates the consciousness. The people discover that the iniquitous phenomenon of exploitation can assume a black or Arab face. They cry treason, but in fact the treason is not national but social, and they need to be taught to cry thief. On their arduous path to rationality the people must also learn to give up their simplistic perception of the oppressor. The species is splitting up before their very eyes. They realize that certain colonists do not succumb to the ambient climate of criminal hysteria and remain apart from the rest of their species. Such men, who were automatically relegated to the monolithic bloc of the foreign presence, condemn the colonial war. The scandal really erupts when pioneers of the species change sides, go "native," and volunteer to undergo suffering, torture, and death.

These examples defuse the overall hatred which the colonized feel toward the foreign settlers. The colonized welcome these men with open arms and in an excess of emotion tend to place absolute confidence in them. In the metropolis, stereotyped as the wicked, bloodthirsty stepmother, numerous and sometimes prominent voices take a stand, condemn unreservedly their government's policy of war and urge that the national will of the colonized finally be taken into consideration. Soldiers desert the colonialist ranks, others explicitly refuse to fight against a people's freedom, are jailed and suffer for the sake of the people's right to independence and the management of their own affairs.

The colonist is no longer simply public enemy number one. Some members of the colonialist population prove to be closer, infinitely closer, to the nationalist struggle than certain native sons. The racial and racist dimension is transcended on both sides. Not every black or Muslim is automatically given a vote of confidence. One no longer grabs a gun or a machete every time a colonist approaches. Consciousness stumbles upon partial, finite, and shifting truths. All this is, one can guess, extremely difficult. The task of bringing the people to maturity is facilitated by rigorous organization as well as the ideological level of their leaders. The power of ideology is elaborated and strengthened as the struggle unfolds, taking into account the enemy's maneuvers and the movement's victories and setbacks. The leadership demonstrates its strength and authority by exposing mistakes and, through experience, learning better ways of going forward every time consciousness takes one step backward. Every regression at a local level is used to take the issue up in every village and throughout the network. The insurrection proves to itself its rationality and demonstrates its maturity every time it uses a specific case to advance the consciousness of the people. In spite of those within the movement, who sometimes are inclined to think that any nuance constitutes a danger and threatens popular solidarity, the leadership stands by the principles worked out in the national struggle and in the universal fight conducted by man for his liberation. There is a brutality and contempt for subtleties and individual cases which is typically revolutionary, but there is another type of brutality with surprising resemblances to the first one which is typically counterrevolutionary, adventurist, and anarchist. If this pure, total brutality is not immediately contained it will, without fail, bring down the movement within a few weeks.

The nationalist militant who fled the town, revolted by the demagogic and reformist maneuvers of the leaders, and disillusioned by "politics," discovers in the field a new political orientation which in no way resembles the old. This new politics is in the hands of cadres and leaders working with the tide of history who use their muscles and their brains to lead the struggle for liberation. It is national, revolutionary, and collective. This new reality, which the colonized are now exposed to, exists by action alone. By exploding the former colonial reality the struggle uncovers unknown facets, brings to light new meanings and underlines contradictions which were camouflaged by this reality. The people in arms, the people whose struggle enacts this new reality, the people who live it, march on, freed from colonialism and forewarned against any attempt at mystification or glorification of the nation. Violence alone, perpetrated by the people, violence organized and guided by the leadership, provides the key for the masses to decipher social reality. Without this struggle, without this praxis there is nothing but a carnival parade and a lot of hot air. All that is left is a slight readaptation, a few reforms at the top, a flag, and down at the bottom a shapeless, writhing mass, still mired in the Dark Ages.

The Trials and Tribulations
of National Consciousness

History teaches us that the anticolonialist struggle is not automatically written from a nationalist perspective. Over a long period of time the colonized have devoted their energy to eliminating iniquities such as forced labor, corporal punishment, unequal wages, and the restriction of political rights. This fight for democracy against man's oppression gradually emerges from a universalist, neoliberal confusion to arrive, sometimes laboriously, at a demand for nationhood. But the unpreparedness of the elite, the lack of practical ties between them and the masses, their apathy and, yes, their cowardice at the crucial moment in the struggle, are the cause of tragic trials and tribulations.

Instead of being the coordinated crystallization of the people's innermost aspirations, instead of being the most tangible, immediate product of popular mobilization, national consciousness is nothing but a crude, empty, fragile shell. The cracks in it explain how easy it is for young independent countries to switch back from nation to ethnic group and from state to tribe—a regression which is so terribly detrimental and prejudicial to the development of the nation and national unity. As we shall see, such shortcomings and dangers derive historically from the incapacity of the national bourgeoisie in underdeveloped countries to rationalize popular praxis, in other words their incapacity to attribute it any reason.

The characteristic, virtually endemic weakness of the underdeveloped countries' national consciousness is not only the consequence of the colonized subject's mutilation by the colonial regime. It can also be attributed to the apathy of the national bourgeoisie, its mediocrity, and its deeply cosmopolitan mentality.

The national bourgeoisie, which takes over power at the end of the colonial regime, is an underdeveloped bourgeoisie. Its economic clout is practically zero, and in any case, no way commensurate with that of its metropolitan counterpart which it intends replacing. In its willful narcissism, the national bourgeoisie has lulled itself into thinking that it can supplant the metropolitan bourgeoisie to its own advantage. But independence, which literally forces it back against the wall, triggers catastrophic reactions and obliges it to send out distress signals in the direction of the former metropolis. The business elite and university graduates, who make up the most educated category of the new nation, are identifiable by their small numbers, their concentration in the capital, and their occupations as traders, landowners and professionals. This national bourgeoisie possesses neither industrialists nor financiers. The national bourgeoisie in the underdeveloped countries is not geared to production, invention, creation, or work. All its energy is channeled into intermediary activities. Networking and scheming seem to be its underlying vocation. The national bourgeoisie has the psychology of a businessman, not that of a captain of industry. And it should go without saying that the rapacity of the colonists and the embargo system installed by colonialism hardly left it any choice.

Under the colonial system a bourgeoisie that accumulates capital is in the realm of the impossible. To our thinking, therefore, the historical vocation of an authentic national bourgeoisie in an underdeveloped country is to repudiate its status as bourgeois and an instrument of capital and to become entirely subservient to the revolutionary capital which the people represent.

In an underdeveloped country, the imperative duty of an authentic national bourgeoisie is to betray the vocation to which it is destined, to learn from the people, and make available to them the intellectual and technical capital it culled from its time in colonial universities. We will see, unfortunately, that the national bourgeoisie often turns away from this heroic and positive path, which is both productive and just, and unabashedly opts for the antinational, and therefore abhorrent, path of a conventional bourgeoisie, a bourgeois bourgeoisie that is dismally, inanely, and cynically bourgeois.

We have seen that the objective of the nationalist parties from a certain period onward is geared strictly along national lines. They mobilize the people with the slogan of independence, and anything else is left to the future. When these parties are questioned on their economic agenda for the nation or the regime they propose to establish they prove incapable of giving an answer because, in fact, they do not have a clue about the economy of their own country.

This economy has always developed outside their control. As for the present and potential resources of their country's soil and subsoil, their knowledge is purely academic and approximate. They can only talk about them in general and abstract terms. After independence, this underdeveloped bourgeoisie, reduced in number, lacking capital and rejecting the road to revolution, stagnates miserably. It cannot give free expression to its genius that was in the past hampered by colonial domination, or so it claims. The precariousness of its resources and the scarcity of managerial talent force it for years into an economy of cottage industries. In its inevitably highly limited perspective, the bourgeoisie's idea of a national economy is one based on what we can call local products. Grandiloquent speeches are made about local crafts. Unable to establish factories which would be more profitable for the country and for themselves, the bourgeoisie cloaks local artisanship in a chauvinistic tenderness which not only ties in with the new national dignity, but also ensures them substantial profits. This cult for local products, this incapacity to invent new outlets is likewise reflected in the entrenchment of the national bourgeoisie in the type of agricultural production typical of the colonial period.

Independence does not bring a change of direction. The same old groundnut harvest, cocoa harvest, and olive harvest. Likewise the traffic of commodities goes unchanged. No industry is established in the country. We continue to ship raw materials, we continue to grow produce for Europe and pass for specialists of unfinished products.

Yet the national bourgeoisie never stops calling for the nationalization of the economy and the commercial sector. In its thinking, to nationalize does not mean placing the entire economy at the service of the nation or satisfying all its requirements. To nationalize does not mean organizing the state on the basis of a new program of social relations. For the bourgeoisie, nationalization signifies very precisely the transfer into indigenous hands of privileges inherited from the colonial period.

Since the bourgeoisie has neither the material means nor adequate intellectual resources such as engineers and technicians, it limits its claims to the takeover of businesses and firms previously held by the colonists. The national bourgeoisie replaces the former European settlers as doctors, lawyers, tradesmen, agents, dealers, and shipping agents. For the dignity of the country and to safeguard its own interests, it considers it its duty to occupy all these positions. Henceforth it demands that every major foreign company must operate through them, if it wants to remain in the country or establish trade. The national bourgeoisie discovers its historical mission as intermediary. As we have seen, its vocation is not to transform the nation but prosaically serve as a conveyor belt for capitalism, forced to camouflage itself behind the mask of neocolonialism. The national bourgeoisie, with no misgivings and with great pride, revels in the role of agent in its dealings with the Western bourgeoisie. This lucrative role, this function as small-time racketeer, this narrow-mindedness and lack of ambition are symptomatic of the incapacity of the national bourgeoisie to fulfil its historic role as bourgeoisie. The dynamic, pioneering aspect, the inventive, discoverer-of-new-worlds aspect common to every national bourgeoisie is here lamentably absent. At the core of the national bourgeoisie of the colonial countries a hedonistic mentality prevails—because on a psychological level it identifies with the Western bourgeoisie from which it has slurped every lesson. It mimics the Western bourgeoisie in its negative and decadent aspects without having accomplished the initial phases of exploration and invention that are the assets of this Western bourgeoisie whatever the circumstances. In its early days the national bourgeoisie of the colonial countries identifies with the last stages of the Western bourgeoisie. Don't believe it is taking short cuts. In fact it starts at the end. It is already senile, having experienced neither the exuberance nor the brazen determination of youth and adolescence.

In its decadent aspect the national bourgeoisie gets considerable help from the Western bourgeoisies who happen to be tourists enamored of exoticism, hunting and casinos. The national bourgeoisie establishes holiday resorts and playgrounds for entertaining the Western bourgeoisie. This sector goes by the name of tourism and becomes a national industry for this very purpose. We only have to look at what has happened in Latin America if we want proof of the way the ex-colonized bourgeoisie can be transformed into "party" organizer. The casinos in Havana and Mexico City, the beaches of Rio, Copacabana, and Acapulco, the young Brazilian and Mexican girls, the thirteen-year-old mestizas, are the scars of this depravation of the national bourgeoisie. Because it is lacking in ideas, because it is inward-looking, cut off from the people, sapped by its congenital incapacity to evaluate issues on the basis of the nation as a whole, the national bourgeoisie assumes the role of manager for the companies of the West and turns its country virtually into a bordello for Europe. Once again we need only to look at the pitiful spectacle of certain republics in Latin America. U.S. businessmen, banking magnates and technocrats jet "down to the tropics," and for a week to ten days wallow in the sweet depravity of their private "reserves."

The behavior of the national landowners is practically the same as that of the urban bourgeoisie. As soon as independence is proclaimed the big farmers demand the nationalization of the agricultural holdings. Through a number of schemes they manage to lay hands on the farms once owned by the colonists, thereby reinforcing their control over the region. But they make no attempt to diversify, increase production or integrate it in a genuinely national economy.

In fact the landowners call on the authorities to increase a hundredfold the facilities and privileges now theirs but once reserved for the foreign colonists. The exploitation of farm workers is intensified and justified. Capitalizing on two or three slogans, these new colonists demand a colossal effort from these farm laborers— in the name of the national interest, of course. There is no modernization of agriculture, no development plan, no initiative, for initiatives imply a degree of risk, and would throw such milieus into a panic, and put to flight a wary, overcautious, landed bourgeoisie which is sinking deeper and deeper into the ruts established by colonialism. In such regions, initiatives are handled by the government. It is the government which approves them, encourages them and finances them. The landed bourgeoisie refuses to take the slightest risk. It is hostile to gambling and ventures. It has no intention of building upon sand. It demands solid investments and quick returns. The profits it pockets are enormous compared to the gross national product, and are not reinvested. Its only mentality is to hoard its savings. This bourgeoisie especially in the aftermath of independence, has no scruples depositing in foreign banks the profits it has made from the national resources. Major sums, however, are invested for the sake of prestige in cars, villas, and all those ostentatious goods described by economists as typical of an underdeveloped bourgeoisie.

We have said that the colonized bourgeoisie which attains power utilizes the aggressiveness of its class to grab the jobs previously held by foreigners. In the aftermath of independence, faced with the human consequences of colonialism, it wages a ruthless struggle against the lawyers, tradespeople, landowners, doctors, and high-ranking civil servants "who insult the national dignity." It frantically brandishes the notions of nationalization and Africanization of the managerial classes. In fact, its actions become increasingly tinged with racism. It bluntly confronts the government with the demand that it must have these jobs. And it does not tone down its virulence until it occupies every single one of them.

The urban proletariat, the unemployed masses, the small artisans, those commonly called small traders, side with this nationalist attitude; but, in all justice, they are merely modeling their attitude on that of their bourgeoisie. Whereas the national bourgeoisie competes with the Europeans, the artisans and small traders pick fights with Africans of other nationalities. In the Ivory Coast, outright race riots were directed against the Dahomeans* and Upper Voltans who controlled much of the business sector and were the target of hostile demonstrations by the Ivorians following independence. We have switched from nationalism to ultranationalism, chauvinism, and racism. There is a general call for these foreigners to leave, their shops are burned, their market booths torn down and some are lynched; consequently, the Ivorian government orders them to leave, thereby satisfying

---

* Translator's Note: Present-day Beninese and Burkinabés

the demands of the nationals. In Senegal it was the anti-Sudanese** demonstrations that caused Mamadou Dia to state: "The people of Senegal owe their blind belief in the Federation of Mali to their affection for its leaders. Their deep attachment to Mali has no other basis but a repeated act of faith in the politics of these leaders. The issue of Senegalese territory was no less alive in their minds, especially as the Sudanese presence in Dakar was far too visible for the problem to be overlooked. This is the reason why, far from causing any regrets, the breakup of the Federation was greeted by the masses with relief and there was no support from any quarter in its favor."[13]

Whereas certain categories of Senegalese jump at the opportunity offered by their own leaders to get rid of the Sudanese, who are unwelcome elements in the business and administrative sectors, the Congolese, who watched in disbelief as the Belgians left en masse, decide to put pressure on the Senegalese established at Léopoldville and Elizabethville and in turn get them to leave.

As we can see, the mechanism is identical in both cases. Whereas the ambitions of the young nation's intellectuals and business bourgeoisie are thwarted by the Europeans, for the majority of the urban population, competition stems mainly from Africans of other nations. In the Ivory Coast it is the Dahomeans; in Ghana, the inhabitants of Niger; and in Senegal, the Sudanese.

Whereas the demand for Africanization and Arabization of management by the bourgeoisie is not rooted in a genuine endeavor at nationalization, but merely corresponds to a transfer of power previously held by the foreigners, the masses make the very same demand at their own level but limit the notion of African or Arab to territorial limits. Between the vibrant calls for African unity and this mass behavior inspired by the managerial class, a number of attitudes emerge. There is a constant pen-

---

** Translator's Note: Present-day Malian
[13] Mamadou Dia, *Nations africaines et solidarité mondiale*, P.U.F., 140.

dulum motion between African unity, which sinks deeper and deeper into oblivion, and a depressing return to the most heinous and virulent type of chauvinism.

"As for the Senegalese leaders who were the main theoreticians of African unification and who, on several occasions, sacrificed their local political organizations as well as their personal careers to this idea, they undeniably bear a great deal of responsibility, although admittedly in all good faith. Their mistake, our mistake, under the pretext of combating Balkanization, was not to take into consideration that pre-colonial factor of territoriality. Our mistake was not to give enough attention in our analyses to this factor, exacerbated by colonialism, but also a sociological fact which no theory on unity, however commendable or appealing, can eliminate. We let ourselves be tempted by the mirage whose configuration is the most satisfying for the mind, and taking our ideal for reality, we believed we only needed to condemn territoriality and its natural offshoot, micro nationalism, to get the better of them and ensure the success of our chimerical endeavor."[14]

From Senegalese chauvinism to Wolof tribalism, there is but one small step. And consequently, wherever the petty-mindedness of the national bourgeoisie and the haziness of its ideological positions have been incapable of enlightening the people as a whole or have been unable to put the people first, wherever this national bourgeoisie has proven to be incapable of expanding its vision of the world, there is a return to tribalism, and we watch with a raging heart as ethnic tensions triumph. Since the only slogan of the bourgeoisie is "Replace the foreigners," and they rush into every sector to take the law into their own hands and fill the vacancies, the petty traders such as taxi drivers, cake sellers, and shoe shiners follow suit and call for the expulsion of the Dahomeans or, taking tribalism to a new level, demand that the Fulani go back to their bush or back up their mountains.

---

[14] *Ibid.*

The triumph of federalism in certain young independent nations must be interpreted along these lines. We know that colonial domination gave preferential treatment to certain regions. The colony's economy was not integrated into that of the nation as a whole. It is still organized along the lines dictated by the metropolis. Colonialism almost never exploits the entire country. It is content with extracting natural resources and exporting them to the metropolitan industries thereby enabling a specific sector to grow relatively wealthy, while the rest of the colony continues, or rather sinks, into underdevelopment and poverty.

In the aftermath of independence the nationals who live in the prosperous regions realize their good fortune and their gut reaction is to refuse to feed the rest of the nation. The regions rich in groundnuts, cocoa, and diamonds stand out against the empty panorama offered by the rest of the country. The nationals of these regions look upon the others with hatred detecting envy, greed, and murderous impulses. The old precolonial rivalries, the old intertribal hatreds resurface. The Balubas refuse to feed the Luluas. Katanga becomes a state on its own and Albert Kalondji crowns himself king of southern Kasai.

African unity, a vague term, but nevertheless one to which the men and women of Africa were passionately attached and whose operative function was to put incredible pressure on colonialism, reveals its true face and crumbles into regionalisms within the same national reality. Because it is obsessed with its immediate interests, because it cannot see further than the end of its nose, the national bourgeoisie proves incapable of achieving simple national unity and incapable of building the nation on a solid, constructive foundation. The national front that drove back colonialism falls apart and licks its wounds.

This ruthless struggle waged by the ethnic groups and tribes, and this virulent obsession with filling the vacancies left by the foreigners also engender religious rivalries. In the interior and the bush, the minor confraternities, the local religions, and *marabout* cults spring back to life and resort once more to the vicious circle of mutual denunciation. In the urban centers the authorities are confronted with a clash between the two major revealed religions: Islam and Catholicism.

Colonialism, which the birth of African unity had trembling on its foundations, is now back on its feet, and now undertakes to break this will to unify by taking advantage of every weak link in the movement. Colonialism will attempt to rally the African peoples by uncovering the existence of "spiritual" rivalries. In Senegal the magazine *Afrique Nouvelle* secretes its weekly dose of hatred against Islam and the Arabs. The Lebanese, who control most of the small businesses along the West Coast of Africa, are publicly vilified. The missionaries opportunely remind the masses that the great African empires were dismantled by the invasion of the Arabs long before the arrival of European colonialism. They even go so far as to say that the Arab occupation paved the way for European colonialism; references are made to Arab imperialism, and the cultural imperialism of Islam is denounced. Muslims are generally kept out of managerial positions. In other regions the reverse is true and it is the indigenous Christians who are the targets and treated as conscious enemies of national independence.

Colonialism shamelessly pulls all these strings, only too content to see the Africans, who were once in league against it, tear at each other's throats. The notion of another Saint Bartholomew's massacre takes shape in some people's minds, and colonialism snickers when it hears the magnificent speeches on African unity. Within the same nation, religion divides the people and sets the spiritual communities, fostered and encouraged by colonialism and its apparatus, at odds with each other. Totally unexpected events break out here and there. In predominantly Catholic or Protestant countries the Muslim minority redoubles its religious fervor. Muslim festivals are revived and Islam defends itself every inch of the way against the violent absolutism of the Catholic religion. Ministers are heard telling certain individuals that if they are not content, they should go and live in Cairo. In some cases American Protestantism transports its anti-Catholic prejudices onto African soil and uses religion to encourage tribal rivalries.

On the scale of the continent this religious tension can take the shape of the crudest form of racism. Africa is divided into a white region and a black region. The substitute names of sub-Saharan Africa and North Africa are unable to mask this latent racism. In some places you hear that White Africa has a thousand-year-old tradition of culture, that it is Mediterranean, an extension of Europe and is part of Greco-Roman civilization. Black Africa is looked upon as a wild, savage, uncivilized, and lifeless region. In other places, you hear day in and day out hateful remarks about veiled women, polygamy, and the Arabs' alleged contempt for the female sex. The aggressiveness of all these remarks recalls those so often attributed to the colonist. The national bourgeoisie of each of these two major regions, who have assimilated to the core the most despicable aspects of the colonial mentality, take over from the Europeans and lay the foundations for a racist philosophy that is terribly prejudicial to the future of Africa. Through its apathy and mimicry it encourages the growth and development of racism that was typical of the colonial period. It is hardly surprising then in a country which calls itself African to hear remarks that are nothing less than racist and to witness paternalistic behavior bitterly reminiscent of Paris, Brussels, or London.

In certain regions of Africa, bleating paternalism toward blacks and the obscene idea drawn from Western culture that the black race is impermeable to logic and science reign in all their nakedness. There are some places where black minorities are confined in semi slavery, which justifies the caution, even distrust, that the countries of Black Africa manifest toward the countries of

White Africa. It is not unusual for a citizen of Black Africa walking in a city of White Africa to hear children call him "nigger" or to find the authorities speaking to him in pidgin.

Unfortunately, alas, it is all too likely that students from Black Africa enrolled in schools north of the Sahara will be asked by their schoolmates whether people live in houses in their home countries, whether they have electricity, and if their family practices cannibalism. Unfortunately, alas, it is all too likely that in certain regions north of the Sahara Africans from the south will encounter fellow countrymen who beg them to take them "anywhere there are blacks." Likewise, in certain newly independent states of Black Africa, members of parliament, even government ministers, solemnly declare that the danger lies not in a reoccupation of their country by a colonial power but a possible invasion by "Arab vandals from the north."

As we have seen, the inadequacies of the bourgeoisie are not restricted to economics. Achieving power in the name of a narrow-minded nationalism, in the name of the race, and in spite of its magnificently worded declarations totally void of content, irresponsibly wielding phrases straight out of Europe's treatises on ethics and political philosophy, the bourgeoisie proves itself incapable of implementing a program with even a minimum humanist content. When it is strong, when it organizes the world on the basis of its power, a bourgeoisie does not hesitate to maintain a pretense of universal democratic ideas. An economically sound bourgeoisie has to be faced with exceptional circumstances to force it to disregard its humanist ideology. Although fundamentally racist, the Western bourgeoisie generally manages to mask this racism by multiplying the nuances, thereby enabling it to maintain intact its discourse on human dignity in all its magnanimity.

Western bourgeoisie has erected enough barriers and safeguards for it to fear no real competition from those it exploits and despises. Western bourgeois racism toward the "nigger" and the "towelhead" is a racism of contempt—a racism that minimizes. But the bourgeois ideology that proclaims all men to be essentially equal, manages to remain consistent with itself by urging the subhuman to rise to the level of Western humanity that it embodies.

The racism of the young national bourgeoisie is a defensive racism, a racism based on fear. Basically it does not differ from common tribalism or even rivalry between clans or confraternities. It is easy to understand why perspicacious international observers never really took the lofty speeches on African unity very seriously. The flagrant flaws are so numerous that one clearly senses that all these contradictions must first be solved before unity can be achieved.

The peoples of Africa have recently discovered each other and, in the name of the continent, have decided to pressure the colonial regimes in a radical way. The national bourgeoisies, however, who, in region after region, are in a hurry to stash away a tidy sum for themselves and establish a national system of exploitation, multiply the obstacles for achieving this "utopia." The national bourgeoisies, perfectly clear on their objectives, are determined to bar the way to this unity, this coordinated effort by 250 million people to triumph over stupidity, hunger, and inhumanity. This is why we must understand that African unity can only be achieved under pressure and through leadership by the people, i.e., with total disregard for the interests of the bourgeoisie.

The national bourgeoisie also proves incompetent in domestic politics and institutionally. In a certain number of underdeveloped countries the parliamentary rules are fundamentally flawed. Economically powerless, unable to establish coherent social relations based on the principle of class domination, the bourgeoisie chooses what seems to be the easiest solution, the single-party system. It does not possess as yet that ease of conscience and serenity that only economic power and control of the state system can give it. It does not establish a reassuring State for the citizen, but one which is troubling.

Instead of inspiring confidence, assuaging the fears of its citizens and cradling them with its power and discretion, the State, on the contrary, imposes itself in a spectacular manner, flaunts its authority, harasses, making it clear to its citizens they are in constant danger. The single party is the modern form of the bourgeois dictatorship—stripped of mask, makeup, and scruples, cynical in every aspect.

Such a dictatorship cannot, in fact, go very far. It never stops secreting its own contradiction. Since the bourgeoisie does not have the economic means both to ensure its domination and to hand out a few crumbs to the rest of the country—so busy is it lining its own pockets not only as fast as it can, but also in the most vulgar fashion—the country sinks ever deeper into stagnation. And in order to hide this stagnation, to mask this regression, to reassure itself and give itself cause to boast, the bourgeoisie has no other option but to erect imposing edifices in the capital and spend money on so-called prestige projects.

The national bourgeoisie increasingly turns its back on the interior, on the realities of a country gone to waste, and looks toward the former metropolis and the foreign capitalists who secure its services. Since it has no intention of sharing its profits with the people or of letting them enjoy the rewards paid by the major foreign companies, it discovers the need for a popular leader whose dual role will be to stabilize the regime and perpetuate the domination of the bourgeoisie. The bourgeois dictatorship of the underdeveloped countries draws its strength from the existence of such a leader. We know that in the developed countries the bourgeois dictatorship is the product of the bourgeoisie's economic power. In the underdeveloped countries, however, the leader represents the moral force behind which the gaunt and destitute bourgeoisie of the young nation decides to grow rich.

The people, who for years have seen him or heard him speak, who have followed from afar, in a kind of dream, the leader's tribulations with the colonial powers, spontaneously place their trust in this patriot. Before independence, the leader, as a rule, personified the aspirations of the people—independence, political freedom, and national dignity. But in the aftermath of independence, far from actually embodying the needs of the people, far from establishing himself as the promoter of the actual dignity of the people, which is founded on bread, land, and putting the country back into their sacred hands, the leader will unmask his inner purpose: to be the CEO of the company of profiteers composed of a national bourgeoisie intent only on getting the most out of the situation.

Honest and sincere though he may often be, in objective terms the leader is the virulent champion of the now combined interests of the national bourgeoisie and the ex-colonial companies. His honesty, which is purely a frame of mind, gradually crumbles. The leader is so out of touch with the masses that he manages to convince himself they resent his authority and question the services he has rendered to the country. The leader is a harsh judge of the ingratitude of the masses and every day a little more resolutely sides with the exploiters. He then knowingly turns into an accomplice of the young bourgeoisie that wallows in corruption and gratification.

The economic channels of the young state become irreversibly mired in a neocolonialist system. Once protected, the national economy is now literally state controlled. The budget is funded by loans and donations. The heads of state themselves or government delegations make quarterly visits to the former metropolis or elsewhere, fishing for capital.

The former colonial power multiplies its demands and accumulates concessions and guarantees, taking fewer and fewer precautions to mask the hold it has over the national government. The people stagnate miserably in intolerable poverty and slowly become aware of the unspeakable treason of their leaders. This awareness is especially acute since the bourgeoisie is incapable of forming a class. Its organized distribution of wealth is not diversfied into sectors, is not staggered, and does not nuance its priorities. This new caste is an insult and an outrage, especially since the immense majority, nine tenths of the population, continue to starve to death. The way this caste gets rich quickly, pitilessly and scandalously, is matched by a determined resurgence of the people and the promise of violent days ahead. This bourgeois caste, this branch of the nation that annexes the entire wealth of the country for its own gain, true to its nature, but nevertheless unexpectedly, casts pejorative aspersions about the other blacks or Arabs, which recall in more ways than one the racist doctrine of the former representatives of the colonial power. It is both this wretchedness of the people and this dissolute enrichment of the bourgeois caste, the contempt it flaunts for the rest of the nation, that will harden thoughts and attitudes.

But the looming threat results in a strengthening of authority and the emergence of a dictatorship. The leader with his militant past as a loyal patriot constitutes a screen between the people and the grasping bourgeoisie because he lends his support to the undertakings of this caste and turns a blind eye to its insolence, mediocrity, and fundamental immorality. He helps to curb the growing awareness of the people. He lends his support to this caste and hides its maneuvers from the people, thus becoming its most vital tool for mystifying and numbing the senses of the masses. Every time he addresses the people he recalls his life, which was often heroic, the battles waged and the victories won in the people's name, thus conveying to the masses they should continue to place their trust in him. There are many examples of African patriots who have introduced into the cautious political struggle of their elders a bold, nationalistic style. These men came from the interior. Scandalizing the colonizer and shaming the nationalists in the capital, they proclaimed loud and clear their origins and spoke in the name of the black masses. These men who have praised the race, who were not ashamed of the past—its debasement and cannibalism—today find themselves, alas, heading a team that turns its back on the interior and proclaims that the vocation of the people is to fall in line, always and forever.

The leader pacifies the people. Years after independence, incapable of offering the people anything of substance, incapable of actually opening up their future, of launching the people into the task of nation building and hence their own development, the leader can be heard churning out the history of independence and recalling the united front of the liberation struggle. Refusing to break up the national bourgeoisie, the leader asks the people to plunge back into the past and drink in the epic that led to independence. The leader objectively places a curb on the people and desperately endeavors either to expel them from history or prevent them from setting foot in it. During the struggle for liberation the leader roused the people and promised them a radical, heroic march forward. Today he repeatedly endeavors to lull them to sleep and three or four times a year asks them to remember the colonial period and to take stock of the immense distance they have covered.

We must point out, however, that the masses are quite incapable of appreciating the immense distance they have covered. The peasant who continues to scratch a living from the soil, the unemployed who never find a job, are never really convinced that their lives have changed, despite the festivities and the flags, however new they might be. No matter how hard the bourgeoisie in power tries to prove it, the masses never manage to delude themselves. The masses are hungry and the police commissioners, now Africans, are not particularly reassuring. The masses begin to keep their distance, to turn their backs on and lose interest in this nation which excludes them.

From time to time, however, the leader rallies his forces, speaks over the radio and tours the country in order to reassure, pacify, and mystify. The leader is even more indispensable since there is no party. During the struggle for independence there was in fact a party headed by the current leader. But since that period the party has sadly disintegrated. Only the party in name, emblem, and motto remains. The organic party, designed to enable the free circulation of an ideology based on the actual needs of the masses, has been transformed into a syndication of individual interests. Since independence the party no longer helps the people to formulate their demands, to better realize their needs and better establish their power. Today the party's mission is to convey to the people the instructions handed down from the top. That productive exchange between the rank and file and the higher echelons and vice versa, the basis and guarantee of democracy in a party, no longer exists. On the contrary, the party now forms a screen between the masses and the leadership. The party has been drained of life. The branches created during the colonial period are today in a state of total demobilization.

The militant is running out of patience. It is now we realize how right certain militants were during the liberation struggle. In fact, during the struggle, a number of militants asked the leading organizations to elaborate a doctrine, to clarify objectives and draw up a program. But under the pretext of safeguarding national unity the leaders categorically refused to address such a task. The doctrine, they retorted, was national unity versus colonialism. And on they forged, armed with only a fiery slogan for a doctrine, reducing any ideological activity to a series of variants on the right of peoples to self-determination and the wind of history that would inevitably sweep away colonialism. When the militants asked that the wind of history be given a little more in-depth analysis, the leaders retorted with the notion of hope, and the necessity and inevitability of decolonization, etc.

After independence the party sinks into a profound lethargy. The only time the militants are called upon to rally is during so-called popular festivals, international conferences, and independence day celebrations. The local cadres of the party are appointed to administrative jobs, the party itself becomes an administration and the militants fall back into line and adopt the hollow title of citizen.

Now that they have fulfilled their historic mission of bringing the bourgeoisie to power, they are firmly asked to withdraw so that the bourgeoisie can quietly fulfill its own mission. We have seen, however, that the national bourgeoisie of the underdeveloped countries is incapable of fulfilling any kind of mission. After a few years the disintegration of the party becomes clear and any observer, however superficial, can see for himself that the only role of the former party, now reduced to a skeleton, is to immobilize the people. The very same party, which during the liberation struggle became the focus of the entire nation, now decomposes. The current behavior of the intellectuals, who on the eve of independence had rallied around the party, is proof that such a rally at the time served no other purpose than to have their share of the independence cake. The party becomes a tool for individual advancement.

Inside the new regime, however, there are varying degrees of enrichment and acquisitiveness. Some are able to cash in on all sides and prove to be brilliant opportunists. Favors abound, corruption triumphs, and morals decline. Today the vultures are too numerous and too greedy, considering the meagerness of the national spoils. The party, which has become a genuine instrument of power in the hands of the bourgeoisie, reinforces the State apparatus and determines the containment and immobilization of the people. The party helps the State keep its grip on the people. It is increasingly an instrument of coercion and clearly antidemocratic. The party is unknowingly, and in some cases knowingly, the accomplice of the mercantile bourgeoisie. Just as the national bourgeoisie sidesteps its formative phase to revel in materialism, likewise, at the institutional level, it skips the parliamentary phase and chooses a national-socialist–type dictatorship. We now know that the shortsighted fascism that has triumphed for half a century in Latin America is the dialectical result of the semicolonial State which has prevailed since independence.

In these poor, underdeveloped countries where, according to the rule, enormous wealth rubs shoulders with abject poverty, the army and the police force form the pillars of the regime; both of which, in accordance with another rule, are advised by foreign experts. The strength of this police force and the power of this army are proportional to the marasmus that afflicts the rest of the nation. The national bourgeoisie sells itself increasingly openly to the major foreign companies. Foreigners grab concessions through kickbacks, scandals abound, ministers get rich, their wives become floozies, members of the legislature line their pockets, and everybody, down to police officers and customs officials, joins hands in this huge caravan of corruption.

The opposition becomes more aggressive and the people are quick to latch on to its propaganda. Hostility toward the bourgeoisie is now manifest. The young bourgeoisie, which seems stricken by premature senility, ignores the advice proffered and proves incapable of understanding that it is in its own interest to veil, even slightly, its exploitation of the people.

The very Christian magazine *La Semaine Africaine* in Brazzaville addresses the barons of the regime thus: "Men in power, and you their wives, today your wealth has afforded you comfort, education perhaps, a beautiful home, contacts and many missions abroad that have opened up new horizons. But all your wealth has encased you in a shell which prevents you from seeing the poverty surrounding you. Beware." This warning from *La Semaine Africaine* addressed to Mr. Youlou's lieutenants is, of course, not revolutionary in the least. What *La Semaine Africaine* wants to convey to those starving the Congolese people is that God will punish them: "If there is no room in your heart for the people under you, there will be no room for you in the house of God."

It is obvious that the national bourgeoisie is little troubled by such denunciations. Focused solely on Europe, it remains firmly resolved to get the most out of the situation. The enormous profits it makes from exploiting the people are shipped abroad. The young national bourgeoisie is very often more wary of the regime it has installed than are the foreign companies. It refuses to invest on home soil and is remarkably ungrateful to the State that protects and feeds it. On the European stock exchanges it buys foreign stocks and spends weekends in Paris and Hamburg. The behavior of the national bourgeoisie of certain underdeveloped countries is reminiscent of members of a gang who, after every holdup, hide their share from their accomplices and wisely prepare for retirement. Such behavior reveals that the national bourgeoisie more or less realizes it will lose out in the long term. It foresees that such a situation cannot last for ever, but intends making the most of it. Such a level of exploitation, however, and such distrust of the State inevitably trigger popular discontent. Under the circumstances the regime becomes more authoritarian. The army thus becomes the indispensable tool for systematic repression. In lieu of a parliament, the army becomes the arbiter. But sooner or later it realizes its influence and intimidates the government with the constant threat of a pronunciamento.

As we have seen, the national bourgeoisie of certain underdeveloped countries has learned nothing from history. If it had looked closer at Latin America it would have no doubt identified the dangers awaiting it. We thus arrive at the conclusion that this microbourgeoisie, despite all the fanfare, is doomed to make no headway. In the underdeveloped countries a bourgeois phase is out of the question. A police dictatorship or a caste of profiteers may very well be the case but a bourgeois society is doomed to failure. The band of gilded profiteers grabbing banknotes against a background of widespread misery will sooner or later be a straw in the hands of the army, which is cleverly manipulated by foreign advisors. The former metropolis therefore governs indirectly both through the bourgeoisie it nurtures and the national army which is trained and supervised by its experts to transfix, immobilize and terrorize the people.

The few remarks we have made concerning the national bourgeoisie lead us to an inevitable conclusion. In the underdeveloped countries the bourgeoisie should not find conditions conducive to its existence and fulfilment. In other words, the combined efforts of the masses, regimented by a party, and of keenly conscious intellectuals, armed with revolutionary principles, should bar the way to this useless and harmful bourgeoisie.

The theoretical question, which has been posed for the last fifty years when addressing the history of the underdeveloped countries, i.e., whether the bourgeois phase can be effectively skipped, must be resolved through revolutionary action and not through reasoning. The bourgeois phase in the underdeveloped countries is only justified if the national bourgeoisie is sufficiently powerful, economically and technically, to build a bourgeois society, to create the conditions for developing a sizeable proletariat, to mechanize agriculture, and finally pave the way for a genuine national culture.

The bourgeoisie, which evolved in Europe, was able to elaborate an ideology while strengthening its own influence. This dynamic, educated, and secular bourgeoisie fully succeeded in its undertaking of capital accumulation and endowed the nation with a minimum of prosperity. In the underdeveloped countries we have seen that there was no genuine bourgeoisie but rather an acquisitive, voracious, and ambitious petty caste, dominated by a small-time racketeer mentality, content with the dividends paid out by the former colonial power. This short-sighted bourgeoisie lacks vision and inventiveness. It has learned by heart what it has read in the manuals of the West and subtly transforms itself not into a replica of Europe but rather its caricature.

* * *

The struggle against the bourgeoisie in the underdeveloped countries is far from being simply theoretical. It is not a question of deciphering the way history has judged and condemned it. The national bourgeoisie in the underdeveloped countries should not be combated because it threatens to curb the overall, harmonious development of the nation. It must be resolutely opposed because literally it serves no purpose. Mediocre in its winnings, in its achievements and its thinking, this bourgeoisie attempts to mask its mediocrity by ostentatious projects for individual prestige, chromium-plated American cars, vacations on the French Riviera and weekends in neon-lit nightclubs.

This bourgeoisie, which increasingly turns its back on the overall population, fails even to squeeze from the West such spectacular concessions as valuable investments in the country's economy or the installation of certain industries. Assembly plants, however, are on the increase, a tendency that confirms the neo-colonialist model in which the national economy is struggling. In no way, therefore, can it be said that the national bourgeoisie slows the country's development, that it is wasting the nation's time or possibly leading it into a dead end. But the truth is that the bourgeois phase in the history of the underdeveloped countries is a useless phase. Once this caste has been eliminated, swallowed up by its own contradictions, it will be clear to everyone that no progress has been made since independence and that everything has to be started over again from scratch. This restructuring of the economy will not be based on the order set in place by the bourgeoisie during its reign, since this caste has done nothing else but prolong the heritage of the colonial economy, thinking, and institutions.

It is that much easier to neutralize this bourgeois class since, as we have seen, it is numerically, intellectually, and economically weak. In the colonized territories after independence the bourgeois caste draws its main strength from agreements signed with the former colonial power. The national bourgeoisie has an even greater chance of taking over from the colonialist oppressor since it has been given every opportunity to maintain its close links with the ex-colonial power. But deep-rooted contradictions shake the ranks of this bourgeoisie, giving the close observer an impression of instability. There is not yet a homogeneity of caste. Many intellectuals, for instance, condemn this regime based on domination by a select few. In the underdeveloped countries there are intellectuals, civil servants, and senior officials who sincerely feel the need for a planned economy, for outlawing profiteers and doing away with any form of mystification. Moreover, such men, to a certain degree, are in favor of maximum participation by the people in the management of public affairs.

In underdeveloped countries that acquire independence there is almost always a small number of upstanding intellectuals, without set political ideas, who instinctively distrust the race for jobs and handouts that is symptomatic of the aftermath of independence. The personal situation of these men (breadwinners for an extended family) or their life story (hardship and strict moral upbringing) explains their clear distrust for the smart alecks and profiteers. These men need to be used intelligently in the decisive struggle to steer the nation in a healthy direction. Barring the way to the national bourgeoisie is a sure way of avoiding the pitfalls of independence, the trials and tribulations of national unity, the decline of morals, the assault on the nation by corruption, an economic downturn and, in the short term, an antidemocratic regime relying on force and intimidation. But it also means choosing the only way to go forward.

The profoundly democratic and progressive elements of the young nation are reluctant and shy about making any decision due to the apparent resilience of the bourgeoisie. The colonial cities of the newly independent underdeveloped countries are teeming with the entire managerial class. For want of any serious analysis of the population as a whole, observers are inclined to believe in the existence of a powerful and perfectly organized bourgeoisie. In fact we now know that there is no bourgeoisie in the underdeveloped countries. What makes a bourgeoisie is not its attitude, taste, or manners. It is not even its aspirations. The bourgeoisie is above all the direct product of precise economic realities.

Economic reality in the colonies, however, is a foreign bourgeois reality. It is the metropolitan bourgeoisie, represented by its local counterparts, which is present in the colonial towns. Before independence the bourgeoisie in the colonies is a Western bourgeoisie, an authentic branch of the metropolitan bourgeoisie from which it draws its legitimacy, its strength and its stability. During the period of unrest preceding independence, indigenous intellectual and business elements within this imported bourgeoisie endeavor to identify themselves with it. Theirs is a wish to identify permanently with the bourgeois representatives from the metropolis.

This bourgeoisie, which has unreservedly and enthusiastically adopted the intellectual reflexes characteristic of the metropolis, which has alienated to perfection its own thought and grounded its consciousness in typically foreign notions, has difficulty swallowing the fact that it is lacking in the one thing that makes a bourgeoisie—money. The bourgeoisie of the underdeveloped countries is a bourgeoisie in spirit only. It has neither the economic power, nor the managerial dynamism, nor the scope of ideas to qualify it as a bourgeoisie. Consequently, it is in its early stages and remains a bourgeoisie of civil servants. Whatever confidence and strength it possesses will derive from the position it occupies in the new national administration. Given time and opportunity by the authorities, it will succeed in amassing a small fortune that will reinforce its domination. But it will still prove incapable of creating a genuine bourgeois society with all the economic and industrial consequences this supposes.

* * *

The national bourgeoisie from the outset is geared toward intermediate activities. Its power base lies in its business sense and petty trading, in its capacity to grab commissions. It is not its money that is working but its sense of business. It does not invest, and cannot achieve that accumulation of capital needed for the formation and expansion of an authentic bourgeoisie. At this rate it would take centuries for it to set up the rudiments of industrialization. In any case it would come up against the implacable opposition of the former metropolis, which will have taken every possible precaution in the framework of neocolonialist agreements.

If the authorities want to lift the country out of stagnation and take great strides toward development and progress, they first and foremost must nationalize the tertiary sector. The bourgeoisie, who wants the spirit of lucre and materialism to prevail as well as its contemptuous attitude toward the masses and the scandalous aspect of profit, or theft we should say, in fact invests massively in this sector. Once dominated by the colonists the tertiary sector is raided by the young national bourgeoisie. In a colonial economy the tertiary sector is by far the most important. For the sake of progress the decision to nationalize this sector must be made in the first few hours. But it is evident that such a nationalization must not take on the aspect of rigid state control. This does not mean putting politically uneducated citizens in managerial positions. Every time this procedure has been adopted it was found that the authorities had in fact contributed to the triumph of a dictatorship of civil servants, trained by the former metropolis, who quickly proved incapable of thinking in terms of the nation as a whole. These civil servants swiftly begin to sabotage the national economy and dismantle the national institutions, while corruption, fraud, misappropriation of goods, and black market trafficking set in. To nationalize the tertiary sector means organizing democratically the cooperatives for buying and selling. It means decentralizing these cooperatives by involving the masses in the management of public affairs. All this obviously cannot succeed unless the people are politically educated. Previously the need to clarify such a paramount issue once and for all would have been recognized. Today the principle of educating the masses politically is generally taken for granted in the underdeveloped countries. But it is apparent that this basic task is not being honestly addressed. The decision to politicize the people implies that the regime expects to make popular support a condition for any action undertaken. A government which declares its intent to politicize the people expresses its desire to govern with the people and for the people. It should not use a language designed to camouflage a bourgeois leadership. The bourgeois governments of the capitalist countries have long since left this infantile phase of power behind. They govern dispassionately using their laws, their economic power, and their police force. Now that their authority is solidly established they are not obliged to waste time with demagogic considerations. They govern in their own interest and make no nonsense about it. They have made themselves legitimate and are strong in their own right.

The bourgeois caste of the newly independent countries has not yet attained either the cynicism or the serenity on which the old bourgeoisies based their power. Hence its concern to hide its deep-rooted convictions, to allay suspicions, in short to demonstrate its popularity. It is not by mobilizing dozens or hundreds of thousands of men and women three or four times a year that you politically educate the masses. These meetings, these spectacular rallies, are similar to the old preindependence tactics whereby you displayed your strength to prove to yourself and to others that you had the people on your side. The political education of the masses is meant to make adults out of them, not to make them infantile.

This brings us to consider the role of the political party in an underdeveloped country. We have seen in the preceding pages that very often simplistic minds, belonging, moreover, to the emerging bourgeoisie, repeatedly argue the need for an underdeveloped country to have a strong authority, even a dictatorship, to head its affairs. With this in mind the party is put in charge of monitoring the masses. The party doubles the administration and the police force, and controls the masses not with the aim of ensuring their actual participation in the affairs of the nation but to remind them constantly that the authorities expect them to be obedient and disciplined. This dictatorship, which believes itself carried by history, which considers itself indispensable in the aftermath of independence, in fact symbolizes the decision of the bourgeois caste to lead the underdeveloped country, at first with the support of the people but very soon against them. The gradual transformation of the party into an intelligence agency is indicative that the authorities are increasingly on the defensive. The shapeless mass of the people is seen as a blind force that must be constantly held on a leash either by mystification or fear instilled by police presence. The party becomes a barometer, an intelligence service. The militant becomes an informer. He is put in charge of punitive missions against the villages. Embryonic opposition parties are eliminated at the stroke of a baton or in a hail of stones. Opposition candidates see their houses go up in flames. The police are increasingly provocative. Under these circumstances, there is, of course, but a single party and the government candidate receives 99 percent of the votes. We have to acknowledge that a certain number of governments in Africa operate along these lines. All the opposition parties who were generally progressive and strove for a greater participation of the masses in the management of public affairs, who wanted to see the arrogant and mercantile bourgeoisie brought to heel, have been bludgeoned and incarcerated into silence and then driven underground.

In many of today's independent regions of Africa the political party is being seriously bloated out of all proportion. In the presence of a party member the people keep mum, behave like sheep, and pay tribute to the government and the leader. But in the street, away from the village of an evening, in the café or on the river, the people's bitter disappointment, their desperation, but also their pent-up anger, can be clearly heard. Instead of letting the people express their grievances, instead of making the free circulation of ideas between the people and the leadership its basic mission, the party erects a screen of prohibitions. The party leaders behave like common sergeants major and constantly remind the people of the need to keep "silence in the ranks." This party, which claimed to be the servant of the people, which claimed to work for the people's happiness, quickly dispatches the people back to their caves as soon as the colonial authorities hand over the country. The party will also commit many mistakes regarding national unity. For example, the so-called national party operates on a tribal basis. It is a veritable ethnic group which has transformed itself into a party. This party which readily proclaims itself national, which claims to speak in the name of the people as a whole, secretly and sometimes openly sets up a genuine ethnic dictatorship. We are no longer witness to a bourgeois dictatorship but to a tribal one. The ministers, private secretaries, ambassadors, and prefects are chosen from the leader's ethnic group, sometimes even directly from his family. These regimes based on the family unit seem to repeat the age-old laws of endogamy and faced with this stupidity, this imposture and this intellectual and spiritual poverty, we are left with a feeling of shame rather than anger. These heads of government are the true traitors of Africa, for they sell their continent to the worst of its enemies: stupidity. This tribalization of power results, much as one would expect, in regionalist thinking and separatism. Decentralizing trends surface and triumph, the nation disintegrates and is dismembered. The leader who once cried: "African unity!" and thought of his own little family awakes to find himself saddled with five tribes who also want their own ambassadors and ministers; and as irresponsible, oblivious, and pathetic as ever he cries "treason."

* * *

We have many times indicated the very often detrimental role of the leader. This is because in certain regions the party is organized like a gang whose toughest member takes over the leadership. The leader's ancestry and powers are readily mentioned, and in a knowing and slightly admiring tone it is quickly pointed out that he inspires awe in his close collaborators. In order to avoid these many pitfalls a persistent battle has to be waged to prevent the party from becoming a compliant instrument in the hands of a leader. *Leader* comes from the English verb "to lead," meaning "to drive" in French.[15] The driver of people no longer exists today. People are no longer a herd and do not need to be driven. If the leader drives me I want him to know that at the same time I am driving him. The nation should not be an affair run by a big boss. Hence the panic that grips government circles every time one of their leaders falls ill, because they are obsessed with the question of succession: What will happen to the country if the leader dies? The influential circles, who in their blind irresponsibility are more concerned with safeguarding their lifestyle, their cocktail parties, their paid travel and their profitable racketeering, have abdicated in favor of a leader and occasionally discover the spiritual void at the heart of the nation.

A country which really wants to answer to history, which wants to develop its towns and the minds of its inhabitants, must possess a genuine party. The party is not an instrument in the hands of the government. Very much to the contrary, the party is an instrument in the hands of the people. It is the party which decides on the policy enacted by the government. The party is not and never should be merely a political bureau where all the members of government and dignitaries of the regime feel free to

---

[15] Translator's Note: In the original, Fanon uses the English word *leader* and compares it to the French verb *conduire*.

congregate. Alas all too often it is the party which makes up the entire political bureau and its members reside permanently in the capital. In an underdeveloped country the leading party members should flee the capital like the plague. With the exception of a few, they should reside in the rural areas. Centralizing everything in the capital should be avoided. No administrative pretext can justify the bustle of the capital already overpopulated and over-developed compared with nine tenths of the territory. The party must be decentralized to the limit. This is the only way to revive regions that are dead, the regions that have not yet woken up to life.

In practice there will be at least one member of the political bureau in each region and care should be taken not to appoint him regional head. He will not handle administrative responsi-bilities. The member of the regional political bureau is not obliged to hold the highest rank in the regional administration. He should not necessarily join forces with the authorities. For the people the party is not the authority but the organization whereby they, the people, exert their authority and will. The less confusion there is, the less duality of powers, the more the party can fulfill its role as guide and the more it will become a decisive guaran-tee for the people. If the party merges with the authorities, then this is the fastest way for the party militant to achieve his selfish ends, obtain a job in the administration, be promoted, change his rank, and make a career for himself.

In an underdeveloped country the creation of dynamic regional bureaus halts the process of urban macrocephaly and the chaotic exodus of the rural masses toward the towns. The establishment, during the very first days of independence, of regional bureaus with the power to stimulate, revive, and accelerate the citizens' con-sciousness is an inevitable prerequisite for any country that wants to progress. Otherwise, the party leaders and dignitaries of the regime congregate around the leader. The administration swells out of all proportion, not because it is expanding or specializing, but because more cousins and more militants expect a position and hope to slip into the works. And the dream of every citizen is to reach the capital, to have his piece of the pie. The towns and villages are deserted, the unaided, uneducated, and untrained rural masses turn their backs on an unrewarding soil and set off for the urban periphery, swelling the lumpenproletariat out of all proportion.

Another national crisis is looming. We believe, on the contrary, that the interior, the back country, should be given priority. In the last resort, moreover, we see no drawback to the government convening elsewhere besides the capital. The myth of the capital must be debunked and the disinherited shown that the decision has been made to work in their interest. To a certain degree this is what the Brazilian government attempted to do with Brasília. The arrogance of Rio de Janeiro was an insult to the Brazilian people. But unfortunately, Brasília is still a new capital, as monstrous as the other one. Its only advantage is that today a road has been built through the forest. No, no serious objection can be made to the choice of a new capital, to relocating the entire government to one of the most destitute regions. The idea of a capital in underdeveloped countries is a commercial notion inherited from the colonial period. In the underdeveloped countries, however, we must increase our contacts with the rural masses. We must apply a national policy, i.e., a policy specifically aimed at the masses. We must never lose contact with the people who fought for their independence and a better life.

Instead of delving into their diagrams and statistics, indigenous civil servants and technicians should delve into the body of the population. They should not bristle every time there is mention of an assignment to the "interior." One should no longer hear their young wives threaten to divorce their husbands if they cannot manage to avoid a rural posting. Hence the party's political bureau should give priority to the disinherited regions, and the artificial and superficial life of the capital, grafted onto the national reality like a foreign body, should occupy as small a place as possible in the life of the nation which, on the contrary, is fundamental and sacred.

In an underdeveloped country the party must be organized in such a way that it is not content merely to stay in touch with the masses. The party must be the direct expression of the masses. The party is not an administration with the mission of transmitting government orders. It is the vigorous spokesperson and the incorruptible defender of the masses. In order to arrive at this notion of party we must first and foremost rid ourselves of the very Western, very bourgeois, and hence very disparaging, idea that the masses are incapable of governing themselves. Experience has proven in fact that the masses fully understand the most complex issues. One of the greatest services the Algerian revolution has rendered to Algerian intellectuals was to put them in touch with the masses, to allow them to see the extreme, unspeakable poverty of the people and at the same time witness the awakening of their intelligence and the development of their consciousness. The Algerian people, that starved, illiterate mass of men and women who for centuries were plunged into incredible darkness, have resisted the tanks and planes, the napalm and the psychological warfare, but above all, the corruption and the brainwashing, the traitors and the "national" armies of General Bellounis. The Algerian people have stood firm in spite of the weak-minded, the fence-sitters, and the would-be dictators. The Algerian people have stood firm because their seven-year struggle has opened up spheres they never even dreamed of. Today arms factories operate deep in the *jebel* several meters underground; today people's tribunals function at every level and local planning commissions carve up the large agricultural estates and draw up the Algeria of tomorrow. An isolated individual can resist understanding an issue, but the group, the village, grasps it with disconcerting speed. Of course if we choose to use a language comprehensible only to law and economics graduates it will be easy to prove that the masses need to have their life run for them. But if we speak in plain language, if we are not obsessed with a perverse determination to confuse the issues and exclude the people, then it will be clear that the masses comprehend all the finer points and every artifice. Resorting to technical language means you are determined to treat the masses as uninitiated. Such language is a poor front for the lecturer's intent to deceive the people and leave them on the sidelines. Language's endeavor to confuse is a mask behind which looms an even greater undertaking to dispossess. The intention is to strip the people of their possessions as well as their sovereignty. You can explain anything to the people provided you really want them to understand. And if you think they can be dispensed with, that on the contrary they would be more of a nuisance to the smooth running of the many private and limited companies whose aim is to push them further into misery, then there is no more to be said.

If you think you can perfectly govern a country without involving the people, if you think that by their very presence the people confuse the issue, that they are a hindrance or, through their inherent unconsciousness, an undermining factor, then there should be no hesitation: The people must be excluded. Yet when the people are asked to participate in the government, instead of being a hindrance they are a driving force. We Algerians during the course of this war have had the opportunity, the good fortune, of fully grasping the reality of a number of things. In some of the rural areas, the politico-military leaders of the revolution found themselves confronted with situations that required radical responses. We shall now address some of these situations.

In 1956 and 1957 French colonialism put certain zones off limits, and travel in these regions was strictly regulated. The peasants were no longer able to travel freely into town to buy fresh provisions. During this period the local grocers made huge profits. Tea, coffee, sugar, tobacco, and salt reached exorbitant prices. The black market flourished and became particularly brazen. The peasants who could not pay cash mortgaged their crops, even their land, or else carved up the family property piece by piece; the next resort was to work solely to pay their bills at the local grocer's. As soon as the political commissioners realized the risks involved they reacted immediately. Consequently a rational system of supplies was established: In town the grocer was obliged to buy from the government wholesalers who gave him an invoice detailing the price of the goods. When the retailer arrived back in the *douar* he had first to report to the political commissioner who checked the invoice, fixed the profit margin, and set the selling price. The resale prices were displayed in the shop and a member of the *douar*, a kind of inspector, was on hand to inform the fellah of the exact price the goods had to be sold. The retailer, however, very quickly discovered a loophole and after three or four days declared he had run out of stock. He resumed his underhand dealings and continued selling on the black market. The reaction by the politico-military authorities was immediate. Large fines were charged and the money collected was paid into the village coffers to finance either charity works or works in the interest of the community. In some cases it was decided to close down the shop for a while. In the event of a second offense the business was immediately taken over and run by an elected management committee, on condition the former owner was paid a monthly allowance.

On the basis of this experience, it was explained to the people how the laws of economics functioned, taking concrete examples. The accumulation of capital turned from a theory into a very real and topical mode of behavior. The people understood how one can get rich from a business and expand it. It was only then that the peasants recounted how their grocer lent them money at usurious rates; others recalled how he had driven them from their land and how they had gone from being landowners to laborers.

The more the people understand, the more vigilant they become, the more they realize in fact that everything depends on them and that their salvation lies in their solidarity, in recognizing their interests and identifying their enemies. The people understand that wealth is not the fruit of labor but the spoils from an organized protection racket. The rich no longer seem respectable men but flesh-eating beasts, jackals and ravens who wallow in the blood of the people. Moreover the political commissioners had to rule that nobody would work for anyone else. The land belongs to those who work it. This is a principle which through an information campaign has become a fundamental law of the Algerian revolution. The peasants who employed agricultural laborers have been obliged to distribute land shares to their former employees.

The yield per acre was thus seen to triple, despite numerous raids and aerial bombardments by the French as well as the difficulty of getting fertilizers. The fellahs who were able to judge and see for themselves the produce they had harvested were eager to understand how it worked. They very quickly realized that work is not a simple notion, that slavery is the opposite of work, and that work presupposes freedom, responsibility, and consciousness.

In the regions where we were able to conduct these enlightening experiments, where we witnessed the edification of man through revolutionary teachings, the peasant clearly grasped the principle whereby the clearer the commitment, the better one works. We were able to convey to the masses that work is not a physical exercise or the working of certain muscles, but that one works more with one's brain and one's heart than with muscles and sweat. Likewise, in liberated regions, cut off from the former distribution channels, we had to modify production which previously was geared solely toward the towns and exports. We established production for consumption by the people and the units of the national liberation army. We quadrupled the production of lentils and organized the making of charcoal. Green vegetables and charcoal were shipped from the northern regions to the south over the mountains, while the southern zones sent meat to the north. It was the FLN (Front de la Libération Nationale) who decided on this coordination and established the communications systems. We did not have technicians or experts from the leading universities of the West. But in the liberated regions, the daily ration reached the hitherto unheard of figure of 3,200 calories. The people were not content merely to celebrate their victory. They asked theoretical questions. For example, why did certain regions never see an orange before the war of liberation, whereas thousands of tons were shipped abroad annually; why had so many Algerians never seen grapes, whereas millions of grapes were dispatched for the enjoyment of Europeans? Today the people have a very clear notion of what belongs to them. The Algerian people now know they are the sole proprietor of their country's soil and subsoil. And if some cannot understand the FLN's relentless refusal to tolerate any infringement of this ownership and its fierce determination not to accept any compromise on principles, then everyone should remember that the Algerian people are now adult, responsible, and conscious. In short, the Algerian people are proprietors.

We have taken the Algerian example to clarify our discourse — not to glorify our own people, but quite simply to demonstrate the important part their struggle has played in achieving consciousness. Obviously other peoples have achieved the same results through other methods. We are now in a better position today to know that the confrontation in Algeria was inevitable, but other regions have led their people to the same results through political struggle and information campaigns by the party. In Algeria we understood that the masses were fully prepared for the problems with which they were confronted. In an underdeveloped country experience proves that the important point is not that three hundred people understand and decide but that all understand and decide, even it if takes twice or three times as long. In fact the time taken to explain, the time "lost" humanizing the worker, will be made up in the execution. People must know where they are going and why. The politician should be aware that the future will remain bleak as long as the people's consciousness remains rudimentary, primary, and opaque. We, African politicians, must have very clear ideas about our peoples' situation. But this lucidity must remain deeply dialectical. The awakening of the people as a whole will not be achieved overnight; their rational commitment to the task of building the nation will be simple and straightforward; first of all, because the methods and channels of communication are still in the development stages; secondly, because the sense of time must no longer be that of the moment or the next harvest but rather that of the rest of the world; and finally, because the demoralization buried deep within the mind by colonization is still very much alive. But we should be aware that victory over the pockets of least resistance—the legacy of the material and spiritual domination of the country—is a requisite that no government can escape. Let us take the example of work under the colonial regime. The colonist never stopped complaining that the "native" was slow. Today in certain independent countries we hear leaders take up the same complaint. What the colonist really wanted was for the slave to be full of enthusiasm. Through a kind of mystification constituting the highest form of alienation, he sought to convince the slave that the land he was working belonged to him and the mines where he was losing his health were his property. The colonist forgot strangely enough that he was getting rich on the agony of the slave. In fact what the colonist was saying to the colonized subject was: "Work yourself to death, but let me get rich!" Today we should proceed differently. We must not say to the people: "Work yourself to death, but let the country get rich!" If we want to increase the gross national income, reduce the imports of certain useless, even harmful, products, improve agricultural production and fight illiteracy, we have to conduct an information campaign. The people must understand what is at stake. Public business must be the business of the public. We arrive therefore at the need to increase the number of local cells among the rank and file. All too often we are content with establishing national bodies such as the Women's Union, the Youth Movement, and the Labor Unions at the top and never outside the capital. But if we venture to investigate behind the offices in the capital, if we go through to the backroom where the records are meant to be, we are aghast at the void, the emptiness, and the bluff. We need a foundation, cells that provide substance and dynamism. The masses must be able to meet, discuss, put forward suggestions and receive instructions. Citizens must have the opportunity to speak, to express themselves and innovate. The meeting of the local cell or the committee meeting is a liturgical act. It is a privileged opportunity for the individual to listen and speak. At every meeting the brain multiplies the association of ideas and the eye discovers a wider human panorama.

The high percentage of young people in the underdeveloped countries poses specific problems for the government that must be addressed lucidly. The idle and often illiterate urban youth is exposed to all kinds of disrupting influences. Youth in the underdeveloped countries is in most cases marketed entertainment from the industrialized countries. As a rule there is some correlation between the mental and material level of a society and the leisure activities it provides. In the underdeveloped countries, however, the young generation has access to entertainment devised for the youth of the capitalist countries: detective stories, slot machines, hard-core photos, pornographic literature, R-rated films and, above all, alcohol. In the West, the family environment, school, and the relatively high standard of living of the working masses, serve as a kind of bulwark against the harmful effects of this entertainment. But in an African country where intellectual development is unequal, where the violent clash of two worlds has seriously shaken up the old traditions and disrupted ways of thinking, the affectivity and sensitivity of the young African are at the mercy of the aggression contained in Western culture. His family very often proves incapable of counteracting this violence with stability and homogeneity.

In this area the government must serve as filter and stabilizer. The commissioners for youth in the underdeveloped countries frequently make one mistake. They see their role as equivalent to that of commissioners for youth in the developed countries. They talk of fortifying the soul, developing the body, and encouraging talent in sports. In our opinion, they should be wary of such ideas. The youth of an underdeveloped country is often an idle youth. It must first of all be occupied. This is why the commissioner for youth must report to the Ministry for Labor. The Ministry for Labor, which is a requirement for an underdeveloped country, works in close collaboration with the Ministry for Planning, another requirement in an underdeveloped country. The youth of Africa should not be oriented toward the stadiums but toward the fields, the fields and the schools. The stadium is not an urban showpiece but a rural space that is cleared, worked, and offered to the nation. The capitalist notion of sports is fundamentally different from that which should exist in an underdeveloped country. The African politician should not be concerned with producing professional sportsmen, but conscious individuals who also practice sports. If sports are not incorporated into the life of the nation, i.e., in the building of the nation, if we produce national sportsmen instead of conscious individuals, then sports will quickly be ruined by professionalism and commercialism. A sport should not be a game or entertainment for the urban bourgeoisie. Our greatest task is to constantly understand what is happening in our own countries. We must not cultivate the spirit of the exceptional or look for the hero, another form of leader. We must elevate the people, expand their minds, equip them, differentiate them, and humanize them.

Once again we turn to the obsession that we would like to see shared by every African politician — the need to shed light on the people's effort, to rehabilitate work, and rid it of its historical opacity. To be responsible in an underdeveloped country is to know that everything finally rests on educating the masses, elevating their minds, and on what is all too quickly assumed to be political education.

It is commonly thought with criminal flippancy that to politicize the masses means from time to time haranguing them with a major political speech. It is thought that for a leader or head of state to speak on major current issues in a pedantic tone of voice is sufficient as obligation to politicize the masses. But political education means opening up the mind, awakening the mind, and introducing it to the world. It is as Césaire said: "To invent the souls of men." To politicize the masses is not and cannot be to make a political speech. It means driving home to the masses that everything depends on them, that if we stagnate the fault is theirs, and that if we progress, they too are responsible, that there is no demiurge, no illustrious man taking responsibility for everything, but that the demiurge is the people and the magic lies in their hands and their hands alone. In order to achieve such things, in order to actually embody them, we must, as we have already mentioned, decentralize to the utmost. The flow of ideas from the upper echelons to the rank and file and vice versa must be an unwavering principle, not for merely formal reasons but quite simply because adherence to this principle is the guarantee of salvation. It is the forces from the rank and file which rise up to energize the leadership and permit it dialectically to make a new leap forward. Once again we Algerians very quickly understood this, for no member of the upper echelons has been able to take precedence in any mission of salvation. It is the rank and file which fights in Algeria and they are fully aware that without their difficult and heroic daily struggle the upper echelons would collapse — just as they are aware that without the upper echelons and leadership the rank and file would disintegrate into chaos and anarchy. The power structure draws its validity and strength solely from the existence of the people's struggle. In practice it is the people who choose a power structure of their own free will and not the power structure that suffers the people.

The masses must realize that the government and the party are at their service. A people worthy of esteem, i.e., conscious of their dignity, is a people who never forget this obvious fact. During the colonial occupation the people were told they had to sacrifice their lives for the sake of dignity. But the African peoples quickly realized that it was not only the occupier who threatened their dignity. The African peoples quickly realized that dignity and sovereignty were exact equivalents. In fact a free people living in dignity is a sovereign people. A people living in dignity is a responsible people. And there is no point "demonstrating" that the African peoples are infantile or retarded. A government and a party get the people they deserve. And in the more or less long term a people gets the government it deserves.

The above arguments are borne out by actual experience in certain regions. It sometimes occurs during a meeting that a militant's answer to a difficult problem is: "All we need do is . . ." This voluntary shortcut, which dangerously combines spontaneity, simplistic syncretism, and little intellectual elaboration, frequently wins the day. Every time we encounter this abdication of responsibility in a militant it is not enough to say he is wrong. He has to be made responsible, encouraged to follow through his chain of reasoning to its conclusion, and taught to grasp the often atrocious, inhuman, and finally sterile nature of this "All you need do is . . . " Nobody has a monopoly on truth, neither the leader nor the militant. The search for truth in local situations is the responsibility of the community. Some militants have a broader experience, are quicker to gather their thoughts, and in the past have succeeded in making a greater number of inferences. But they should avoid overshadowing the people, for the successful outcome of any decision depends on the conscious, coordinated commitment of the people as a whole. We are all in the same boat. Everybody will be slaughtered or tortured, and within the context of the independent nation everyone will suffer the same hunger and marasmus. The collective struggle presupposes a collective responsibility from the rank and file and a collegial responsibility at the top. Yes, everyone must be involved in the struggle for the sake of the common salvation. There are no clean hands, no innocent bystanders. We are all in the process of dirtying our hands in the quagmire of our soil and the terrifying void of our minds. Any bystander is a coward or a traitor.

The duty of a leadership is to have the masses on their side. Any commitment, however, presupposes awareness and understanding of the mission to be accomplished, in short a rational analysis, no matter how embryonic. The people should not be mesmerized, swayed by emotion or confused. Only underdeveloped countries led by a revolutionary elite emanating from the people can today empower the masses to step onto the stage of history. But once again on the condition that we vigorously and decisively reject the formation of a national bourgeoisie, a caste of privileged individuals. To politicize the masses is to make the nation in its totality a reality for every citizen. To make the experience of the nation, the experience of every citizen. As President Sékou Touré so aptly reminded us in his address to the Second Congress of African Writers: "In the realm of thought, man can claim to be the brain of the world, but in reality, where every action affects spiritual and physical being, the world is still the brain of mankind for it is here that are concentrated the totalization of powers and elements of thought, the dynamic forces of development and improvement, and it is here too that energies are merged and the sum total of man's intellectual values is finally inscribed." Since individual experience is national, since it is a link in the national chain, it ceases to be individual, narrow and limited in scope, and can lead to the truth of the nation and the world. Just as every fighter clung to the nation during the period of armed struggle, so during the period of nation building every citizen must continue in his daily purpose to embrace the nation as a whole, to embody the constantly dialectical truth of the nation, and to will here and now the triumph of man in his totality. If the building of a bridge does not enrich the consciousness of those working on it, then don't build the bridge, and let the citizens continue to swim across the river or use a ferry. The bridge must not be pitchforked or foisted upon the social landscape by a deus ex machina, but, on the contrary, must be the product of the citizens' brains and muscles. And there is no doubt architects and engineers, foreigners for the most part, will probably be needed, but the local party leaders must see to it that the techniques seep into the desert of the citizen's brain so that the bridge in its entirety and in every detail can be integrated, redesigned, and reappropriated. The citizen must appropriate the bridge. Then, and only then, is everything possible.

A government that proclaims itself national must take responsibility for the entire nation, and in underdeveloped countries the youth represents one of the most important sectors. The consciousness of the younger generation must be elevated and enlightened. It is this younger generation that will compose the national army. If they have been adequately informed, if the National Youth Movement has done its work of integrating the youth into the nation then the mistakes that have compromised, even undermined, the future of the Latin American republics, will have been avoided. The army is never a school for war, but a school for civics, a school for politics. The soldier in a mature nation is not a mercenary but a citizen who defends the nation by the use of arms. This is why it is paramount that the soldier knows he is at the service of his country and not of an officer, however illustrious he may be. Military and civilian national service must be used to raise the level of national consciousness, to detribalize and unify. In an underdeveloped country the mobilization of men and women should be undertaken as

quickly as possible. The underdeveloped country must take precautions not to perpetuate feudal traditions that give priority to
men over women. Women shall be given equal importance to
men, not in the articles of the consitution, but in daily life, at the
factory, in the schools, and in assemblies. If the countries of the
West station their soldiers in barracks, this does not mean this is
the best solution. We are not obliged to militarize recruits. National service can be civilian or military, and in any case every able-
bodied citizen should be able to join his fighting unit at a moment's
notice to defend the freedom of the nation and its civil liberties.

The major public works projects of national interest should
be carried out by the recruits. This is a highly effective way of
stimulating stagnant regions and getting the greatest number of
citizens to learn of the country's realities. We should avoid trans-
forming the army into an autonomous body that sooner or later,
idle and aimless, will "go into politics" and threaten the authorities. By dint of haunting the corridors of power, armchair gener-
als dream of pronunciamentos. The only way of avoiding this is
to politicize the army, i.e., nationalize it. Likewise there is an
urgent need to strengthen the militia. In the event of war, it is
the entire nation which fights or works. There should be no professional soldiers, and the number of career officers should be
kept to a minimum; first of all, because very often the officers
are selected from university graduates who would be much more
useful elsewhere—an engineer is a thousand times more indispensable to the nation than an officer—and secondly, because
any hint of a caste consciousness should be eliminated. We have
seen in the preceding pages how nationalism, that magnificent
hymn which roused the masses against the oppressor, disintegrates in the aftermath of independence. Nationalism is not a
political doctrine, it is not a program. If we really want to safeguard our countries from regression, paralysis, or collapse, we
must rapidly switch from a national consciousness to a social and
political consciousness. The nation can only come into being

in a program elaborated by a revolutionary leadership and enthusiastically and lucidly appropriated by the masses. The national effort must be constantly situated in the general context of the underdeveloped countries. The front line against hunger and darkness, the front line against poverty and stunted consciousness, must be present in the minds and muscles of the men and women. The work of the masses, their determination to conquer the scourges that for centuries have excluded them from the history of the human mind, must be connected to the work and determination of all the underdeveloped peoples. There is a kind of collective endeavor, a common destiny among the underdeveloped masses. The peoples of the Third World are not interested in news about King Baudoin's wedding or the affairs of the Italian bourgeoisie. What we want to hear are case histories in Argentina or Burma about the fight against illiteracy or the dictatorial behavior of other leaders. This is the material that inspires us, educates us, and greatly increases our effectiveness. As we have seen, a government needs a program if it really wants to liberate the people politically and socially. Not only an economic program but also a policy on the distribution of wealth and social relations. In fact there must be a concept of man, a concept about the future of mankind. Which means that no sermon, no complicity with the former occupier can replace a program. The people, at first unenlightened and then increasingly lucid, will vehemently demand such a program. The Africans and the underdeveloped peoples, contrary to what is commonly believed, are quick to build a social and political consciousness. The danger is that very often they reach the stage of social consciousness before reaching the national phase. In this case the underdeveloped countries' violent calls for social justice are combined, paradoxically enough, with an often primitive tribalism. The underdeveloped peoples behave like a starving population—which means that the days of those who treat Africa as their playground are strictly numbered. In other words, their power cannot last forever. A bourgeoisie that has only nationalism to feed the people fails in its mission and inevitably gets tangled up in a series of trials and tribulations. If nationalism is not explained, enriched, and deepened, if it does not very quickly turn into a social and political consciousness, into humanism, then it leads to a dead end. A bourgeois leadership of the underdeveloped countries confines the national consciousness to a sterile formalism. Only the massive commitment by men and women to judicious and productive tasks gives form and substance to this consciousness. It is then that flags and government buildings cease to be the symbols of the nation. The nation deserts the false glitter of the capital and takes refuge in the interior where it receives life and energy. The living expression of the nation is the collective consciousness in motion of the entire people. It is the enlightened and coherent praxis of the men and women. The collective forging of a destiny implies undertaking responsibility on a truly historical scale. Otherwise there is anarchy, repression, the emergence of tribalized parties and federalism, etc. If the national government wants to be national it must govern by the people and for the people, for the disinherited and by the disinherited. No leader, whatever his worth, can replace the will of the people, and the national government, before concerning itself with international prestige, must first restore dignity to all citizens, furnish their minds, fill their eyes with human things and develop a human landscape for the sake of its enlightened and sovereign inhabitants.

On National Culture

It is not enough to write a revolutionary hymn to be a part of the African revolution, one has to join with the people to make this revolution. Make it with the people and the hymns will automatically follow. For an act to be authentic, one has to be a vital part of Africa and its thinking, part of all that popular energy mobilized for the liberation, progress and happiness of Africa. Outside this single struggle there is no place for either the artist or the intellectual who is not committed and totally mobilized with the people in the great fight waged by Africa and suffering humanity.

Sékou Touré[16]

Each generation must discover its mission, fulfill it or betray it, in relative opacity. In the underdeveloped countries preceding generations have simultaneously resisted the insidious agenda of colonialism and paved the way for the emergence of the current struggles. Now that we are in the heat of combat, we must shed the habit of decrying the efforts of our forefathers or feigning incomprehension at their silence or passiveness. They fought as best they could with the weapons they possessed at the time, and if their struggle did not reverberate throughout the international arena, the reason should be attributed not so much to a

---

[16] "The Political Leader as Representative of a Culture." Paper presented at the Second Congress of Black Writers and Artists, Rome, 1959.

lack of heroism but to a fundamentally different international situation. More than one colonized subject had to say, "We've had enough," more than one tribe had to rebel, more than one peasant revolt had to be quelled, more than one demonstration to be repressed, for us today to stand firm, certain of our victory.

For us who are determined to break the back of colonialism, our historic mission is to authorize every revolt, every desperate act, and every attack aborted or drowned in blood.

In this chapter we shall analyze the fundamental issue of the legitimate claim to a nation. The political party that mobilizes the people, however, is little concerned with this issue of legitimacy. Political parties are concerned solely with daily reality, and it is in the name of this reality, in the name of this immediacy, which influences the present and future of men and women, that they make their call to action. The political party may very well speak of the nation in emotional terms, but it is primarily interested in getting the people who are listening to understand that they must join in the struggle if they want quite simply to exist.

We now know that in the first phase of the national struggle colonialism attempts to defuse nationalist demands by manipulating economic doctrine. At the first signs of a dispute, colonialism feigns comprehension by acknowledging with ostentatious humility that the territory is suffering from serious underdevelopment that requires major social and economic reforms.

And it is true that certain spectacular measures such as the opening of work sites for the unemployed here and there delay the formation of a national consciousness by a few years. But sooner or later colonialism realizes it is incapable of achieving a program of socio-economic reforms that would satisfy the aspirations of the colonized masses. Even when it comes to filling their bellies, colonialism proves to be inherently powerless. The colonialist state very quickly discovers that any attempt to disarm the national parties at a purely economic level would be tantamount to practicing in the colonies what it did not want to do on its own territory. And it is no coincidence that today the doctrine of Cartierism is on the rise just about everywhere.

Cartier's bitter disillusionment with France's stubborn determination to retain ties with people it will have to feed, whereas so many French citizens are in dire straits, reflects colonialism's inability to transform itself into a nonpartisan aid program. Hence once again no need to waste time repeating "Better to go hungry with dignity than to eat one's fill in slavery." On the contrary we must persuade ourselves that colonialism is incapable of procuring for colonized peoples the material conditions likely to make them forget their quest for dignity. Once colonialism has understood where its social reform tactics would lead it, back come the old reflexes of adding police reinforcements, dispatching troops, and establishing a regime of terror better suited to its interests and its psychology.

Within the political parties, or rather parallel to them, we find the cultured class of colonized intellectuals. The recognition of a national culture and its right to exist represent their favorite stamping ground. Whereas the politicians integrate their action in the present, the intellectuals place themselves in the context of history. Faced with the colonized intellectual's debunking of the colonialist theory of a precolonial barbarism, colonialism's response is mute. It is especially mute since the ideas put forward by the young colonized intelligentsia are widely accepted by metropolitan specialists. It is in fact now commonly recognized that for several decades numerous European researchers have widely rehabilitated African, Mexican, and Peruvian civilizations. Some have been surprised by the passion invested by the colonized intellectuals in their defense of a national culture. But those who consider this passion exaggerated are strangely apt

to forget that their psyche and their ego are conveniently safeguarded by a French or German culture whose worth has been
proven and which has gone unchallenged.

I concede the fact that the actual existence of an Aztec civilization has done little to change the diet of today's Mexican peasant. I concede that whatever proof there is of a once mighty
Songhai civilization does not change the fact that the Songhais
today are undernourished, illiterate, abandoned to the skies and
water, with a blank mind and glazed eyes. But, as we have said
on several occasions, this passionate quest for a national culture
prior to the colonial era can be justified by the colonized intellectuals' shared interest in stepping back and taking a hard look
at the Western culture in which they risk becoming ensnared.
Fully aware they are in the process of losing themselves, and
consequently of being lost to their people, these men work away
with raging heart and furious mind to renew contact with their
people's oldest, inner essence, the farthest removed from colonial times.

Let us delve deeper; perhaps this passion and this rage are
nurtured or at least guided by the secret hope of discovering
beyond the present wretchedness, beyond this self-hatred, this
abdication and denial, some magnificent and shining era that
redeems us in our own eyes and those of others. I say that I have
decided to delve deeper. Since perhaps in their unconscious the
colonized intellectuals have been unable to come to loving terms
with the present history of their oppressed people, since there is
little to marvel at in its current state of barbarity, they have decided to go further, to delve deeper, and they must have been
overjoyed to discover that the past was not branded with shame,
but dignity, glory, and sobriety. Reclaiming the past does not only
rehabilitate or justify the promise of a national culture. It triggers a change of fundamental importance in the colonized's
psycho-affective equilibrium. Perhaps it has not been sufficiently

demonstrated that colonialism is not content merely to impose its law on the colonized country's present and future. Colonialism is not satisfied with snaring the people in its net or of draining the colonized brain of any form or substance. With a kind of perverted logic, it turns its attention to the past of the colonized people and distorts it, disfigures it, and destroys it. This effort to demean history prior to colonization today takes on a dialectical significance.

When we consider the resources deployed to achieve the cultural alienation so typical of the colonial period, we realize that nothing was left to chance and that the final aim of colonization was to convince the indigenous population it would save them from darkness. The result was to hammer into the heads of the indigenous population that if the colonist were to leave they would regress into barbarism, degradation, and bestiality. At the level of the unconscious, therefore, colonialism was not seeking to be perceived by the indigenous population as a sweet, kindhearted mother who protects her child from a hostile environment, but rather a mother who constantly prevents her basically perverse child from committing suicide or giving free rein to its malevolent instincts. The colonial mother is protecting the child from itself, from its ego, its physiology, its biology, and its ontological misfortune.

In this context there is nothing extravagant about the demands of the colonized intellectual, simply a demand for a coherent program. The colonized intellectual who wants to put his struggle on a legitimate footing, who is intent on providing proof and accepts to bare himself in order to better display the history of his body, is fated to journey deep into the very bowels of his people.

This journey into the depths is not specifically national. The colonized intellectual who decides to combat these colonialist lies does so on a continental scale. The past is revered. The culture which has been retrieved from the past to be displayed in all its splendor is not his national culture. Colonialism, little troubled by nuances, has always claimed that the "nigger" was a savage, not an Angolan or a Nigerian, but a "nigger." For colonialism, this vast continent was a den of savages, infested with superstitions and fanaticism, destined to be despised, cursed by God, a land of cannibals, a land of "niggers." Colonialism's condemnation is continental in scale. Colonialism's claim that the precolonial period was akin to a darkness of the human soul refers to the entire continent of Africa. The colonized's endeavors to rehabilitate himself and escape the sting of colonialism obey the same rules of logic. The colonized intellectual, steeped in Western culture and set on proving the existence of his own culture, never does so in the name of Angola or Dahomey. The culture proclaimed is African culture. When the black man, who has never felt as much a "Negro" as he has under white domination, decides to prove his culture and act as a cultivated person, he realizes that history imposes on him a terrain already mapped out, that history sets him along a very precise path and that he is expected to demonstrate the existence of a "Negro" culture.

And it is all too true that the major responsibility for this racialization of thought, or at least the way it is applied, lies with the Europeans who have never stopped placing white culture in opposition to the other noncultures. Colonialism did not think it worth its while denying one national culture after the other. Consequently the colonized's response was immediately continental in scope. In Africa, colonized literature over the last twenty years has not been a national literature but a "Negro" literature. The concept of negritude for example was the affective if not logical antithesis of that insult which the white man had leveled at the rest of humanity. This negritude, hurled against the contempt of the white man, has alone proved capable in some sectors of lifting taboos and maledictions. Because the Kenyan and

Guinean intellectuals were above all confronted with a generalized ostracism and the syncretic contempt of the colonizer, their reaction was one of self-regard and celebration. Following the unconditional affirmation of European culture came the unconditional affirmation of African culture. Generally speaking the bards of negritude would contrast old Europe versus young Africa, dull reason versus poetry, and stifling logic versus exuberant Nature; on the one side there stood rigidity, ceremony, protocol, and skepticism, and on the other, naïveté, petulance, freedom, and, indeed, luxuriance. But also irresponsibility.

The bards of negritude did not hesitate to reach beyond the borders of the continent. Black voices from America took up the refrain on a larger scale. The "black world" came into being, and Busia from Ghana, Birago Diop from Senegal, Hampaté Ba from Mali and Saint-Clair Drake from Chicago were quick to claim common ties and identical lines of thought.

This might be an appropriate time to look at the example of the Arab world. We know that most of the Arab territories came under colonial domination. Colonialism used the same tactics in these regions to inculcate the notion that the precolonial history of the indigenous population had been steeped in barbarity. The struggle for national liberation was linked to a cultural phenomenon commonly known as the awakening of Islam. The passion displayed by contemporary Arab authors in reminding their people of the great chapters of Arab history is in response to the lies of the occupier. The great names of Arabic literature have been recorded and the past of the Arab civilization has been brandished with the same zeal and ardor as that of the African civilizations. The Arab leaders have tried to revive that famous Dar el Islam, which exerted such a shining influence in the twelfth, thirteenth and fourteenth centuries.

Today, at a political level, the Arab League is a concrete example of this determination to revive the legacy of the past and carry it to a conclusion. Today Arab physicians and poets hail each other across borders in their endeavor to launch a new Arab culture, a new Arab civilization. They join forces in the name of Arabism, which is the guiding light for their thoughts. In the Arab world, however, even under colonial domination, nationalist feeling has been kept alive at an intensity unknown in Africa. As a result the Arab League shows no signs of that spontaneous solidarity between members of the group. On the contrary, paradoxically, each member endeavors to praise the achievements of his nation. Although the cultural element has been freed from that lack of differentiation that is characteristic of the African world, the Arabs do not always manage to forget their common identity when faced with an objective. Their actual cultural experience is not national but Arab. The issue at stake is not yet to secure a national culture, not yet to plunge into the groundswell of nations, but rather to pit an Arab or African culture against the universal condemnation of the colonizer. From both the Arab and African perspectives, the claims of the colonized intellectual are syncretic, continental in scope and, in the case of the Arabs, global.

This historical obligation to racialize their claims, to emphasize an African culture rather than a national culture leads the African intellectuals into a dead end. Let us take as an example the African Society for Culture. This Society was created by African intellectuals for a mutual exchange of ideas, experiences, and research. The aim of the Society was therefore to establish the existence of an African culture, to detail it nation by nation and reveal the inner dynamism of each of the national cultures. But at the same time this Society was responding to another demand: the need to take its place within the ranks of the European Society for Culture that threatened to turn into the Universal Society for Culture. At the root of this decision there was therefore the preoccupation with taking its place on an equal footing in the universal arena, armed with a culture sprung from the very bowels of the African continent. Very quickly, however, this Society proved incapable of handling these assignments and members' behavior was reduced to window-dressing operations such as proving to the Europeans that an African culture did exist and pitting themselves against the narcissism and ostentation of the Europeans. We have demonstrated that such an attitude was normal and drew its legitimacy from the lie propagated by the European intellectuals. But the aims of this Society were to deteriorate seriously once the concept of negritude had been elaborated. The African Society for Culture was to become the Cultural Society for the Black World and was forced to include the black diaspora, i.e., the dozens of millions of blacks throughout the Americas.

The blacks who lived in the United States, Central, and Latin America in fact needed a cultural matrix to cling to. The problem they were faced with was not basically any different from that of the Africans. The whites in America had not behaved any differently to them than the white colonizers had to the Africans. We have seen how the whites were used to putting all "Negroes" in the same basket. During the First Congress of the African Society for Culture in Paris in 1956 the black Americans spontaneously considered their problems from the same standpoint as their fellow Africans. By integrating the former slaves into African civilization the African intellectuals accorded them an acceptable civil status. But gradually the black Americans realized that their existential problems differed from those faced by the Africans. The only common denominator between the blacks from Chicago and the Nigerians or Tanganyikans[17] was that they all defined themselves in relation to the whites. But once the initial comparisons had been made and subjective feelings had settled down, the black Americans realized that the objective problems were fundamentally different. The principle and purpose of the

---

[17] Translator's Note: Present-day Tanzanians

freedom rides whereby black and white Americans endeavor to combat racial discrimination have little in common with the heroic struggle of the Angolan people against the iniquity of Portuguese colonialism. Consequently, during the Second Congress of the African Society for Culture the black Americans decided to create the American Society for African Culture.

Negritude thus came up against its first limitation, namely, those phenomena that take into account the historicizing of men. "Negro" or "Negro-African" culture broke up because the men who set out to embody it realized that every culture is first and foremost national, and that the problems for which Richard Wright or Langston Hughes had to be on the alert were fundamentally different from those faced by Léopold Senghor or Jomo Kenyatta. Likewise certain Arab states, who had struck up the glorious hymn to an Arab renaissance, were forced to realize that their geographical position and their region's economic interdependence were more important than the revival of their past. Consequently the Arab states today are organically linked to Mediterranean societies and cultures. The reason being that these states are subject to modern pressures and new commercial channels, whereas the great trade routes of the days of Arab expansion have now disappeared. But above all there is the fact that the political regimes of certain Arab states are so heterogenous and alien to each other that any encounter, even cultural, between these states proves meaningless.

It is clear therefore that the way the cultural problem is posed in certain colonized countries can lead to serious ambiguities. Colonialism's insistence that "niggers" have no culture, and Arabs are by nature barbaric, inevitably leads to a glorification of cultural phenomena that become continental instead of national, and singularly racialized. In Africa, the reasoning of the intellectual is Black-African or Arab-Islamic. It is not specifically national. Culture is increasingly cut off from reality. It finds safe haven in a refuge of smoldering emotions and has difficulty cutting a straightforward path that would, nevertheless, be the only one likely to endow it with productiveness, homogeneity, and substance.

Though historically limited the fact remains that the actions of the colonized intellectual do much to support and justify the action of the politicians. And it is true the attitude of the colonized intellectual sometimes takes on the aspect of a cult or religion. But under closer analysis it clearly reflects he is only too aware that he is running the risk of severing the last remaining ties with his people. This stated belief in the existence of a national culture is in fact a burning, desperate return to anything. In order to secure his salvation, in order to escape the supremacy of white culture the colonized intellectual feels the need to return to his unknown roots and lose himself, come what may, among his barbaric people. Because he feels he is becoming alienated, in other words the living focus of contradictions which risk becoming insurmountable, the colonized intellectual wrenches himself from the quagmire which threatens to suck him down, and determined to believe what he finds, he accepts and ratifies it with heart and soul. He finds himself bound to answer for everything and for everyone. He not only becomes an advocate, he accepts being included with the others, and henceforth he can afford to laugh at his past cowardice.

This painful and harrowing wrench is, however, a necessity. Otherwise we will be faced with extremely serious psycho-affective mutilations: individuals without an anchorage, without borders, colorless, stateless, rootless, a body of angels. And it will come as no surprise to hear some colonized intellectuals state: "Speaking as a Senegalese and a Frenchman. . . . Speaking as an Algerian and a Frenchman." Stumbling over the need to assume two nationalities, two determinations, the intellectual who is Arab and French, or Nigerian and English, if he wants to be sincere with himself, chooses the negation of one of these two determinations. Usually, unwilling or unable to choose, these intellectuals collect all the historical determinations which have conditioned them and place themselves in a thoroughly "universal perspective."

The reason being that the colonized intellectual has thrown himself headlong into Western culture. Like adopted children who only stop investigating their new family environment once their psyche has formed a minimum core of reassurance, the colonized intellectual will endeavor to make European culture his own. Not content with knowing Rabelais or Diderot, Shakespeare or Edgar Allen Poe, he will stretch his mind until he identifies with them completely.

La dame n'était pas seule
Elle avait un mari
Un mari très comme il faut
Qui citait Racine et Corneille
Et Voltaire et Rousseau
Et le Père Hugo et le jeune Musset
Et Gide et Valéry
Et tant d'autres encore.[18]

In some cases, however, at the very moment when the nationalist parties mobilize the people in the name of national independence, the colonized intellectual rejects his accomplishments, suddenly feeling them to be alienating. But this is easier said than done. The intellectual who has slipped into Western civilization through a cultural back door, who has managed to embody, or rather change bodies with, European civilization, will realize that the cultural model he would like to integrate for authenticity's

---

[18] "The lady was not alone/She had a husband/A fine, upstanding husband/ Who recited Racine and Corneille/And Voltaire and Rousseau/And old Hugo and the young Musset/And Gide and Valéry/And so many others as well." René Depestre, *"Face à la nuit."*

sake offers little in the way of figureheads capable of standing up to comparison with the many illustrious names in the civilization of the occupier. History, of course, written by and for Westerners, may periodically enhance the image of certain episodes of the African past. But faced with his country's present-day status, lucidly and "objectively" observing the reality of the continent he would like to claim as his own, the intellectual is terrified by the void, the mindlessness, and the savagery. Yet he feels he must escape this white culture. He must look elsewhere, anywhere; for lack of a cultural stimulus comparable to the glorious panorama flaunted by the colonizer, the colonized intellectual frequently lapses into heated arguments and develops a psychology dominated by an exaggerated sensibility, sensitivity, and susceptibility. This movement of withdrawal, which first of all comes from a petitio principi in his psychological mechanism and physiognomy, above all calls to mind a muscular reflex, a muscular contraction.

The foregoing is sufficient to explain the style of the colonized intellectuals who make up their mind to assert this phase of liberating consciousness. A jagged style, full of imagery, for the image is the drawbridge that lets out the unconscious forces into the surrounding meadows. An energetic style, alive with rhythms bursting with life. A colorful style too, bronzed, bathed in sunlight and harsh. This style, which Westerners once found jarring, is not, as some would have it, a racial feature, but above all reflects a single-handed combat and reveals how necessary it is for the intellectual to inflict injury on himself, to actually bleed red blood and free himself from that part of his being already contaminated by the germs of decay. A swift, painful combat where inevitably the muscle had to replace the concept.

Although this approach may take him to unusual heights in the sphere of poetry, at an existential level it has often proved a dead end. When he decides to return to the routine of daily life, after having been roused to fever pitch by rubbing shoulders with his people, whoever they were and whoever they may be, all he brings back from his adventures are terribly sterile clichés. He places emphasis on customs, traditions, and costumes, and his painful, forced search seems but a banal quest for the exotic. This is the period when the intellectuals extol every last particular of the indigenous landscape. The flowing dress of the *boubou* is regarded as sacred and shoes from Paris or Italy are shunned for Muslim slippers, *babouches*. The language of the colonizer suddenly scorches his lips. Rediscovering one's people sometimes means in this phase wanting to be a "nigger," not an exceptional "nigger," but a real "nigger," a "dirty nigger," the sort defined by the white man. Rediscovering one's people means becoming a "filthy Arab,"of going as native as possible, becoming unrecognizable; it means clipping those wings which had been left to grow.

The colonized intellectual decides to draw up a list of the bad old ways characteristic of the colonial world, and hastens to recall the goodness of the people, this people who have been made guardians of truth. The scandal this approach triggers among the colonists strengthens the determination of the colonized. Once the colonists, who had relished their victory over these assimilated intellectuals, realize that these men they thought saved have begun to merge with the "nigger scum," the entire system loses its bearings. Every colonized intellectual won over, every colonized intellectual who confesses, once he decides to revert to his old ways, not only represents a setback for the colonial enterprise, but also symbolizes the pointlessness and superficiality of the work accomplished. Every colonized intellectual who crosses back over the line is a radical condemnation of the method and the regime, and the uproar it causes justifies his abdication and encourages him to persevere.

If we decide to trace these various phases of development in the works of colonized writers, three stages emerge. First, the colonized intellectual proves he has assimilated the colonizer's culture. His works correspond point by point with those of his metropolitan counterparts. The inspiration is European and his works can be easily linked to a well-defined trend in metropolitan literature. This is the phase of full assimilation where we find Parnassians, Symbolists, and Surrealists among the colonized writers.

In a second stage, the colonized writer has his convictions shaken and decides to cast his mind back. This period corresponds approximately to the immersion we have just described. But since the colonized writer is not integrated with his people, since he maintains an outsider's relationship to them, he is content to remember. Old childhood memories will surface, old legends be reinterpreted on the basis of a borrowed aesthetic, and a concept of the world discovered under other skies. Sometimes this precombat literature is steeped in humor and allegory, at other times in anguish, malaise, death, and even nausea. Yet underneath the self-loathing, the sound of laughter can be heard.

Finally, a third stage, a combat stage where the colonized writer, after having tried to lose himself among the people, with the people, will rouse the people. Instead of letting the people's lethargy prevail, he turns into a galvanizer of the people. Combat literature, revolutionary literature, national literature emerges. During this phase a great many men and women who previously would never have thought of writing, now that they find themselves in exceptional circumstances, in prison, in the resistance or on the eve of their execution, feel the need to proclaim their nation, to portray their people and become the spokesperson of a new reality in action.

Sooner or later, however, the colonized intellectual realizes that the existence of a nation is not proved by culture, but in the people's struggle against the forces of occupation. No colonialism draws its justification from the fact that the territories it occupies are culturally nonexistent. Colonialism will never be put to shame by exhibiting unknown cultural treasures under its nose.

The colonized intellectual, at the very moment when he undertakes a work of art, fails to realize he is using techniques and a language borrowed from the occupier. He is content to cloak these instruments in a style that is meant to be national but which is strangely reminiscent of exoticism. The colonized intellectual who returns to his people through works of art behaves in fact like a foreigner. Sometimes he will not hesitate to use the local dialects to demonstrate his desire to be as close to the people as possible, but the ideas he expresses, the preoccupations that haunt him are in no way related to the daily lot of the men and women of his country. The culture with which the intellectual is preoccupied is very often nothing but an inventory of particularisms. Seeking to cling close to the people, he clings merely to a visible veneer. This veneer, however, is merely a reflection of a dense, subterranean life in perpetual renewal. This reification, which seems all too obvious and characteristic of the people, is in fact but the inert, already invalidated outcome of the many, and not always coherent, adaptations of a more fundamental substance beset with radical changes. Instead of seeking out this substance, the intellectual lets himself be mesmerized by these mummified fragments which, now consolidated, signify, on the contrary, negation, obsolescence, and fabrication. Culture never has the translucency of custom. Culture eminently eludes any form of simplification. In its essence it is the very opposite of custom, which is always a deterioration of culture. Seeking to stick to tradition or reviving neglected traditions is not only going against history, but against one's people. When a people support an armed or even political struggle against a merciless colonialism, tradition changes meaning. What was a technique of passive resistance may, in this phase, be radically doomed. Traditions in an underdeveloped country undergoing armed struggle are fundamentally unstable and crisscrossed by centrifugal forces. This is why the intellectual often risks being out of step. The peoples who have waged the struggle are increasingly impermeable to demagoguery, and by seeking to follow them too closely, the intellectual turns out to be nothing better than a vulgar opportunist, even behind the times.

In the field of visual arts, for example, the colonized creator who at all costs wants to create a work of art of national significance confines himself to stereotyping details. These artists, despite having been immersed in modern techniques and influenced by the major contemporary trends in painting and architecture, turn their backs on foreign culture, challenge it, and, setting out in search of the true national culture, they give preference to what they think to be the abiding features of national art. But these creators forget that modes of thought, diet, modern techniques of communication, language, and dress have dialectically reorganized the mind of the people and that the abiding features that acted as safeguards during the colonial period are in the process of undergoing enormous radical transformations.

This creator, who decides to portray national truth, turns, paradoxically enough, to the past, and so looks at what is irrelevant to the present. What he aims for in his inner intentionality is the detritus of social thought, external appearances, relics, and knowledge frozen in time. The colonized intellectual, however, who strives for cultural authenticity, must recognize that national truth is first and foremost the national reality. He must press on until he reaches that place of bubbling trepidation from which knowledge will emerge.

Before independence the colonized painter was insensitive to the national landscape. He favored therefore the nonrepresentational or, more often, specialized in still life. After independence his desire to reunite with the people confines him to a point by point representation of national reality which is flat, untroubled, motionless, reminiscent of death rather than life. The educated circles go ecstatic over such careful renditions of truth, but we have every right to ask ourselves whether this truth is real, whether in fact it is not outmoded, irrelevant, or called into question by the heroic saga of the people hacking their way into history.

Much the same could be said about poetry. After the assimilation period of rhyming verse, the beat of the poetic drum bursts onto the scene. Poetry of revolt, but which is also analytical and descriptive. The poet must, however, understand that nothing can replace the rational and irreversible commitment on the side of the people in arms. Let us quote Depestre once again:

> La dame n'était pas seule
> Elle avait un mari
> Un mari qui savait tout
> Mais à parler franc qui ne savait rien
> Parce que la culture ne va pas sans concessions
> Une concession de sa chair et de son sang
> Une concession de soi-même aux autres
> Une concession qui vaut le
> Classicisme et le romantisme
> Et tout ce dont on abreuve notre esprit.[19]

The colonized poet who is concerned with creating a work of national significance, who insists on describing his people, misses his mark, because before setting pen to paper he is in no fit state to make that fundamental concession which Depestre mentions. The French poet René Char fully understood this when he reminds us that "the poem emerges from a subjective imposition and an objective choice. The poem is a moving assembly of

---

[19] "The lady was not alone/She had a husband/A husband who knew everything/But to tell the truth knew nothing/Because culture does not come without making concessions/Without conceding your flesh and blood/Without conceding yourself to others/A concession worth just as much as/Classicism or Romanticism/And all that nurtures our soul." René Depestre, *"Face à la nuit."*

decisive original values, in topical relation with someone whom such an undertaking brings to the foreground."[20]

Yes, the first duty of the colonized poet is to clearly define the people, the subject of his creation. We cannot go resolutely forward unless we first realize our alienation. We have taken everything from the other side. Yet the other side has given us nothing except to sway us in its direction through a thousand twists, except lure us, seduce us, and imprison us by ten thousand devices, by a hundred thousand tricks. To take also means on several levels being taken. It is not enough to try and disengage ourselves by accumulating proclamations and denials. It is not enough to reunite with the people in a past where they no longer exist. We must rather reunite with them in their recent counter move which will suddenly call everything into question; we must focus on that zone of hidden fluctuation where the people can be found, for let there be no mistake, it is here that their souls are crystallized and their perception and respiration transfigured.

Keita Fodeba, minister for internal affairs of the Republic of Guinea, when he was director of the African Ballet, did not trifle with the reality of the people of Guinea. He reinterpreted all the rhythmic images of his country from a revolutionary perspective. But he did more than this. In his little-known poetical work there is a constant obsession with identifying the exact historical moment of the struggle, with defining the place of action and the ideas around which the will of the people will crystallize. Here is a poem by Keita Fodeba, a genuine invitation for us to reflect on demystification and combat.

AFRICAN DAWN

(*Guitar music*)
It was dawn. The little village which had danced half the night away to the sound of the drums was slowly awakening. The shepherds dressed

---

[20] René Char, "*Partage Formel.*"

in rags were driving their flocks down to the valley to the sound of their flutes. The young girls, carrying their water pots on their heads, wound their way in single file to the well. In the marabout's compound a group of children were chanting in unison verses from the Koran.

(*Guitar music*)

It was dawn. The combat between day and night. Exhausted from the struggle the night slowly breathed its last sigh. A few rays of sun heralding the victory of daylight hovered timid and pale on the horizon while the last stars slipped under a bank of clouds the color of flame trees in flower.

(*Guitar music*)

It was dawn. And there at the edge of the vast, purple-contoured plain was the silhouette of a man bent over as he cleared the ground: the silhouette of Naman, the peasant farmer. Every time he wielded his hoe, a frightened flock of birds flew up and swiftly made their way to the peaceful banks of the Joliba, the great Niger river. His grey cotton trousers, soaked in dew, brushed the grass on either side. Sweating, untiring, constantly bent, he skilfully worked with his hoe for his seeds had to be sown before the next rains.

(*Kora music*)

It was dawn. Dawn was still breaking. The millet birds flitted among the foliage announcing the coming day. A child carrying over his shoulder a small bag of arrows was running out of breath along the damp track over the plain in the direction of Naman. "Brother Naman," he called, "the head of the village wants you under the palaver tree."

(*Kora music*)

Surprised at such an early summons, Naman laid down his hoe and walked towards the village which now shone in the glow of the rising sun. The elders, looking more solemn than ever, were already seated. Beside them was a man in uniform, a district guard quietly smoking his pipe unperturbed.

(*Kora music*)

Naman sat down on a sheepskin. The griot of the village head stood up to convey to the assembly the elders' decision: "The whites have sent a district guard to request that a man from the village be sent to fight in the war in their country. After deliberating, the elders have decided to send the young man who best represents our race so that he can prove to the white man the courage which we Mandingos have always been known for."

(*Guitar music*)

Naman, whose imposing build and muscular frame were the subject of nightly songs by the young girls of the village, was chosen unanimously. Gentle Kadia, his young wife, distraught by the news, suddenly stopped her pounding, placed the mortar under the granary, and without saying a word, shut herself up in her hut to weep in muffled sobs over her misfortune. Since death had taken her first husband, she could not believe that the whites would take Naman in whom she had placed all her hopes.

(*Guitar music*)

The next morning, in spite of her tears and lamentations, the solemn beat of the war drums accompanied Naman to the little village harbor where he boarded a barge headed for the district capital. That night, instead of dancing in the open as usual, the young girls came to keep watch in Naman's antechamber where they told their tales around a wood fire until morning.

(*Guitar music*)

Several months went by without news from Naman. Little Kadia became so worried she went to consult the fetish priest in the neighboring village. Even the elders met in secret counsel on the subject, but nothing came of it.

(*Kora music*)

At last one day a letter arrived addressed to Kadia. Concerned about her husband's situation she left that night and after walking for many long hours arrived in the district capital where a translator read her letter.

Naman was in North Africa in good health and was asking for news of the harvest, the fishing festival, the dances, the palaver tree and the village . . .

(*Balafon*)

That night the old women of the village allowed the young Kadia to attend their traditional evening palaver in the compound of their most senior member. The village head, overjoyed at the news, offered a huge banquet to all the beggars in the neighborhood.

(*Balafon*)

Several months went by once more and everyone became anxious again for there was still no news of Naman. Kadia was planning on going to consult the fetish priest again when she received a second letter. After Corsica and Italy Naman was now in Germany and was proud of having been decorated.

(*Balafon*)

The next time it was just a card which said that Naman had been taken prisoner by the Germans. This news threw the village into consternation. The elders held counsel and decided that henceforth Naman was authorized to dance the Douga, the sacred dance of the vulture, reserved for those who had performed an exceptional feat, the dance of the Mandingo emperors whose every step represents a period in the history of Mali. Kadia found consolation in seeing her husband raised to the dignity of a national hero.

(*Guitar music*)

Time went by. . . . One year followed the next . . . Naman was still in Germany. He no longer wrote.

(*Guitar music*)

One day the head of the village received word from Dakar that Naman would soon be home.

Immediately the drums began to beat. They danced and sang until dawn. The young girls composed new songs to welcome him for the old ones dedicated to him made no mention of the Douga, that famous dance of the Mandingos.

(*Drums*)

But one month later Corporal Moussa, a great friend of Naman's, sent this tragic letter to Kadia: "It was dawn. We were at Tiaroye-sur-Mer. In the course of a major dispute between us and our white chiefs in Dakar, a bullet struck Naman. He lies in Senegalese soil."

(*Guitar music*)

In fact it was dawn. The first rays of the sun lightly brushing the surface of the sea tipped the little foam-flecked waves with gold. Stirred by the breeze the palm trees gently bent their trunks towards the ocean as if sickened by this morning's battle. The noisy flocks of crows cawed to the neighborhood the news of the tragedy which had bloodied the dawn at Tiaroye. . . . And in the scorched blue of the sky, right above the body of Naman, a gigantic vulture slowly hovered. It seemed to say to him: "Naman! You have not danced the dance that bears my name. Others will dance it."

(*Kora music*)

The reason I have chosen this long poem is because of its undeniable pedagogical value. Here things are clear. It is a meticulous account that develops progressively. Understanding the poem is not only an intellectual act, but also a political one. To understand this poem is to understand the role we have to play, to identify our approach and prepare to fight. There is not one colonized subject who will not understand the message in this poem. Naman, hero of the battlefields of Europe, Naman who vouched for the power and the continuity of the metropolis, Naman mowed down by the police at the very moment he returns home; this is Sétif in 1945, Fort-de-France, Saigon, Dakar, and Lagos. All the "niggers" and all the "filthy Arabs" who fought to defend France's liberty or British civilization will recognize themselves in this poem by Keita Fodeba.

But Keita Fodeba sees further. After having utilized the native peoples on its battle fields, colonialism uses them as veterans in its colonies to break up the independence movement. The veterans associations in the colonies are some of the most anti-nationalist forces that exist. The poet Keita Fodeba was preparing the minister for internal affairs of the Republic of Guinea to thwart the plots organized by French colonialism. It was in fact with the help of the veterans that the French secret service intended, among other things, to bring down the newly independent Guinea.

When the colonized intellectual writing for his people uses the past he must do so with the intention of opening up the future, of spurring them into action and fostering hope. But in order to secure hope, in order to give it substance, he must take part in the action and commit himself body and soul to the national struggle. You can talk about anything you like, but when it comes to talking about that one thing in a man's life that involves opening up new horizons, enlightening your country and standing tall alongside your own people, then muscle power is required.

The colonized intellectual is responsible not to his national culture, but to the nation as a whole, whose culture is, after all, but one aspect. The colonized intellectual should not be concerned with choosing how or where he decides to wage the national struggle. To fight for national culture first of all means fighting for the liberation of the nation, the tangible matrix from which culture can grow. One cannot divorce the combat for culture from the people's struggle for liberation. For example, all the men and women fighting French colonialism in Algeria with their bare hands are no strangers to the national culture of Algeria. The Algerian national culture takes form and shape during the fight, in prison, facing the guillotine, and in the capture and destruction of the French military positions.

We should not therefore be content to delve into the people's past to find concrete examples to counter colonialism's endeavors to distort and depreciate. We must work and struggle in step with the people so as to shape the future and prepare the ground where vigorous shoots are already sprouting. National culture is no folklore where an abstract populism is convinced it has uncovered the popular truth. It is not some congealed mass of noble gestures, in other words less and less connected with the reality of the people. National culture is the collective thought process of a people to describe, justify, and extol the actions whereby they have joined forces and remained strong. National culture in the underdeveloped countries, therefore, must lie at the very heart of the liberation struggle these countries are waging. The African intellectuals who are still fighting in the name of "Negro-African" culture and who continue to organize conferences dedicated to the unity of that culture should realize that they can do little more than compare coins and sarcophagi.

There is no common destiny between the national cultures of Guinea and Senegal, but there is a common destiny between the nations of Guinea and Senegal dominated by the same

French colonialism. If we want the national culture of Senegal to resemble the national culture of Guinea it is not enough for the leaders of the two countries to address the problems of independence, labor unions, and the economy from a similar perspective. Even then they would not be absolutely identical since the people and the leaders operate at a different pace.

There can be no such thing as rigorously identical cultures. To believe one can create a black culture is to forget oddly enough that "Negroes" are in the process of disappearing, since those who created them are witnessing the demise of their economic and cultural supremacy.[21] There will be no such thing as black culture because no politician imagines he has the vocation to create a black republic. The problem is knowing what role these men have in store for their people, the type of social relations they will establish and their idea of the future of humanity. That is what matters. All else is hot air and mystification.

In 1959 the African intellectuals meeting in Rome constantly spoke of unity. But one of the leading bards of this cultural unity is Jacques Rabemananjara, today a minister in the government of Madagascar, who toed his government's line to vote against the Algerian people at the United Nations General Assembly. Rabe, if he had been sincere with himself, should have resigned from the government and denounced those men who claim to represent the will of the Malagasy people. The ninety thousand dead of Madagascar did not authorize Rabe to oppose the aspirations of the Algerian people at the UN General Assembly.

---

[21] At the last school prize-giving ceremony in Dakar, the president of the Republic of Senegal, Léopold Senghor, announced that negritude should be included in the school curriculum. If this decision is an exercise in cultural history, it can only be approved. But if it is a matter of shaping black consciousness it is simply turning one's back on history which has already noted the fact that most "Negroes" have ceased to exist.

* * *

"Negro-African" culture grows deeper through the people's struggle, and not through songs, poems, or folklore. Senghor, who is also a member of the African Society for Culture and who has worked with us on this issue of African culture, had no scruples either about instructing his delegation to back the French line on Algeria. Support for "Negro-African" culture and the cultural unity of Africa is first contingent on an unconditional support for the people's liberation struggle. One cannot expect African culture to advance unless one contributes realistically to the creation of the conditions necessary for this culture, i.e., the liberation of the continent.

Once again, no speech, no declaration on culture will detract us from our fundamental tasks which are to liberate the national territory; constantly combat the new forms of colonialism; and, as leaders, stubbornly refuse to indulge in self-satisfaction at the top.

MUTUAL FOUNDATIONS FOR NATIONAL CULTURE AND LIBERATION STRUGGLES

The sweeping, leveling nature of colonial domination was quick to dislocate in spectacular fashion the cultural life of a conquered people. The denial of a national reality, the new legal system imposed by the occupying power, the marginalization of the indigenous population and their customs by colonial society, expropriation, and the systematic enslavement of men and women, all contributed to this cultural obliteration.

Three years ago at our first congress I demonstrated that in a colonial situation any dynamism is fairly rapidly replaced by a reification of attitudes. The cultural sphere is marked out by safety railings and signposts, every single one of them defense mechanisms of the most elementary type, comparable in more ways than one to the simple instinct of self-preservation. This period is interesting because the oppressor is no longer content with the objective nonexistence of the conquered nation and culture. Every effort is made to make the colonized confess the inferiority of their culture, now reduced to a set of instinctive responses, to acknowledge the unreality of their nation and, in the last extreme, to admit the disorganized, half-finished nature of their own biological makeup.

The reactions of the colonized to this situation vary. Whereas the masses maintain intact traditions totally incongruous with the colonial situation, whereas the style of artisanship ossifies into an increasingly stereotyped formalism, the intellectual hurls himself frantically into the frenzied acquisition of the occupier's culture, making sure he denigrates his national culture, or else confines himself to making a detailed, methodical, zealous, and rapidly sterile inventory of it.

What both reactions have in common is that they both result in unacceptable contradictions. Renegade or substantialist, the colonized subject is ineffectual precisely because the colonial situation has not been rigorously analyzed. The colonial situation brings national culture virtually to a halt. There is no such thing as national culture, national cultural events, innovations, or reforms within the context of colonial domination, and there never will be. There are scattered instances of a bold attempt to revive a cultural dynamism, and reshape themes, forms, and tones. The immediate, tangible, and visible effects of these minor convulsions is nil. But if we follow the consequences to their very limit there are signs that the veil is being lifted from the national consciousness, oppression is being challenged and there is hope for the liberation struggle.

National culture under colonial domination is a culture under interrogation whose destruction is sought systematically. Very quickly it becomes a culture condemned to clandestinity. This notion of clandestinity can immediately be perceived in the reactions of the occupier who interprets this complacent attachment to traditions as a sign of loyalty to the national spirit and a refusal to submit. This persistence of cultural expression condemned by colonial society is already a demonstration of nationhood. But such a demonstration refers us back to the laws of inertia. No offensive has been launched, no relations redefined. There is merely a desperate clinging to a nucleus that is increasingly shriveled, increasingly inert, and increasingly hollow.

After one or two centuries of exploitation the national cultural landscape has radically shriveled. It has become an inventory of behavioral patterns, traditional costumes, and miscellaneous customs. Little movement can be seen. There is no real creativity, no ebullience. Poverty, national oppression, and cultural repression are one and the same. After a century of colonial domination culture becomes rigid in the extreme, congealed, and petrified. The atrophy of national reality and the death throes of national culture feed on one another. This is why it becomes vital to monitor the development of this relationship during the liberation struggle. Cultural denial, the contempt for any national demonstration of emotion or dynamism and the banning of any type of organization help spur aggressive behavior in the colonized. But this pattern of behavior is a defensive reaction, nonspecific, anarchic, and ineffective. Colonial exploitation, poverty, and endemic famine increasingly force the colonized into open, organized rebellion. Gradually, imperceptibly, the need for a decisive confrontation imposes itself and is eventually felt by the great majority of the people. Tensions emerge where previously there were none. International events, the collapse of whole sections of colonial empires and the inherent contradictions of the colonial system stimulate and strengthen combativity, motivating and invigorating the national consciousness.

These new tensions, which are present at every level of the colonial system, have repercussions on the cultural front. In literature, for example, there is relative overproduction. Once a pale imitation of the colonizer's literature, indigenous production now shows greater diversity and a will to particularize. Mainly consumer during the period of oppression, the intelligentsia turns productive. This literature is at first confined to the genre of poetry and tragedy. Then novels, short stories, and essays are tackled. There seems to be a kind of internal organization, a law of expression, according to which poetic creativity fades as the objectives and methods of the liberation struggle become clearer. There is a fundamental change of theme. In fact, less and less do we find those bitter, desperate recriminations, those loud, violent outbursts that, after all, reassure the occupier. In the previous period, the colonialists encouraged such endeavors and facilitated their publication. The occupier, in fact, likened these scathing denunciations, outpourings of misery, and heated words to an act of catharsis. Encouraging these acts would, in a certain way, avoid dramatization and clear the atmosphere.

But such a situation cannot last. In fact the advances made by national consciousness among the people modify and clarify the literary creation of the colonized intellectual. The people's staying power stimulates the intellectual to transcend the lament. Complaints followed by indictments give way to appeals. Then comes the call for revolt. The crystallization of the national consciousness will not only radically change the literary genres and themes but also create a completely new audience. Whereas the colonized intellectual started out by producing work exclusively with the oppressor in mind—either in order to charm him or to denounce him by using ethnic or subjectivist categories—he gradually switches over to addressing himself to his people.

It is only from this point onward that one can speak of a national literature. Literary creation addresses and clarifies typically nationalist themes. This is combat literature in the true sense of the word, in the sense that it calls upon a whole people to join in the struggle for the existence of the nation. Combat literature, because it informs the national consciousness, gives it shape and contours, and opens up new, unlimited horizons. Combat literature, because it takes charge, because it is resolve situated in historical time.

At another level, oral literature, tales, epics, and popular songs, previously classified and frozen in time, begin to change. The storytellers who recited inert episodes revive them and introduce increasingly fundamental changes. There are attempts to update battles and modernize the types of struggle, the heroes' names, and the weapons used. The method of allusion is increasingly used. Instead of "a long time ago," they substitute the more ambiguous expression "What I am going to tell you happened somewhere else, but it could happen here today or perhaps tomorrow." In this respect the case of Algeria is significant. From 1952–53 on, its storytellers, grown stale and dull, radically changed both their methods of narration and the content of their stories. Once scarce, the public returned in droves. The epic, with its standardized forms, reemerged. It has become an authentic form of entertainment that once again has taken on a cultural value. Colonialism knew full well what it was doing when it began systematically arresting these storytellers after 1955.

The people's encounter with this new song of heroic deeds brings an urgent breath of excitement, arouses forgotten muscular tensions and develops the imagination. Every time the storyteller narrates a new episode, the public is treated to a real invocation. The existence of a new type of man is revealed to the public. The present is no longer turned inward but channeled in every direction. The storyteller once again gives free rein to his imagination, innovates, and turns creator. It even happens that unlikely characters for such a transformation, social misfits such as outlaws or drifters, are rediscovered and rehabilitated. Close attention should be paid to the emergence of the imagination and the inventiveness of songs and folk tales in a colonized country. The storyteller responds to the expectations of the people by trial and error and searches for new models, national models, apparently on his own, but in fact with the support of his audience. Comedy and farce disappear or else lose their appeal. As for drama, it is no longer the domain of the intellectual's tormented conscience. No longer characterized by despair and revolt, it has become the people's daily lot, it has become part of an action in the making or already in progress.

In artisanship, the congealed, petrified forms loosen up. Wood carving, for example, which turned out set faces and poses by the thousands, starts to diversify. The expressionless or tormented mask comes to life, and the arms are raised upwards in a gesture of action. Compositions with two, three, or five figures emerge. An avalanche of amateurs and dissidents encourages the traditional schools to innovate. This new stimulus in this particular cultural sector very often goes unnoticed. Yet its contribution to the national struggle is vital. By bringing faces and bodies to life, by taking the group set on a single socle as creative subject, the artist inspires concerted action.

The awakening national consciousness has had a somewhat similar effect in the sphere of ceramics and pottery. Formalism is abandoned. Jugs, jars, and trays are reshaped, at first only slightly and then quite radically. Colors, once restricted in number, governed by laws of traditional harmony, flood back, reflecting the effects of the revolutionary upsurge. Certain ochers, certain blues that were apparently banned for eternity in a given cultural context, emerge unscathed. Likewise, the taboo of representing the human face, typical of certain clearly defined regions according to sociologists, is suddenly lifted. The metropolitan anthropologists and experts are quick to note these changes and denounce them all, referring rather to a codified artistic style and culture developing in tune with the colonial situation. The colonialist experts do not recognize these new forms and rush to the rescue of indigenous traditions. It is the colonialists who become the defenders of indigenous style. A memorable example, and one that takes on particular significance because it does not quite involve a colonial reality, was the reaction of white jazz fans when after the Second World War new styles such as bebop established themselves. For them jazz could only be the broken, desperate yearning of an old "Negro," five whiskeys under his belt, bemoaning his own misfortune and the racism of the whites. As soon as he understands himself and apprehends the world differently, as soon as he elicits a glimmer of hope and forces the racist world to retreat, it is obvious he will blow his horn to his heart's content and his husky voice will ring out loud and clear. The new jazz styles are not only born out of economic competition. They are one of the definite consequences of the inevitable, though gradual, defeat of the Southern universe in the USA. And it is not unrealistic to think that in fifty years or so the type of jazz lament hiccuped by a poor, miserable "Negro" will be defended by only those whites believing in a frozen image of a certain type of relationship and a certain form of negritude.

We would also uncover the same transformations, the same progress and the same eagerness if we enquired into the fields of dance, song, rituals, and traditional ceremonies. Well before the political or armed struggle, a careful observer could sense and feel in these arts the pulse of a fresh stimulus and the coming combat. Unusual forms of expression, original themes no longer invested with the power of invocation but the power to rally and mobilize with the approaching conflict in mind. Everything conspires to stimulate the colonized's sensibility, and to rule out and reject attitudes of inertia or defeat. By imparting new meaning and dynamism to artisanship, dance, music, literature, and the oral epic, the colonized subject restructures his own perception. The world no longer seems doomed. Conditions are ripe for the inevitable confrontation.

We have witnessed the emergence of a new energy in the cultural sphere. We have seen that this energy, these new forms, are linked to the maturing of the national consciousness, and now become increasingly objectivized and institutionalized. Hence the need for nationhood at all costs.

A common mistake, hardly defensible, moreover, is to attempt cultural innovations and reassert the value of indigenous culture within the context of colonial domination. Hence we arrive at a seemingly paradoxical proposition: In a colonized country, nationalism in its most basic, most rudimentary, and undifferentiated form is the most forceful and effective way of defending national culture. A culture is first and foremost the expression of a nation, its preferences, its taboos, and its models. Other taboos, other values, other models are formed at every level of the entire society. National culture is the sum of all these considerations, the outcome of tensions internal and external to society as a whole and its multiple layers. In the colonial context, culture, when deprived of the twin supports of the nation and the state, perishes and dies. National liberation and the resurrection of the state are the preconditions for the very existence of a culture.

The nation is not only a precondition for culture, its ebullition, its perpetual renewal and maturation. It is a necessity. First of all it is the struggle for nationhood that unlocks culture and opens the doors of creation. Later on it is the nation that will provide culture with the conditions and framework for expression. The nation satisfies all those indispensable requirements for culture which alone can give it credibility, validity, dynamism, and creativity. It is also the national character that makes culture permeable to other cultures and enables it to influence and penetrate them. That which does not exist can hardly have an effect on reality or even influence it. The restoration of the nation must therefore give life in the most biological sense of the term to national culture.

We have thus traced the increasingly essential fissuring of the old cultural strata, and on the eve of the decisive struggle for national liberation, grasped the new forms of expression and the flight of the imagination.

There now remains one fundamental question. What is the relationship between the struggle, the political or armed conflict, and culture? During the conflict is culture put on hold? Is the national struggle a cultural manifestation? Must we conclude that the liberation struggle, though beneficial for culture a posteriori, is in itself a negation of culture? In other words, is the liberation struggle a cultural phenomenon?

We believe the conscious, organized struggle undertaken by a colonized people in order to restore national sovereignty constitutes the greatest cultural manifestation that exists. It is not solely the success of the struggle that consequently validates and energizes culture; culture does not go into hibernation during the conflict. The development and internal progression of the actual struggle expand the number of directions in which culture can go and hint at new possibilities. The liberation struggle does not restore to national culture its former values and configurations. This struggle, which aims at a fundamental redistribution of relations between men, cannot leave intact either the form or substance of the people's culture. After the struggle is over, there is not only the demise of colonialism, but also the demise of the colonized.

This new humanity, for itself and for others, inevitably defines a new humanism. This new humanism is written into the objectives and methods of the struggle. A struggle, which mobilizes every level of society, which expresses the intentions and expectations of the people, and which is not afraid to rely on their support almost entirely, will invariably triumph. The merit of this type of struggle is that it achieves the optimal conditions for cultural development and innovation. Once national liberation has been accomplished under these conditions, there is none of that tiresome cultural indecisiveness we find in certain newly independent countries, because the way a nation is born and functions exerts a fundamental influence on culture. A nation born of the concerted action of the people, which embodies the actual aspirations of the people and transforms the state, depends on exceptionally inventive cultural manifestations for its very existence.

The colonized who are concerned for their country's culture and wish to give it a universal dimension should not place their trust in a single principle—that independence is inevitable and automatically inscribed in the people's consciousness—in order to achieve this aim. National liberation as objective is one thing, the methods and popular components of the struggle are another. We believe that the future of culture and the richness of a national culture are also based on the values that inspired the struggle for freedom.

And now the moment has come to denounce certain pharisees. Humanity, some say, has got past the stage of nationalist claims. The time has come to build larger political unions, and consequently the old-fashioned nationalists should correct their mistakes. We believe on the contrary that the mistake, heavy with consequences, would be to miss out on the national stage. If culture is the expression of the national consciousness, I shall have no hesitation in saying, in the case in point, that national consciousness is the highest form of culture.

Self-awareness does not mean closing the door on communication. Philosophy teaches us on the contrary that it is its guarantee. National consciousness, which is not nationalism, is alone capable of giving us an international dimension. This question of national consciousness and national culture takes on a special dimension in Africa. The birth of national consciousness in Africa strictly correlates with an African consciousness. The responsibility of the African toward his national culture is also a responsibility toward "Negro-African" culture. This joint responsibility does not rest upon a metaphysical principle but mindfulness of a simple rule which stipulates that any independent nation in an Africa where colonialism still lingers is a nation surrounded, vulnerable, and in permanent danger.

If man is judged by his acts, then I would say that the most urgent thing today for the African intellectual is the building of his nation. If this act is true, i.e., if it expresses the manifest will of the people, if it reflects the restlessness of the African peoples, then it will necessarily lead to the discovery and advancement of universalizing values. Far then from distancing it from other nations, it is the national liberation that puts the nation on the stage of history. It is at the heart of national consciousness that international consciousness establishes itself and thrives. And this dual emergence, in fact, is the unique focus of all culture.

Paper presented at the Second Congress of Black Writers and Artists, Rome, 1959.

Colonial War
and Mental Disorders

But the war goes on. And for many years to come we shall be bandaging the countless and sometimes indelible wounds inflicted on our people by the colonialist onslaught.

Imperialism, which today is waging war against a genuine struggle for human liberation, sows seeds of decay here and there that must be mercilessly rooted out from our land and from our minds.

We shall deal here with the problem of mental disorders born out of the national war of liberation waged by the Algerian people.

Perhaps the reader will find these notes on psychiatry out of place or untimely in a book like this. There is absolutely nothing we can do about that.

We had no control over the fact that the psychiatric phenomena, the mental and behavioral disorders emerging from this war, have loomed so large among the perpetrators of "pacification" and the "pacified" population. The truth is that colonization, in its very essence, already appeared to be a great purveyor of psychiatric hospitals. Since 1954 we have drawn the attention of French and international psychiatrists in scientific works to the difficulty of "curing" a colonized subject correctly, in other words making him thoroughly fit into a social environment of the colonial type.

Because it is a systematized negation of the other, a frenzied determination to deny the other any attribute of humanity, colonialism forces the colonized to constantly ask the question: "Who am I in reality?"

The defensive positions born of this violent confrontation between the colonized and the colonial constitute a structure which then reveals the colonized personality. In order to understand this "sensibility" we need only to study and appreciate the scope and depth of the wounds inflicted on the colonized during a single day under a colonial regime. We must remember in any case that a colonized people is not just a dominated people. Under the German occupation the French remained human beings. Under the French occupation the Germans remained human beings. In Algeria there is not simply domination but the decision, literally, to occupy nothing else but a territory. The Algerians, the women dressed in haiks, the palm groves, and the camels form a landscape, the *natural* backdrop for the French presence.

A hostile, ungovernable, and fundamentally rebellious Nature is in fact synonymous in the colonies with the bush, the mosquitoes, the natives, and disease. Colonization has succeeded once this untamed Nature has been brought under control. Cutting railroads through the bush, draining swamps, and ignoring the political and economic existence of the native population are in fact one and the same thing.

When colonization remains unchallenged by armed resistance, when the sum of harmful stimulants exceeds a certain threshold, the colonized's defenses collapse, and many of them end up in psychiatric institutions. In the calm of this period of triumphant colonization, a constant and considerable stream of mental symptoms are direct sequels of this oppression.

Today the all-out national war of liberation waged by the Algerian people for seven years has become a breeding ground for mental disorders.[22] We include here cases of Algerian and French patients under our care which we think particularly meaningful. We need hardly add that our approach here is not that of a scientific work, and we have avoided any semiological, nosological, or therapeutic discussion. The few technical terms used here are solely meant as points of reference. We must, however, insist on two points:

As a general rule, clinical psychiatry classifies the various disorders presented by our patients under the heading "psychotic reaction." In doing so, priority is given to the situation that triggered the disorder, although here and there mention is made of the role played by the subject's psychological, affective, and biological history, and that of his milieu. We believe that in the cases presented here the triggering factor is principally the bloody, pitiless atmosphere, the generalization of inhuman practices, of people's lasting impression that they are witnessing a veritable apocalypse.

Case no. 2 of Series A is a typical psychotic reaction, but case nos. 1, 2, 4, and 5 of Series B suppose a much vaguer causality, although we cannot really point to a particular triggering situation. Here it is the war, this colonial war that very often takes on the aspect of a genuine genocide, this war which radically disrupts and shatters the world, which is in fact the triggering

---

[22] In the unpublished introduction of the first two editions of *L'an V de la révolution algérienne* (Studies in a Dying Colonialism), we already indicated that an entire generation of Algerians, steeped in collective, gratuitous homicide with all the psychosomatic consequences this entails, would be France's human legacy in Algeria. The French who condemn torture in Algeria constantly adopt a strictly French point of view. This is not a reproach, merely an affirmation: they want to safeguard the conscience of present and potential torturers and try and protect French youth from moral degradation. We, for our part, can but approve such an approach. Some of the observations collected here, notably case histories nos. 4 and 5 of series A, sadly illustrate and justify this obsessive fear of French democrats. Our purpose, in any case, is to demonstrate that any torture deeply dislocates, as might be expected, the personality of the tortured.

situation. These are brief psychotic disorders, if we want to use the official term, but putting particular emphasis on war in general and the specific circumstances of a colonial war. After the two major world wars there was a host of publications on the mental pathology of soldiers engaged in action as well as the civilian refugees and bombing victims. The novel physiognomy of some of the case histories mentioned here provides confirmation, if we still needed it, that this colonial war is a new phenomenon even in the pathology it produces.

Another well-established notion that deserves in our opinion to be reevaluated is that these psychotic reactions are relatively benign. Anniversary reactions, i.e., cases where the entire personality has been definitively dislocated, have of course been described, but always as exceptional cases. We believe on the contrary that the pathological processes tend as a rule to be frequently malignant. These disorders last for months, wage a massive attack on the ego, and almost invariably leave behind a vulnerability virtually visible to the naked eye. In all evidence the future of these patients is compromised. The following example will illustrate our standpoint.

In a certain African country, independent for some years now, we have had the opportunity of treating a patriot and former resistance fighter. The man, in his thirties, would come and ask us for advice and help, since he was afflicted with insomnia together with anxiety attacks and obsession with suicide around a certain date in the year. The critical date corresponded to the day he had been ordered to place a bomb somewhere. Ten people had perished during the attack.[23]

---

[23] The circumstances surrounding the symptoms are interesting for several reasons. Several months after his country had gained independence he had made the acquaintance of nationals from the former colonizing nation. They became friends. These men and women welcomed the newly acquired independence and unhesitatingly paid tribute to the courage of the patriots in the national liberation struggle. The militant was then overcome by a kind of vertigo. He anxiously asked himself whether among the victims of his bomb

This militant, who never for a moment had thought of recant-
ing, fully realized the price he had had to pay in his person for
national independence. Such borderline cases pose the question
of responsibility in the context of the revolution.

The observations quoted here cover the period 1954 to 1959.
Certain patients were examined in Algeria either in hospitals or
private practice. The others were treated in the National Liberation Army's medical facilities.

SERIES A

Five cases have been collected here, all involving Algerians
or Europeans who had clearly defined symptoms of severe reactive disorders.

*Case No. 1—Impotence in an Algerian following the rape of
his wife*

B— —is a twenty-six-year-old man. He has been referred to us
by the Medical Services of the National Liberation Front for persistent migraines and insomnia. A former taxi driver, he has been
a militant in the nationalist parties since the age of eighteen. In
1955 he became a member of an FLN (Front de Libération
Nationale) unit. On several occasions he used his taxi to carry
propaganda leaflets and political leaders. Confronted with a
widening crackdown, the FLN decided to wage war in the urban

---

there might have been individuals similar to his new acquaintances. It was
true the bombed café was known to be the haunt of notorious racists, but
nothing could stop any passerby from entering and having a drink. From that
day on the man tried to avoid thinking of past events. But paradoxically a few
days before the critical date the first symptoms would break out. They have
been a regular occurrence ever since.

In other words, our actions never cease to haunt us. The way they are ordered, organized, and reasoned can be a posteriori radically transformed. It is
by no means the least of the traps history and its many determinations set for
us. But can we escape vertigo? Who dares claim that vertigo does not prey on
every life?

centers; B— —was then assigned to driving commandos close to the points of attack, and fairly often having to wait for them.

One day, however, right in the middle of the European sector, following a fairly extensive commando raid, the sector was sealed off, forcing him to abandon his taxi and compelling the commando unit to break up and disperse. B— —, who managed to escape the enemy's surveillance, took refuge at a friend's house, and a few days later, on orders from his superiors, went underground to join the nearest resistance unit without ever going home.

For several months he went without news of his wife and his twenty-month-old daughter. He did learn, however, that the police had been looking for him for weeks in the city. After two years in the resistance movement he received a message from his wife asking him to forget her. She had brought shame on herself. He must no longer think of coming back to live with her. Extremely worried, he requested permission from his commander to make a secret trip back home. It was refused. However, steps were taken for a member of the FLN to contact B— —'s wife and parents.

Two weeks later a detailed report reached the commander of B— —'s unit.

Soon after his abandoned taxi had been discovered (with two machine gun magazines inside) a group of French soldiers and policemen had gone to his home. Finding him absent, they took away his wife and kept her for over a week.

She was interrogated about the company her husband kept and slapped fairly violently for two days. On the third day a French soldier—she was unable to say whether he was an officer— ordered the others out and raped her. Shortly afterward a second soldier, this time in the presence of the others, raped her, telling her: "If you ever see that bastard your husband again, don't you forget to tell him what we did to you." She remained another week without undergoing further interrogation. She was then escorted home. When she told her story to her mother, the latter convinced her to tell B — — everything. So as soon as her husband got in touch with her again, she confessed her disgrace.

Once the initial shock was over, B — — soon recovered by devoting every minute of his life to the cause. For several months he took reports from Algerian women who had been tortured or raped; he had the opportunity of meeting with the husbands of abused women and his personal misfortune, his dignity as an injured husband took second place.

In 1958 he was assigned to a mission abroad. Just before rejoining his unit an unusual distraction and insomnia worried his comrades and his superiors. His departure was delayed and a medical examination ordered. This was when he was referred to us. Our first impression was good. A lively face, a bit too lively perhaps. His smile was slightly forced, his exuberance superficial: "I'm okay . . . I'm okay. I feel better now. Give me a fortifier, some vitamins, and let me go back." He was obviously anxious deep down. He was immediately hospitalized.

On the second day the smoke screen of optimism vanished and we had on our hands a bedridden anorexic suffering from melancholic depression. He avoided any political discussion and manifested a marked disinterest for anything concerning the national struggle. He avoided listening to news about the war of liberation. Identifying his problems was extremely laborious, but after several days we managed to reconstruct his story:

During his stay abroad he had tried to have sexual intercourse but failed. Thinking it was merely fatigue, normal after forced marches and periods of malnutrition, he tried again two weeks later and failed again. Spoke to a comrade about it who advised him to take vitamin B_{12}. Took it in tablet form. New attempt, new failure. Furthermore, a few moments before the act he had an irresistible impulse to tear up a photo of his little girl. Such a symbolic connection could raise the possibility of unconscious incestuous drives. However, several conversations and a dream in which the patient witnessed the rapid putrefying of a kitten giving off a nauseating smell, led us in a completely new direction.

"This girl," he told us one day, referring to his daughter, "has something rotten inside her." From that moment on his insomnia became extremely troubling, and despite a fairly large dose of neuroleptics, he developed a state of nervous anxiety that was particularly alarming. He then spoke to us for the first time about his wife and said laughingly: "She got a bit of French meat." It was then we were able to reconstruct the whole story. The fabric of events became clear. He told us that every time he tried to have sexual intercourse, he thought of his wife. What he confided to us seemed to be of fundamental interest.

"I married this girl whereas I was in love with my cousin. But the cousin's parents had arranged to marry their daughter to someone else. So I accepted the first girl my parents offered me. She was nice, but I didn't love her. I kept telling myself: you're young . . . wait a bit, and when you've found the right girl, you'll divorce and make a happy marriage. So I wasn't very attached to my wife. With the war, we moved even further apart. In the end, I used to come and eat my meals and go to bed with hardly a word between us.

"When I learned during my time with the freedom fighters that she had been raped by some French soldiers I first of all felt angry with the bastards. Then I said, 'Oh, it's nothing serious; she wasn't killed. She can start her life over again.' And then several weeks later it dawned on me that she had been raped *because they had been looking for me*. In fact she had been raped to punish her for keeping quiet. She could have easily given them at least one militant's name, which would have enabled them to discover and eliminate the network, and perhaps even have me arrested. It was not therefore a simple rape for want of anything better to do or out of sadism, as I had often seen in the *douars*; it was the rape of a tenacious woman who was prepared to accept anything rather than give up her husband. And that husband *was me*. That woman had saved my life and had protected the network. It was my fault she had been dishonored. Yet she didn't say: 'This is what I endured for you.' On the contrary, she said: 'Forget me, start a new life, I have been disgraced.'

"It was then that I made up my mind to take her back after the war; I have to tell you I've seen peasants dry the tears of their wives who had been raped under their very eyes. That shook me up quite a bit and I have to confess that at first I couldn't understand their attitude. But we had to intervene increasingly in such circumstances to explain things to the civilians and I've seen civilians volunteer to marry a young girl who had been raped and made pregnant by French soldiers. All that made me think again about my wife.

"I've made up my mind to take her back, but I still don't know how I'll react when I see her. And when I look at the picture of my daughter I often think she was dishonored as well. As if everything that had to do with my wife was rotten. If they had tortured her, if they had broken all her teeth or an arm, I wouldn't have minded so much. But that thing, how can you ever get over it? And did she have to tell me about it?"

He then asked me whether his "sexual failing" in my opinion was caused by his worrying.

Answer: "It's quite likely."

He then sat up in bed.

"What would you do if it happened to you?"

"I don't know . . ."

"Would you take your wife back?"

"I think I would . . ."

"Ah, you see . . . you're not quite sure."

He put his head in his hands and after a few moments left the room.

From that day on, he gradually accepted to listen to political discussions while his migraines and anorexia lessened considerably.

After two weeks he rejoined his unit telling me: "On independence, I'll take my wife back. If it doesn't work out, I'll come and see you again in Algiers."

Case No. 2—Random homicidal impulses in a survivor of a massacre

S——, thirty-seven years old, a fellah. Lives in a *douar* in the region of Constantine. Has never been involved in politics. Since the beginning of the war his region has been the scene of violent battles between the Algerian forces and the French army. S——therefore has had occasion to see the dead and the wounded. But he continued to keep his distance. Like the general population, the peasants from his village had occasionally come to the aid of Algerian fighters as they passed through. But one day in early 1958 a deadly ambush occurred not far from the *douar*. The enemy forces went into action and surrounded the village where there was not a single soldier. All the inhabitants were rounded up and interrogated. Everyone kept silent. A few hours later a French officer arrived by helicopter and declared: 'There's too much fuss over this *douar*; destroy it!' The soldiers began to set fire to the houses while the women who were trying to collect a few clothes or save some provisions were driven back with rifle butts. Some of the peasants took advantage of the confusion to escape. The officer gave orders to round up the remaining men and had them brought to a neighboring wadi where the massacre began. Twenty-nine men were killed at point-blank range. S——was wounded by two bullets that passed through his right thigh and left arm respectively, the latter wound causing a fractured humerus.

S—— fainted and regained consciousness in the midst of a group of ALN (Armée de Libération Nationale) soldiers. He was treated by their medical personnel and evacuated once he was able to walk. En route his increasingly abnormal behavior was a constant source of concern for the escort. He demanded a gun, although he was a helpless civilian, and refused to walk in front of anybody. He refused to have anyone behind him. One night he grabbed one of the soldier's guns and clumsily fired on the sleeping soldiers. He was disarmed by force. From then on his hands were tied and that is how he arrived at the Center.

He began by telling us he was not dead and he had played a trick on the others. Gradually we managed to reconstruct the story of his failed assassination attempt. S— — is not anxious, but overexcited with violent mood swings and shouting. He did not break anything, but wore everyone out by his constant chatter and the Service was on permanent alert because of his declared intention to 'kill everybody.' During his hospitalization he would attack roughly eight patients, with makeshift weapons. The nurses and doctors were not spared either. We even wondered whether we were not facing one of those latent forms of epilepsy characterized by a general aggressiveness that was almost constantly on edge.

We started narcotherapy. After the third day a daily cross-examination allowed us to better understand the dynamics of the pathological process. His intellectual confusion gradually cleared up. The following are extracts from the patient's statements:

"God is with me . . . but he can't have been with those who died. . . . I was damn lucky. . . . In life, it's kill or be killed. . . . When I think I knew nothing about all that business. . . . There are some French among us. . . . They're disguised as Arabs. . . . They've all got to be killed. . . . Give me a machine gun. All these so-called Algerians are French . . . and they won't leave me alone. As soon as I try to get some sleep, they come into my room. But now I know what they're up to. Everyone wants to kill me. But I'll fight back. I'll kill them all, every one of them. I'll slit their thoats, one after the other, and yours as well. You all want to take me out, but you'll have to think of other ways. Killing you won't affect me in the slightest. The little ones, the grown-ups, the women, the children, the dogs, the birds, the donkeys . . . nobody will be spared. . . . Afterwards, I'll be able to sleep in peace . . ."

All that was said in fits and starts and he remained hostile, aloof and scornful.

After three weeks his agitated state disappeared, but there was a disinclination to communicate and a tendency to keep to himself, which made us fear the worst. However, after a month he asked to leave so that he could learn a trade compatible with his disability. He was then entrusted to the care of the FLN's social services. Saw him again six months later. Doing well.

Case No. 3—Major depressive disorder with mood-congruent psychotic features following the murder of a woman while briefly psychotic

D——, former student, ALN fighter, nineteen years old. When he arrived at the Center he had already been ill for several months. His symptoms were characteristic: deeply depressed, dry lips, and constantly moist hands. Heaved constant sighs. Persistent insomnia. Two suicide attempts since the onset of the disorder. During the conversation showed signs of auditory hallucination. Sometimes his gaze fixed for a few moments at a point in space while his face lit up, giving the impression he was seeing something. Incoherent thoughts. Behavior known in psychiatry as blocking where the start of a gesture or phrase is suddenly interrupted for no apparent reason. But one feature in particular caught our attention: The patient talked of his blood being spilled, his arteries drained, and an abnormal heartbeat. He begged us to stop the hemorrhage and not let them come into the hospital to "suck the lifeblood" out of him. From time to time, could no longer speak and asked for a pencil. Wrote: "Have lost my voice, my whole life is fading away." This display of depersonalization led us to believe he had reached a serious stage.

Several times in the course of our conversations the patient mentioned a woman who would come and persecute him when night fell. Having previously learned that his mother, whom he adored, had died and that he would never get over his loss (at that moment his voice became muffled and a few tears appeared) I turned the cross-examination to the mother image. When I asked him to describe this woman who was haunting, even persecuting, him he told me she was no stranger, that he knew her very well and he was the one who had killed her. The question was then of knowing whether we were in the presence of an unconscious guilt complex after his mother's death, as Freud describes in his "Mourning and Melancholia." We asked him to tell us more about this woman since he knew her so well and was supposed to have killed her. That is how we managed to reconstruct the following story:

"I left the town where I had been a student to join the underground resistance movement. After several months I received news of home. I learned that my mother had been killed at point-blank range by a French soldier, and two of my sisters taken to the barracks. To this day I don't know where they are. I was terribly shaken by my mother's death. My father had died some years back, I was the only man in the family, and my sole ambition had always been to do something to make life easier for my mother and sisters. One day we went to a large estate owned by white settlers where the manager, a notorious colonial, had already killed two Algerian civilians. It was night when we arrived at his house. But he wasn't at home. Only his wife was in the house. On seeing us, she begged us not to kill her: 'I know you have come for my husband,' she said, 'but he isn't here . . . How many times have I told him not to get mixed up in politics.' We decided to wait for the husband. But I kept looking at the woman and thinking of my mother. She was sitting in an armchair and her thoughts seemed to be elsewhere. I was asking myself why we didn't kill her. And then she noticed I was looking at her. She threw herself on me screaming: 'Please . . . don't kill me . . . I've got children.' The next minute she was dead. I'd killed her with my knife. My commander disarmed me and gave me orders to leave. I was interrogated by the district commander a few days later. I thought I was going to be shot, but I didn't give a damn.[24] And then I began to vomit after eating and I slept badly. After that this woman would come every night asking for my blood. And what about my mother's blood?"

---

[24] After the medical and legal reports had stressed the pathological nature of the act, the legal proceedings initiated by the ALN's staff headquarters were dropped.

As soon as the patient went to bed at night the room was "invaded by women," all the same. It was the same woman duplicated over and over again. They all had a gaping hole in their stomachs. They were bloodless, sickly pale, and terribly thin. The women tormented the young man and demanded their blood back. At that moment the sound of rushing water filled the room and grew so loud it seemed like a thundering waterfall, and the young patient saw the floor of his room soaked in blood, his blood, while the women slowly got their color back and their wounds began to close. Soaked in sweat and filled with anxiety, the patient would wake up and remain agitated until dawn.

The young patient has been treated now for several weeks and the oneiroid (nightmare) symptoms have virtually disappeared. His personality, however, remains seriously flawed. As soon as he thinks of his mother, this disemboweled woman looms up disconcertingly in her place. As unscientific as it may seem, we believe only time may heal the dislocated personality of this young man.

Case No. 4—A European police officer suffering from depression while at the hospital meets one of his victims, an Algerian patriot suffering from stupor

A——, twenty-eight years old, married without children. We have learned that he and his wife have been undergoing treatment for several years to try and have children. He is referred to us by his superiors because of behavioral problems.

The immediate rapport proved to be fairly good. The patient spoke to us spontaneously about his problems. On good terms with his wife and parents-in-law. Good relations with his colleagues at work and well thought of by his superiors. What troubled him was having difficulty sleeping at night because he kept hearing screams. In fact, he told us that for the last few weeks before going to bed he closes all the shutters and stops up the windows (it is summer) to the utter despair of his wife who is suffocating from the heat. He also stuffs cotton in his ears so as to muffle the screams. Sometimes in the middle of the night he switches on the radio or puts on some music so as not to hear the nightly din. He consequently explained to us his tribulations in great detail:

A few months ago he was transferred to an anti-FLN brigade. To begin with he was assigned to watching a few buildings and cafés. But after a few weeks he was working almost full time at the police headquarters. That was where he came to be involved in interrogations which always implied some form of "roughing up." "The thing is they never wanted to confess anything."

"Sometimes," he went on to explain, "you feel like telling them that if they had any consideration for us, they'd cough up and not force us to spend hours on end squeezing the information out of them word by word. But you might as well talk to the wall. Every question gets the answer: 'I don't know.' Even when we ask for their names. If we ask them where they live, they answer, 'I don't know.' So of course we had to give them the works. But they scream too much. At first it made me laugh. But then it began to unnerve me. Today I can tell just which stage the interrogation has reached by the sound of the screams. The guy who has been punched twice and given a blow behind the ear has a certain way of talking, screaming, and saying that he is innocent. After he has been hanging by his wrists for two hours, his voice changes. After the bathtub, a different voice. And so on. But it's after the electricity that it becomes unbearable. You'd think he was going to die at any moment. Of course there are those who don't scream: those are the hardliners. But they imagine we are going to kill them immediately. But we're not interested in killing them. What we want is information. We first try and get them to scream, and sooner or later they give in. That's already a victory. Then we continue. Mind you, we'd prefer not to. But they don't make things easy for us. Now I can hear those screams even at home. Especially the screams of the ones who died at the police headquarters. Doctor, I'm sick of this job. If you can cure me, I'll request a transfer to France. If they refuse, I'll resign."

Under the circumstances I put him on sick leave. Since he refused to be admitted to hospital, I treated him as a private patient. One day just before our session was due to begin, I was called back to the ward for an emergency. When he arrived at my house, my wife told A— —he could wait, but he said he preferred to go for a walk in the hospital grounds, thinking he might find me there. A few minutes later, on my way back home, I found him leaning against a tree, covered in sweat and having a panic attack. I put him in the car and drove home. Once we had settled him on the sofa, he told me he had encountered one of my patients (an Algerian patriot) who had been tortured at police headquarters and who was being treated for post-traumatic stress. I then learned that this police officer had been actively involved in torturing this patient. I gave him some sedatives, which calmed his anxiety. After he had left, I visited the ward where the Algerian was being treated. The staff hadn't noticed anything. The patient, however, was nowhere to be found. We eventually discovered him hiding in a bathroom where he was trying to commit suicide. The patient had recognized the police officer and was convinced he had come looking for him to take him back to police headquarters.

A— — came back to see me several times, and after his condition improved rapidly he was eventually repatriated on medical grounds. As for the Algerian patriot, it took a long time for the staff to convince him he had been deluding himself, that policemen were not allowed inside the hospital, that he was tired, and he was here to be cared for, etc. . . .

Case No. 5—A European police inspector tortures his wife and children

R— —, thirty years old, referred himself to us of his own free will. He is a police inspector who for some weeks realized that "something was wrong." Married with three children. Smokes a lot: three packs a day. He has lost his appetite and his sleep is disturbed by nightmares. These nightmares have no particular distinguishing features. What bothers him most is what he calls his "fits of madness." First of all he does not like to be contradicted: "Doctor, tell me why as soon as someone confronts me, I feel like hitting him. Even outside work I feel like punching the guy who gets in my way. For nothing at all. Take for example when I go to buy the paper. There's a line. So you have to wait. I hold out my hand to take the paper (the guy who runs the newsstand is an old friend of mine) and someone in the line calls out aggressively: 'Wait your turn.' Well, I feel like beating him up and I tell myself: 'If I could get you, pal, for a few hours, you wouldn't mess with me.'"

He can't put up with noise. At home he has a constant desire to give everyone a beating. And he violently assaults his children, even his twenty-month-old baby.

But what frightened him was one evening when his wife had bitterly protested he was being too hard on the children (she had even said to him: "For goodness sake, you're crazy . . .") he turned on her, beat her, and tied her to a chair shouting: "I'm going to teach you once and for all who's the boss around here."

Fortunately his children began to cry and scream. He then realized the full gravity of his behavior, untied his wife, and the next morning decided to consult a "nerve specialist." He had never been like that, he says; he seldom punished his children and never quarreled with his wife. The present problem had occurred since "the troubles." "The fact is," he said, "we're now being used as foot soldiers. Last week, for example, we operated as if we were in the army. Those guys in the government say there's no war in Algeria and the police force must restore law and order, but there *is* a war in Algeria, and when they realize it, it'll be too late. The thing that gets me the most is the torture. Does that mean anything to you? . . . Sometimes I torture for ten hours straight."

"How does torturing make you feel?"

"It wears you out, of course . . . It's true we take turns, but the question is knowing when to let your colleague have a go. Everyone thinks he's just about to get the information and is careful not to hand over the customer all nice and ready for the other guy to take all the glory. So sometimes we hand him over and sometimes we don't.

"We even offer the guy money, our own pocket money, to get him to squeal. Our problem is, are we able to get the guy to talk? It's a matter of personal success; we're sort of competing. We eventually messed up our fists. So we brought in the 'Senegalese.' But they either hit too hard and mess up the guy in thirty minutes, or not enough and nothing happens. In fact, you need to use your head in this kind of work. You need to know when to tighten your grip and when to loosen it. You have to have a feel for it. When the guy is ripe, there's no point continuing to hit him. That's why it's best to do your own work, you can judge better how you're doing. I'm against those who get others to work the guy over and then pop in every so often to see how he's doing. The golden rule is never give the guy the impression he won't get out alive. He'll then wonder what's the use of talking if it won't save his life. In that case you'll have no chance at all of getting anything out of him. He has to go on hoping: It's hope that makes them talk.

"But what bothers me most, is this business with my wife. I must have a screw loose somewhere. You've got to straighten me out, doctor."

Since his administration refused to give him a sick leave and the patient did not wish for certification from a psychiatrist, we treated him "while on duty." It is easy to imagine the disadvantages of such a procedure. This man knew perfectly well that all his problems stemmed directly from the type of work conducted in the interrogation rooms, though he tried to blame everything on "the troubles." As he had no intention of giving up his job as a torturer (this would make no sense since he would then have to resign) he asked me in plain language to help him torture Algerian patriots without having a guilty conscience, without any behavioral problems, and with a total peace of mind.[25]

SERIES B

Here we have collected cases or groups of cases where the triggering factor is first and foremost the atmosphere of outright war that reigns in Algeria.

Case No. 1—The murder by two thirteen- and fourteen-year-old Algerians of their European playmate
This involves a medical and legal examination. Two thirteen- and fourteen-year-olds, Algerian schoolboys, are accused of killing one of their European playmates. They have admitted to the act. The crime has been reconstructed and photos included in the file. They show one of the children holding their victim while the other stabs him with a knife. The accused did not go back on their statements. We have long conversations with them. The relevant extracts read as follows:
a. The thirteen-year-old:
"We were not angry with him. Every Thursday we used to go and hunt together with a slingshot up on the hill behind the village. He was our best friend. He had left school because he wanted to become a mason like his father. One day we decided to kill him because the Europeans want to kill all the Arabs. We can't kill the 'grown-ups,' but we can kill someone like him because he's our own age. We didn't know how to go about it. We

---

[25] This case revealed the existence of a coherent system that leaves nothing intact. The torturer who loves birds or quietly enjoys a symphony or a sonata is simply one stage. The next stage is nothing more than radical and absolute sadism.

wanted to throw him into a ditch, but this might only have injured him. So we took a knife from home and we killed him."

"But why did you pick on him?"

"Because he used to play with us. Another boy wouldn't have gone up the hill with us."

"But he was a friend of yours?"

"So, why do they want to kill us? His father's in the militia and says we all ought to have our throats slit."

"But he didn't say anything like that to you?"

"Him? No."

"You know he's dead now."

"Yes."

"What does being dead mean?"

"It means it's all over, you go to Heaven."

"Did you kill him?"

"Yes."

"Are you sorry you killed someone?"

"No, because they want to kill us, so . . ."

"Do you mind being in prison?"

"No."

b. The fourteen-year-old:

This boy is very different from his classmate. He is almost a man, an adult, judging from his muscular control, his physiognomy, and the tone and content of his answers. He does not deny killing either. Why did he do it? He does not answer the question, but asks me if I have ever seen a European in prison. Has there ever been a European arrested and imprisoned for the murder of an Algerian? I replied that in fact I had never seen any Europeans in prison.

"And yet there are Algerians killed every day, aren't there?"

"Yes."

"So why are there only Algerians in prison? How do you explain that?"

"I can't, but tell me why you killed this boy who was your friend?"

"I'll tell you. . . . Have you heard about the Rivet business?"[26]

"Yes."

"Two of my family were killed that day. At home they say the French had sworn to kill us all, one after the other. Has any Frenchman been arrested for all those Algerians that were killed?"

"I don't know."

"Well, no one has been arrested. I wanted to take to the mountains, but I'm too young. So [the other boy] and I said . . . we would kill a European."

"Why?"

"In your opinion, what do you think we should have done?"

"I don't know. But you are a child and the things that are going on are for grown-ups."

"But they kill children too."

"But that's no reason for killing your friend."

"Well, I killed him. Now you can do what you like."

"Did this friend do anything to you?"

"No. He didn't do anything."

"Well?"

"That's all there is to it."

Case No. 2 — Paranoid delusions and suicidal behavior disguised as "terrorist act" in a young twenty-two-year-old Algerian

This patient was referred to the hospital by the French judiciary authorities following a medical and legal examination by French psychiatrists practicing in Algeria.

The patient was emaciated and in a state of confusion. His body was covered in ecchymoses and he was unable to absorb any food owing to two fractures of the jaw. For over two weeks the patient was fed intravenously.

---

[26] Rivet is a village in the region around Algiers which became headline news one day in 1956. One evening the village was raided by French militia who dragged forty men from their beds and murdered them.

After two weeks his thinking became less blank and we were able to establish contact. We managed to reconstruct the young man's dramatic story.

During adolescence he had been an ardent scout and became one of the leaders in the Muslim scout movement. But at age nineteen he completely abandoned the scouts to devote himself entirely to his profession. A passionate student of mechanical data processing he dreamed of becoming a leading specialist in the field. November 1, 1954, found him absorbed in strictly professional matters. At the time he showed no interest in the national liberation struggle. He had already forsaken his former friends. He said he was at the time "entirely devoted to improving his technical abilities."

In mid-1955, however, during a family reunion he suddenly got the impression his parents considered him a traitor. After a few days this fleeting impression lost its edge, but deep down he felt strangely anxious and uneasy.

He decided, therefore, to spend as little time as possible eating and talking with his family and locked himself up in his room. Avoided any contact. It was under these circumstances that the catastrophe occurred. One day, in the middle of the street, around half past twelve, he distinctly heard a voice call him a traitor. He turned around, but saw nobody. He hurried on and decided to stay away from work. He stayed in his room and did not have any dinner. It was during the night he suffered the attack. For three hours he heard all kinds of insults, voices crying in his head and in the darkness: "Traitor . . . coward . . . all your brothers are dying . . . traitor . . . traitor."

He was gripped by an indescribable anxiety: "For eighteen hours my heart beat at one hundred and thirty beats per minute. I thought I was going to die."

From that moment on the patient could no longer swallow a thing. He got thinner by the minute, kept himself in pitch darkness and refused to see his parents. Around the third day he isolated himself in prayer. He told me he remained kneeling seventeen to eighteen hours a day. On the fourth day, acting on impulse, "like a madman" with "a beard which must have made him look even more like a madman," he went out without his usual jacket or tie. Once he stepped into the street he had no idea where to go, but he walked and after a while found himself in the European sector. His physical appearance (he could be taken for a European) seems to have protected him from being stopped and questioned by the French police, whereas, next to him, Algerian men and women were being arrested, roughed up, insulted, and searched. Paradoxically he had no identity papers on him. The fact that the enemy patrols instinctively showed him consideration confirmed his delusion that "everyone knows he's on the side of the French. The soldiers themselves have orders to leave him alone."

Moreover, the looks of the Algerians arrested with their hands behind their necks, waiting to be searched, seemed to him to be full of contempt. Stricken by an uncontrollable agitation he quickly strode away. It was then he found himself in front of the French staff headquarters. At the gate stood several soldiers armed with machine guns. He walked over toward the soldiers, hurled himself onto one of them and tried to grab his machine gun, shouting: "I am an Algerian!"

Quickly brought under control he was led into the police offices where they stubbornly tried to make him confess the names of the leaders and various members of the network for which he was supposedly working. After a few days the police and the soldiers realized they were dealing with a sick individual. An examination was ordered that concluded he was suffering from mental disorders and should be admitted to a hospital. "All I wanted to do," he told us, "was to die. Even at the police station I believed and hoped that after they had tortured me they would kill me. I was happy to be beaten because that proved they considered me to be one of the enemy as well. I couldn't go on hearing those accusations and do nothing. I'm not a coward. I'm not a sissy. I'm not a traitor."[27]

Case No. 3—Anxiety disorder in a young Frenchwoman whose
father, a senior civil servant, was killed in an ambush
This twenty-one-year-old student came to consult me for minor anxiety symptoms that were interfering with her studies and social life. Hands constantly clammy and at times presented truly alarming symptoms when water "dripped from her hands." Chest constrictions accompanied by nocturnal migraine. Bit her nails. But what caught our attention especially was the clearly overdesirous way to make contact whereas there was a sense of considerable underlying anxiety. She brushed aside her father's death, which was recent judging by the date, in such an off-hand way that we quickly turned our investigation to her relationship with her father. We were given a clear, absolutely lucid description, so lucid as to be almost insensitive, which revealed by its very rationality the nature and origin of this young woman's disorder.

"My father was a senior civil servant. He was in charge of a vast rural area. As soon as the troubles broke out, he threw himself like a maniac into a frenzied manhunt for Algerians. Sometimes he could neither eat nor sleep, he was so worked up about quelling the rebellion. I watched helplessly as my father slowly changed. In the end I decided not to go and see him anymore and stay in town. In fact every time I went home the screams coming from downstairs kept me awake at night. They were torturing Algerians in the cellar and the disused rooms so as to get information out of them. You can't imagine how horrible it is to

---

[27] During the year 1955 cases of this sort were extremely numerous in Algeria. Unfortunately, not all of them had the good fortune to be admitted to a hospital.

hear screams like that all through the night. Sometimes I wonder how a human being can put up with it, I don't mean torturing but simply hearing someone scream in pain. And it went on and on. Eventually I never went back. The few times my father came to see me in town I couldn't look him in the face I was so horribly frightened and embarrassed. I found it increasingly difficult to kiss him.

"You see I'd lived for a long time in the village. I know almost all the families. I had played with the young Algerians of my age when we were little. Every time I went home my father would tell me a new batch of people had been arrested. In the end I no longer dared go out in the street, I was so sure I'd encounter hatred everywhere I looked. Deep down I knew the Algerians were right. If I were Algerian I'd join the resistance movement."

One day, however, she received a telegram announcing that her father had been seriously injured. She went to the hospital and found her father in a coma. He died shortly afterward. Her father had been wounded during a reconnaissance mission with a military detachment. The patrol had fallen into an ambush laid by the Algerian National Army.

"The funeral sickened me," she said. "All those officials mourning over the death of my father whose 'high moral qualities had won over the native population' made me feel nauseous. Everyone knew it wasn't true. Nobody could remain ignorant of the fact that my father had ruled all the interrogation centers in the area with an iron fist. They knew that ten people were killed every day under torture, and yet they came to recite their lies about his devotion, his self-sacrifice, his love for his country, etc. . . . . I have to confess that words don't mean much to me now, well not very much. I went straight back to town and avoided the authorities. They offered me financial support but I refused. For me it was bought with the blood my father had spilled. I don't want any of it. I intend to work."

Case No. 4—Adjustment disorders with mixed behavioral and emotional features in young Algerians under ten

These cases are refugees, sons of freedom fighters or civilians killed by the French. They have been allocated to centers in Tunisia and Morocco. They are provided with schooling, and games and outings are organized. They are examined regularly by doctors. This is how we came to meet a certain number of them.

a. All the children presented a very marked love for parental images. Anything which resembles a father or a mother is doggedly sought after and jealously guarded.

b. Generally speaking they all show signs of a phobia to noise. They are deeply affected by the slightest reprimand. A great craving for calm and affection.

c. Many of them suffer from insomnia and sleepwalking.

d. Sporadic enuresis.

e. Sadistic tendencies. One of their favorite games is to angrily pierce holes in a stretched sheet of paper. All their pencils are chewed and they bite their nails with distressing regularity. Quarrels often break out despite their deep affection for each other.

Case No. 5—Puerperal psychoses in refugees

Puerperal psychosis refers to those mental disorders which occur in women during maternity. Such disorders can occur immediately before or several weeks after childbirth. Their psychological determinism is highly complex. The two major causes are thought to be a disruption to the endocrine glands and the occurrence of a "psychological shock"—a term that, although vague, corresponds roughly to what is commonly known as a "bad fright."

Ever since the French government's decision to apply their scorched earth policy and establish a buffer zone over hundreds of kilometers there are almost 300,000 refugees along the Tunisian and Moroccan borders. The state of dire poverty they live in is no secret. International Red Cross commissions have paid them a number of visits and on ascertaining their extreme poverty and precarious living conditions, they recommended increased aid by international organizations. Given the malnutrition that is rampant in these camps it is therefore inevitable that the pregnant women are particularly prone to developing puerperal psychoses.

These refugees live in an atmosphere of permanent insecurity, the combined effects of frequent raids by French troops applying the "right to hunt and pursue," aerial bombardments—there is no end to the bombing of Moroccan and Tunisian territories by the French army, and Sakiet-Sidi-Youssef, the martyred village in Tunisia is the bloodiest example—machine gun raids as well as the breakup of the family unit as a result of flight. In truth, there are few Algerian women refugees who do not suffer from mental disorders following childbirth.

There are various symptoms: agitation sometimes accompanied by furor; deep asthenic depression coupled with multiple suicide attempts; symptoms of anxiety accompanied by tears, lamentations, and appeals for mercy, etc. Likewise, the delusional disorders present many different characteristics: a delusion of vague persecution, aimed at anyone; a delirious aggressivity aimed at the French, who want to kill the unborn or newborn child; an impression of imminent death in which the mothers beg the invisible killers to spare their children.

Once again we must point out that the underlying problem is not solved by sedation or a reversal of the symptoms. Even after the patient has been cured, her predicament maintains and nurtures these pathological complications.

SERIES C
AFFECTIVE AND MENTAL CHANGES AND EMOTIONAL DISTURBANCES AFTER TORTURE

This series groups patients in a fairly serious condition whose disorders appeared immediately after or during torture. We have classified them into sub-groups because we realized that their characteristic symptoms of morbidity corresponded to different methods of torture irrespective of the superficial or profound effects on the personality.

Group No. 1—After indiscriminate torture as a so-called precautionary measure

Here we refer to the brutal methods used to get the victim to speak rather than actual torture. The principle according to which above a certain limit the suffering becomes unbearable here takes on a particular significance. The aim therefore is to reach this limit as quickly as possible. There is no meticulous attention to details. It is brute force using a variety of methods: several policemen beat the victim simultaneously; four policemen stand around the prisoner in a circle juggling with him like a punchball while one burns his chest with a cigarette and another hits the soles of his feet with a stick. Some of the methods of torture used in Algeria seemed to us to be particularly horrifying as described to us by the victims:

a. Water is forced through the mouth accompanied by an enema of soapy water injected at high pressure.[28]

b. A bottle is rammed into the anus.

Two types of so-called "forced immobility" torture:

c. The prisoner is forced to his knees, arms parallel to the ground, palms upward, keeping his torso and head straight. He is not allowed to move. A policeman sitting behind the prisoner forces him to remain motionless with blows from a billy club.

d. The prisoner stands facing a wall, arms raised, his hands placed against the wall. Here again at the slightest move or sign of weakening he is dealt a series of blows.

---

[28] This type of torture is the cause of a great many deaths. The high pressure of the enema causes multiple lesions and minute perforations to the mucous membrane of the intestine. Gaseous embolism and peritonitis commonly result.

We must now point out there are two categories of tortured victims:

    a. Those who know something.

    b. Those who know nothing.

    a. Those who know something are seldom seen in the medical centers. We may know for a fact that a particular patriot has been tortured in the French prisons, but we never encounter him as a patient.[29]

    b. Those who know nothing, however, very often come to consult us. We do not mean those Algerians who have been beaten up during a police roundup or spot check. They never come to see us as patients either. We mean those Algerians belonging to no organization who are arrested and taken to police barracks or interrogation centers to be questioned.

Psychiatric Symptoms Encountered

    a. Clinical depression: Four cases

    These are melancholic patients, totally devoid of anxiety, depressed and most of the time bedridden, who avoid contact and then very suddenly become extremely violent for no apparent reason.

    b. Anorexia nervosa: Five cases

    These patients pose serious problems since their anorexia nervosa is accompanied by a phobia of any physical contact. The nurse who approaches the patient and tries to touch him or take his hand, for example, is vigorously pushed away. Impossible to practice intravenous feeding or administer medication.[30]

---

[29] We are speaking of course of those Algerians who know something and have not confessed under torture for it is a fact that an Algerian who confesses is killed immediately afterward.

[30] The medical staff have to take turns attending the patient night and day and explaining things to him. The idea that "the patient needs a little bullying" is understandably of little use here.

c. Restlessness: Eleven cases

These are patients who cannot stay in one place. They insist on being alone and have difficulty accepting confinement with a doctor in his consulting room.

Two feelings frequently emerged in this first batch of tortured victims:

First of all, *that of injustice*. Having been tortured day in and day out for nothing seems to have broken something in these men. One of these martyred victims had a particularly painful experience: After several days of unsuccessful torturing, the policemen came to realize they were dealing with a peace-loving individual who had nothing to do with any of the FLN networks. In spite of this conviction a police inspector reportedly said: "Don't let him go like that. Work him over a bit more so that when he gets out he'll keep quiet."[31]

Secondly, *an indifference to any moral argument*. For these patients there is no just cause. A tortured cause is a weak cause. The first thing to do is to increase one's power and not pose the question of the merits of a cause. Power is the only thing that counts.

Group No. 2—After torture by electricity

In this batch we have grouped the Algerian patriots who have been mainly tortured by electricity. Whereas electricity was once just one method of torture in a series, from September 1956 onward certain interrogations were conducted exclusively with electricity.

---

[31] This precautionary torture in certain regions becomes "precautionary repression." At Rivet, for example, although the place was totally calm, the colonists were determined not to be taken by surprise (the neighboring regions had begun to show signs of unrest) and decided to eliminate purely and simply any member of the FLN. Over forty Algerians were killed in a single day.

Psychiatric Symptoms Encountered
    a. Local or systemic somatic delusions: Three cases
    These patients feel pins and needles throughout the body and get the impression their hands are being torn off, their heads are bursting, and they are swallowing their tongue.
    b. Apathy, lack of will, and loss of interest: Seven cases
    These patients suffer from apathy, a lack of motivation and energy, and live from day to day.
    c. Phobia of electricity
    Fear of touching a light switch, fear of switching on the radio, fear of using the telephone. Absolutely impossible for the doctor to even mention the possibility of electroshock treatment.

Group No. 3 — After administration of the truth serum
    This drug is used in a patient who apparently suffers from an unconscious mental block such that no cross examination can induce him to talk freely. Methods of chemical exploration are used. Intravenous injection of Pentothal is the most common method with the aim of liberating the patient from an inner conflict he is unable to surmount. The doctor intervenes in order to liberate the patient from this "foreign body."[32] Nevertheless there have been difficulties controlling the gradual disintegration of the psychological agencies, and it is not unusual to witness a spectacular deterioration or the emergence of new and quite inexplicable symptoms. Generally speaking this method, therefore, has been more or less abandoned.
    In Algeria the military doctors and psychiatrists have discovered further possibilities for experimenting with this method in the police detention centers. If Pentothal can release repression in the case of neuroses, then, in the case of Algerian patriots, it

---

[32] In fact it is not foreign at all. The conflict is nothing more than the result of the changing dynamics of his personality where there is no question of "foreign body." It would be better defined as being poorly assimilated.

must also be able to break the political barrier and get the prisoner to confess without recourse to electricity—for according to medical tradition any suffering must be avoided. This is the medical equivalent of "psychological warfare."

The scene goes as follows: First of all, the psychiatrist states, "I am a doctor, not a policeman. I'm here to help you." Thus the prisoner's trust is won after a few days.[33] Then: "I'm going to give you a few shots to clear your head." For several days all kinds of vitamins, heart stimulants and other placebos are administered. On the fourth or fifth day the Pentothal is injected intravenously. The interrogation begins.

Psychiatric Symptoms Encountered

a. Verbal stereotypy

The patient continually repeats phrases such as: "I didn't tell them anything. You have to believe me, I didn't talk." This stereotypy is accompanied by a permanent anxiety. Very often in fact the patient is unaware of whether he has given any information away. Guilt toward the cause he stands for and the comrades whose names and addresses he might have given, here takes on dramatic proportions. No reassurance can restore peace of mind to these ruined consciences.

b. Blurred mental and sensory perception

The patient cannot ascertain the existence of an object. Reasoning is assimilated without making any distinctions. There is a basic indistinction between true and false. Everything is both true and false.

c. A phobia of any one-on-one conversation

---

[33] We can also mention the case of psychiatrists running the "Présence française" groups who, appointed to examine the prisoner, started off boasting they were great friends with the defense lawyer and claiming both of them (the lawyer and the psychiatrist) would get the prisoner out. All the prisoners examined by this method were guillotined. These psychiatrists boasted in front of us of this neat method of overcoming "resistance."

This fear stems from the acute impression that he can be interrogated again at any time.

d. Inhibition

The patient is on his guard. He registers a question word by word and elaborates his answer word by word. Hence the impression of virtual inhibition together with psychological slowing down, interrupted sentences, and repetition, etc. . . .

It is obvious these patients stubbornly refuse any type of intravenous injection.

Group No. 4—After brainwashing

There has been much talk recently about "psychological warfare" in Algeria. We have no intention of conducting a critical study of these methods. We shall merely highlight here their psychiatric consequences. There are two categories of brainwashing centers in Algeria.

I. For Intellectuals

The principle here is to induce the intellectual into role-playing. It is clear to which psychotherapy school this refers.[34]

a. Play the game of collaborator.

The intellectual is induced to collaborate by establishing a justification for his collaboration. He is therefore obliged to live a dual personality and play the part of a well-known patriot who has been taken out of circulation as a precautionary measure. The aim of the operation is to attack from the inside those

---

[34] In the U.S. there is a trend toward social therapy. Supporters of this school believe that the plight of contemporary man lies in the fact that he no longer has a role to play and that he is nothing but a cog in the social mechanism. Social therapy, therefore, allows man to play several roles as part of a genuine recreational activity. Anyone can play any role and even change roles during the course of the day, symbolically substituting for anybody. Occupational therapists in the U.S. apparently achieve miracles in group social therapy among factory workers. The workers are allowed to identify with role models and employer-employee relations are considerably less strained.

elements that constitute the national consciousness. Not only must he collaborate, but he is given orders to discuss "freely" with opponents and holdouts in order to win them over. This is an efficient way of getting him to give leads on patriots and using him, therefore, as an informer. If by chance he claims he didn't find any opponents, they are designated for him or else he is asked to behave as if they were.

b. Give talks on the value of French accomplishments and the merits of colonization.

In order to achieve his job effectively, the intellectual is counseled by a broad spectrum of "political advisors" such as officers for Native Affairs or better still psychologists, therapists and sociologists, etc.

c. Take the arguments for the Algerian Revolution and eliminate them one by one.

Algeria is not a nation, has never been a nation, and never will be.

There is no such thing as the "Algerian people."

Algerian patriotism is devoid of meaning.

The *fellagas* are schemers, criminals, and have had the wool pulled over their eyes.

The intellectuals have to take turns giving a presentation on these topics and each has to be convincing. Grades (the infamous "awards") are allocated and totalled at the end of the month. They are used to evaluate whether the intellectual will be released.

d. Lead an absolutely pathological communal life.

To remain alone is an act of rebellion. The individual must always be in the presence of somebody. Silence is also prohibited. The individual must think out loud.

Testimony

This is the case of an academic who was interned and subjected to months of brainwashing. One day the camp officials congratulated him on his progress and announced he would soon be set free.

Familiar with the enemy's tactics, he was wary of taking the news too seriously. The stratagem, in fact, was to announce to the prisoners they were going to be freed and a few days before the set date organize a group session of self-criticism. At the end of the session it was often decided to postpone release since the prisoner showed no signs of being definitely cured. The session, according to the psychologists present, highlighted a single-minded nationalist virus.

This time, however, there was no subterfuge. The prisoner was well and truly freed. Once outside, in town and with his family, the former prisoner congratulated himself on having played his role so well. He was overjoyed at the idea of taking part again in the national struggle and endeavored to get back in touch with the leaders. It was then that a terrible, nagging idea crossed his mind. Perhaps nobody had been duped—neither his captors, nor his co-inmates, nor even himself.

Where was the game supposed to end?

Once again we had to reassure the patient and free him from the burden of guilt.

Psychiatric Symptoms Encountered

a. Phobia of any collective discussion. As soon as three or four people got together, the inhibition reappeared, and mistrust and reticence reasserted themselves.

b. The subject finds it impossible to explain and defend a given viewpoint. An antithetical thought process. Anything which is affirmed can be simultaneously denied with the same force. This is certainly the most painful legacy we have encountered in this war. The obsessive personality is the fruit of the "psychological warfare" used in the service of colonialism in Algeria.

II.—For Nonintellectuals

In centers like Berrouaghia, subjectivity is no longer taken as the starting point for modifying the individual's attitude. On the contrary, emphasis is on the body, which is broken in the hope that the national consciousness will disintegrate. The individual is "knocked" into shape. The individual's reward is being spared torture or being allowed to eat.

a. You must confess you are not a member of the FLN. It has to be shouted collectively and repeated for hours.

b. Then you have to confess to being in the FLN and now admit it was wrong. Down with the FLN.

Then comes the next stage: the future of Algeria is French, it can only be French. Without France, Algeria would return to the Dark Ages.

Finally, you are French. Long live France.

The disorders encountered here are not serious. It is the bruised, suffering body which cries out for peace and calm.

SERIES D
PSYCHOSOMATIC DISORDERS

The increasing occurrence of mental illness and the rampant development of specific pathological conditions are not the only legacy of the colonial war in Algeria. Apart from the pathology of torture, the pathology of the tortured and that of the perpetrator, there is a pathology of the entire atmosphere in Algeria, a condition which leads the attending physician to say when confronted with a case they cannot understand: "This will all be cleared up once the damned war is over."

We propose grouping in this fourth series the illnesses encountered in Algerians some of whom were sent to internment camps. They can all be characterized as being psychosomatic.

The name psychosomatic pathology is given to the general body of organic disorders developed in response to a situation of conflict.[35] Psychosomatic, because its determinism is psychic in

---

[35] This term which expresses an idealist notion is being used less and less. The cortico-visceral terminology, in fact a legacy of Soviet research—especially Pavlov—has at least the advantage of putting the brain back in its place, i.e., of considering it the matrix where precisely the psyche is elaborated.

origin. This pathology is considered a way the organism can respond, in other words how it adapts to the conflict, the disorder being both a symptom and a cure. More exactly it is generally agreed that the organism (here again it is the former psychosomatic, cortico-visceral body) outwits the conflict using the wrong, but nevertheless economic, channels. The organism chooses the lesser evil in order to avoid a complete breakdown.

On the whole this pathology is widely accepted today, although the various therapeutic methods such as relaxation and suggestion are highly uncertain. During the Second World War air raids on England and the siege of Stalingrad, for example, in the Soviet Union, the number of disorders reported increased dramatically. We now know perfectly well that there is no need to be wounded by a bullet to suffer from the effects of war in body and soul. Like any war, the war in Algeria has created its contingent of cortico-visceral illnesses. Except for group g below all the disorders encountered in Algeria have been reported during "conventional" wars. We found group g specific to the colonial war in Algeria. This particular form of pathology (systemic muscular contraction) already caught our attention before the revolution began. But the doctors who described it turned it into a congenital stigma of the "native," an original feature of his nervous system, manifest proof of a predominant extrapyramidal system in the colonized.[36] This contraction, in fact, is quite simply a postural concurrence and evidence in the colonized's muscles of their rigidity, their reticence and refusal in the face of the colonial authorities.

Psychosomatic Symptoms Encountered
  a. Stomach ulcers
  Very numerous. The pain is mainly felt at night accompanied by severe vomiting, loss of weight, melancholia and depression;

---

[36] The higher one is on the neurological scale, the less one is extrapyramidal. Manifestly everything seems to tally.

irritability is rare. Most of the patients are very young, between eighteen and twenty-five years old. As a rule we never advise surgery. A gastrectomy was conducted twice and each time we had to reoperate within the year.

b. Renal colic

Here again the pain reaches its height during the night. Obviously there are never any kidney stones. These colics can occur in fourteen- to sixteen-year-olds, but this is rare.

c. Disturbed menstrual cycles

These symptoms are very common and we will be brief. Either the women go three to four months without their periods, or menstruation is so painful it affects the women's character and behavior.

d. Hypersomnia due to idiopathic tremors

These are cases of young adults who are denied any rest owing to tiny systemic tremors resembling Parkinson's disease. Here again, some "great scientific minds" might be tempted to suggest an extrapyramidal determinism.

e. Premature whitening of hair

The hair of survivors of the interrogation centers suddenly turns white in patches, in specific areas or all over. Very often this disorder is accompanied by deep asthenia plus loss of interest and impotence.

f. Paroxysmal tachycardia

The heart rate suddenly accelerates to 120, 130, and 140 beats per minute. This tachycardia is accompanied by panic attacks, an impression of imminent death, and the end of the attack is marked by heavy sweating.

g. Systemic contraction, muscular stiffness

These are male patients who slowly have difficulty making certain movements such as climbing stairs, walking quickly, or running (in two cases it was very sudden). The cause of this difficulty lies in a characteristic rigidity which inevitably suggests an attack on certain areas of the brain (central gray matter). Walking becomes contracted and turns into a shuffle. Passive bending of the lower limbs is practically impossible. No relaxation can be achieved. Immediately rigid and incapable of relaxing of his own free will, the patient seems to be made in one piece. The face is set, but expresses a marked degree of bewilderment.

The patient does not seem to be able to "demobilize his nerves." He is constantly tense, on hold, between life and death. As one of them told us: "You see, I'm as stiff as a corpse."[37]

FROM THE NORTH AFRICAN'S CRIMINAL IMPULSIVENESS TO THE WAR OF NATIONAL LIBERATION

Fighting for the freedom of one's people is not the only necessity. As long as the fight goes on you must reenlighten not only the people but also, and above all, yourself on the full measure of man. You must retrace the paths of history, the history of man damned by other men, and initiate, bring about, the encounter between your own people and others.

In fact the aim of the militant engaged in armed combat, in a national struggle, is to assess the daily humiliations inflicted on man by colonial oppression. The militant sometimes has the grueling impression he has to drag his people back, up from the pit and out of the cave. The militant very often realizes that not only must he hunt down the enemy forces but also the core of despair crystallized in the body of the colonized. The period of oppression is harrowing, but the liberation struggle's rehabilitation of man fosters a process of reintegration that is extremely productive and decisive. The victorious combat of a people is not just the crowning triumph of their rights. It procures them substance, coherence, and homogeneity. For colonialism has not simply depersonalized the colonized. The very structure of society has been depersonalized on a collective level. A colonized

---

[37] It is irrelevant to add this is not a case of hysterical contraction.

people is thus reduced to a collection of individuals who owe their very existence to the presence of the colonizer.

The combat waged by a people for their liberation leads them, depending on the circumstances, either to reject or to explode the so-called truths sown in their consciousness by the colonial regime, military occupation, and economic exploitation. And only the armed struggle can effectively exorcize these lies about man that subordinate and literally mutilate the more conscious-minded among us.

How many times in Paris or Aix, in Algiers or Basse-Terre have we seen the colonized vehemently protest the so-called indolence of the black, the Algerian, and the Vietnamese. And yet in a colonial regime if a fellah were a zealous worker or a black were to refuse a break from work, they would be quite simply considered pathological cases. The colonized's indolence is a conscious way of sabotaging the colonial machine; on the biological level it is a remarkable system of self-preservation and, if nothing else, a positive curb on the occupier's stranglehold over the entire country.

The resistance of the forests and swamps to foreign penetration is the natural ally of the colonized. Put yourself in his shoes and stop reasoning and claiming that the "nigger" is a hard worker and the "towelhead" great at clearing land. In a colonial regime the reality of the "towelhead," the reality of the "nigger," is not to lift a finger, not to help the oppressor sink his claws into his prey. The duty of the colonized subject, who has not yet arrived at a political consciousness or a decision to reject the oppressor, is to have the slightest effort literally dragged out of him. This is where non-cooperation or at least minimal cooperation clearly materializes.

These observations regarding the colonized's disposition to work could also be applied to the colonized's attitude toward the colonizer's laws, his taxes, and the colonial system. Under a colonial regime, gratitude, sincerity, and honor are hollow words.

Over recent years I have had the opportunity to verify the fundamental fact that honor, dignity and integrity are only truly evident in the context of national and international unity. As soon as you and your fellow men are cut down like dogs there is no other solution but to use every means available to reestablish your weight as a human being. You must therefore weigh as heavily as possible on your torturer's body so that his wits, which have wandered off somewhere, can at last be restored to their human dimension. During the course of recent years I have had the opportunity to witness the extraordinary examples of honor, self-sacrifice, love of life, and disregard for death in an Algeria at war. No, I am not going to sing the praises of the freedom fighters. A common observation the most hard-lined colonialists have not failed to note is that the Algerian fighter has an unusual way of fighting and dying, and no reference to Islam or Paradise can explain this spirit of self-sacrifice when it comes to protecting his people or shielding his comrades. Then there is this deathly silence — the body of course cries out — the silence that suffocates the torturer. Here we find the old law stating that anything alive cannot afford to remain still while the nation is set in motion, while man both demands and claims his infinite humanity.

One of the characteristics of the Algerian people established by colonialism is their appalling criminality. Prior to 1954 magistrates, police, lawyers, journalists, and medical examiners were unanimous that the Algerian's criminality posed a problem. The Algerian, it was claimed, was a born criminal. A theory was elaborated and scientific proof was furnished. This theory was taught at universities for more than twenty years. Algerian medical students received this education, and slowly and imperceptibly the elite, after having consented to colonialism, consented to the natural defects of the Algerian people: born idlers, born liars, born thieves, and born criminals.

We propose here to expound this official theory, to recall its basis and scientific reasoning. In a second stage we shall review the facts and endeavor to reinterpret them.

The Algerian is an habitual killer: It's a fact, the magistrates will tell you, that four fifths of the cases heard involve assault and battery. The crime rate in Algeria is one of the highest in the world, they claim. There are no petty delinquents. When the Algerian, and this applies to all North Africans, puts himself on the wrong side of the law, he always goes to extremes.

The Algerian is a savage killer: And his weapon of choice is the knife. The magistrates "who know the country" have elaborated their own theory on the subject. The Kabyles, for example, prefer a revolver or shotgun. The Arabs from the plains have a preference for the knife. Some magistrates wonder whether the Algerian does not have a need to see blood. The Algerian, they will tell you, needs to feel the heat of blood and steep himself in his victim's blood. These magistrates and police officers very seriously hold forth on the connections between the Muslim psyche and blood.[38] A number of magistrates even go so far as to say that killing a man for an Algerian means first and foremost slitting his throat. The savagery of the Algerian manifests itself in particular by the number of wounds, many of them inflicted unnecessarily after the victim's death. Autopsies undeniably establish this fact: the killer gives the impression he wanted to kill an incalculable number of times given the equal deadliness of the wounds inflicted.

The Algerian is a senseless killer: Very often the magistrates and police officers are stunned by the motives for the murder: a gesture, an allusion, an ambiguous remark, a quarrel over the ownership of an olive tree or an animal that has strayed a few feet. The search for the cause, which is expected to justify and pin down the murder, in some cases a double or triple murder, turns up a hopelessly trivial motive. Hence the frequent impression that the community is hiding the real motives.

---

[38] We know for a fact that Islam forbids eating meat from an animal that has not been drained of its blood. This is why the animals have their throats cut.

Finally, *robbery by an Algerian is always breaking and entering*, in some cases involving murder, in every case involving assault of the owner.

All these elements focalizing on Algerian criminality appeared sufficiently evident to support an attempt at systematization.

Since similar, though less implicit, observations had been conducted in Tunisia and Morocco, reference was increasingly made to a North African criminality. For more than thirty years, under the constant direction of Professor Porot, professor of psychiatry at the Faculty of Algiers, several teams worked on defining this criminality's modes of expression and offering a sociological, functional, and anatomical interpretation.

The main research work on the question conducted by the psychiatric school of the Faculty of Algiers will be the basis for our conclusions. Research findings conducted over more than a twenty year period were the subject, we recall, of lectures given by the chair of psychiatry.

Consequently the Algerian doctors who graduated from the Faculty of Algiers were forced to hear and learn that the Algerian is a born criminal. Moreover I remember one of us in all seriousness expounding these theories he had learned and adding: "It's hard to swallow, but it's been scientifically proved."

The North African is a criminal, his predatory instinct a known fact and his unwieldy aggressiveness visible to the naked eye. The North African loves extremes so you can never entirely trust him. Today, your best friend, tomorrow your worst enemy. He is immune to nuances, Cartesianism is fundamentally foreign to him and moderation, a sense of proportion and level-headedness, are contrary to his inner nature. The North African is violent, hereditarily violent. He finds it impossible to discipline himself and channel his instincts. Yes, the Algerian is congenitally impulsive.

But, they tell us, this impulsiveness is highly aggressive and generally homicidal. This explains, they say, the unorthodox behavior of the melancholic Algerian. French psychiatrists in Algeria were faced with a difficult problem. They had been trained to fear suicidal tendencies in a patient suffering from melancholia. The melancholic Algerian, however, kills. This disorder of the moral conscience, which is always accompanied by self-accusation and suicidal tendencies, in the Algerian takes the shape of homicidal instincts. The Algerian suffering from melancholia does not commit suicide. He kills. This is the homicidal melancholia elaborated by Professor Porot in the thesis of his pupil Monserrat.

How does the Algerian school account for this anomaly? Firstly, according to the school of Algiers, killing oneself is tantamount to examining one's own feelings, looking at oneself and practicing introspection. The Algerian, however, rebels against his inner feelings. There is no inner life in the North African. On the contrary, the North African rids himself of his troubles by attacking the people around him. He has no sense of analysis. Since by definition melancholia is a disorder of the moral conscience it is obvious the Algerian can only develop pseudo-melancholias given the unreliability of his conscience and the fickleness of his moral sense. This incapacity of the Algerian to analyze a situation, to organize a mental panorama, makes perfect sense if we refer to the two types of causality proposed by the French psychiatrists.

First of all, his mental capacity. The Algerian is mentally retarded. If we want to fully understand this basic point of departure, we must recall the semiology elaborated by the school of Algiers. The "native," it says, presents the following characteristics:

- complete or almost complete lack of emotivity
- highly credulous and suggestible
- doggedly stubborn
- childlike mentality minus the curiosity of the European child
- prone to accidents and pithiatic reactions[39]

---

[39] Professor A. Porot, *Annales Médico-Psychologiques*, 1918.

The Algerian is unable to grasp an overall picture. The questions he asks himself are always concerned with details and rule out any synthesis. Pointillistic, attracted to objects, lost in details, insensitive to ideas, and closed to concepts. Verbal expression is reduced to a minimum. His movements are always impulsive and aggressive. Incapable of interpreting details on the basis of the overall picture, the Algerian absolutizes the component and takes one part for the whole. As a consequence his reactions are generalizing when confronted with minor provocations or trivialities such as a fig tree, a gesture, or a sheep on his land. The congenital aggressiveness looks for outlets and is content with the slightest pretext. It is aggressiveness in a pure state.[40]

The school of Algiers abandoned the phase of description for the next stage of clarification. It was in 1935 at the Congress of French-Speaking Psychiatrists and Neurologists in Brussels that Professor Porot was to define the scientific bases for his theory. Discussing Baruk's report on hysteria he indicated that "the North African native whose cortex and reflexes are poorly developed, is a primitive being whose essentially vegetative and instinctive life is primarily governed by his diencephalon."

In order to gauge the importance of this discovery by Professor Porot we should recall that the characteristic which differentiates the human species from other vertebrates is the cortex. The diencephalon is one of the most primitive parts of the brain and man is above all the vertebrate governed by the cortex.

For Professor Porot the life of the North African is governed by the diencephalic agents. This is tantamount to saying that the North African in a certain way is deprived of a cortex. Professor

---

[40] In the words of a senior magistrate at a court in Algiers this aggressiveness of the Algerian is expressed in his love for "fantasia." "All this unrest," he said in 1955, "we'd be wrong to think it was political. From time to time this love they have for knocking themselves about has to come out!" For the anthropologist the elaboration of a series of projective tests and games capable of channeling the overall aggressive instincts of the colonized would have stopped the revolution in the Aurès in 1955–56.

Porot does not evade this contradiction and in the April 1939 issue of *Sud Médical et Chirurgical* he states, in collaboration with his pupil Sutter, currently professor of psychiatry in Algiers: "Primitivism is not a lack of maturity, an interrupted development of the mental psyche. It is a social condition which has reached the end of its evolution and is a logical adaptation to a life different from ours." Lastly, the professors address the very basis of the doctrine: "This primitivism is not only a condition resulting from a specific upbringing, its foundations go far deeper, and we believe its substratum must lie in a specific configuration of the architectonics, or at least of the dynamic hierarchical organization of the nervous system. We have observed that the impulsiveness of the Algerian, the frequency and nature of his murders, his permanent criminal tendencies and his primitivism are no coincidences. We are in the presence of a coherent pattern of behavior and a coherent lifestyle which can be explained scientifically. The Algerian has no cortex, or to be more exact, like the inferior vertebrates he is governed by his diencephalon. The cortical functions, if they exist, are extremely weak, virtually excluded from the brain's dynamics. There is therefore neither mystery nor paradox. The colonizer's reluctance to entrust the native with any kind of responsibility does not stem from racism or paternalism but quite simply from a scientific assessment of the colonized's limited biological possibilities."

Let us end this overview by requesting Dr. Carothers, an expert from the World Health Organization, to conclude with his findings throughout Africa. This international expert collected his primary observations in a book published in 1954.[41]

Dr. Carothers practiced in Central and East Africa but his findings match those of the North African school. For the international expert, "The African uses his frontal lobes very little. All

---

[41] J. C. Carothers, *The African Mind in Health and Disease: A Study in Ethnopsychiatry* (World Health Organization).

the peculiarities of African psychiatry can be envisaged in terms of frontal idleness."[42]

In order to make his point clear Dr. Carothers establishes a very vivid comparison. He puts forward the idea that the normal African is a *lobotomized European*. We know that the English-speaking school believed they had found a radical therapy for treating certain serious mental illnesses by practicing surgical incision in the front of the brain. This method has been abandoned since discovering the major damage it caused to the personality. According to Dr. Carothers the similarity between the normal African and the lobotomized European is striking.

After having studied the work of various researchers practicing throughout Africa, Dr. Carothers gives us a conclusion that establishes a uniform concept of the African. "These are," he writes, "the data of the cases that do not fit the European categories. They are culled from several parts of Africa—east, west, and south—and, on the whole, the writers had little or no knowledge of each other's work. Their essential similarity is therefore quite remarkable."[43]

Before concluding it is worth pointing out that Dr. Carothers defined the Mau-Mau revolt as the expression of an unconscious frustration complex whose recurrence could be scientifically treated by radical psychologically appropriate methods.

So it was the unusual behavior such as the Algerian's recurring criminality, the triviality of the motives and the murderous and always highly bloody nature of the quarrels that posed a problem for observers. The proposed explanation, which is now taught as part of the curriculum, seems in the last analysis to be as follows: The configuration of the North African's brain structure accounts for the indolence of "the native," his mental and social inaptitude as well as his virtual animal impulsiveness. The criminal impulsiveness of the North African is the transcription

---

[42] *Ibid.*, p. 157.
[43] *Ibid.*, p. 158.

of a certain configuration of the nervous system into his pattern of behavior. It is a neurologically comprehensible reaction, written into the nature of things, of *the thing* which is biologically organized. The idleness of the frontal lobes explains his indolence, his crimes, his thefts, his rapes, and his lies. And the conclusion was given to me by a *sous-préfet* now *préfet*: "These instinctive beings," he told me, "who blindly obey the laws of their nature must be strictly and pitilessly regimented. Nature must be tamed, not talked into reason." Discipline, tame, subdue, and now pacify are the common terms used by the colonialists in the territories occupied.

The reason why we have dealt at length with the theories by the colonialist scholars is not so much to demonstrate their paucity and absurdity as to address an extremely important theoretical and practical question. Algerian criminality, in fact, was given relatively little attention among the questions which the revolution was confronted with and the issues which were raised during discussions on political enlightenment and demystification. But the few debates on the subject were so constructive that they enabled us to examine further and better identify the notion of individual and social freedom. When the question of Algerian criminality is broached with leaders and militants in the heat of revolution, when the average number of crimes, misdemeanors and thefts in the period prior to the revolution are brought to light, when it is explained that the physiognomy of a crime and the occurrence of misdemeanors are based on the relationships between men and women, between man and the State, and everyone gets the message; when we see the notion of the Algerian or North African as born criminal dislodged before our very eyes, a notion which was also planted in the Algerian's consciousness because after all "we are a bad, quick-tempered, aggressive people . . . and that's the way we are . . . " then yes, we can say the revolution is making progress.

The major theoretical problem is that the insult to man which is in ourselves must be identified, demystified and hunted down at all times and in all places. We must not expect the nation to produce new men. We must not expect men to change imperceptibly as the revolution constantly innovates. It is true both processes are important, but it is the consciousness that needs help. If the revolution in practice is meant to be totally liberating and exceptionally productive, everything must be accounted for. The revolutionary feels a particularly strong need to totalize events, to handle everything, to settle everything, to assume responsibility for everything. The consciousness then does not balk at thinking back or marking time, if need be. This is the reason why as a combat unit progresses in the field the end of an ambush does not mean cause for respite but the very moment for the consciousness to go one step further since everything must work in unison.

Yes, the Algerian spontaneously acknowledged the magistrates and police officers were right.[44] This narcissistic aspect of Algerian criminality as a manifestation of genuine virility had to be tackled again and reconsidered in the light of colonial history. By showing, for example, how the criminality of the Algerians in France fundamentally differed from the criminality of the Algerians directly subjected to colonial exploitation.

A second aspect caught our attention: in Algeria, criminality among Algerians occurred practically in a closed circle. The Algerians robbed each other, tore each other to pieces, and killed each other. In Algeria, the Algerian seldom attacked the

---

[44] It is evident, moreover, that this identification with the image invented by the European was highly ambivalent. The European in fact seemed to be paying an equally ambivalent tribute to the violent, excitable, brutal, jealous, proud, and arrogant Algerian who stakes his life on a detail or a word, etc. Let us mention in passing that in their confrontations with the French from metropolitan France, the Europeans in Algeria increasingly tend to identify with this image of the Algerian in their opposition to the French.

French and avoided quarreling with them. In France, however, the immigrant's criminality crossed boundaries between communities and social categories.

In France Algerian criminality is diminishing. It is mainly directed at the French and the motives are entirely new. One paradox, however, helped us considerably to get the militants to understand that since 1954 common law crimes have virtually disappeared. Gone are the quarrels, the disputes over minor details ending in homicide. Gone the explosive fits of rage because the neighbor caught sight of my wife's forehead or left shoulder. The national struggle appears to have channeled all this anger and nationalized every affective and emotional reaction. The French magistrates and lawyers had already noted this, but the militant had to be made aware of it and understand the reasons.

We now had to find an explanation.

Could it be said that the war, the privileged terrain for expressing finally a collective aggressiveness, directs congenitally murderous acts at the occupier? It is common knowledge that significant social upheavals lessen the occurrence of misdemeanors and mental disorders. The existence of a war which was breaking Algeria in two and rejecting the judicial and administrative machine onto the side of the enemy was therefore a perfectly good explanation for this decline in Algerian criminality.

In the countries of the Maghreb already liberated, however, this was true during the liberation struggles and remains so to an even greater degree during independence. It is therefore apparent that the colonial context is sufficiently original to afford a reinterpretation of criminality. This is what we have done for the militants. Today everyone on our side knows that criminality is not the result of the Algerian's congenital nature nor the configuration of his nervous system. The war in Algeria and wars of national liberation bring out the true protagonists. We have demonstrated that in the colonial situation the colonized are confronted with themselves. They tend to use each other as a screen. Each prevents his neighbor from seeing the national enemy. And when exhausted after a sixteen-hour day of hard work the colonized subject collapses on his mat and a child on the other side of the canvas partition cries and prevents him from sleeping, it just so happens it's a little Algerian. When he goes to beg for a little semolina or a little oil from the shopkeeper to whom he already owes several hundred francs and his request is turned down, he is overwhelmed by an immense hatred and desire to kill—and the shopkeeper happens to be an Algerian. When, after weeks of keeping a low profile, he finds himself cornered one day by the *kaid* demanding "his taxes," he is not even allowed the opportunity to direct his hatred against the European administrator; before him stands the *kaid* who excites his hatred—and he happens to be an Algerian.

Exposed to daily incitement to murder resulting from famine, eviction from his room for unpaid rent, a mother's withered breast, children who are nothing but skin and bone, the closure of a worksite and the jobless who hang around the foreman like crows, the colonized subject comes to see his fellow man as a relentless enemy. If he stubs his bare feet on a large stone in his path it is a fellow countryman who has put it there, and the meager olives he was about to pick, here are X's children who have eaten them during the night. Yes, during the colonial period in Algeria and elsewhere a lot of things can be committed for a few pounds of semolina. One can kill. You need to use your imagination to understand these things. Or your memory. In the concentration camps men killed each other for a morsel of bread. I can recall one horrible scene. It was in Oran in 1944. From the military camp where we were waiting to embark, the soldiers threw bits of bread to some Algerian children who fought for them in a frenzy of rage and hatred. A veterinarian could no doubt explain these events in terms of the famous "pecking order"* noted in farmyards where the corn

---

*Translator's Note: Fanon uses the phrase "peck order" in English in the original text.

is bitterly fought over. The strongest birds gobble up all the grain while the less aggressive grow visibly thinner. Any colony tends to become one vast farmyard, one vast concentration camp where the only law is that of the knife.

In Algeria, everything has changed since the war of national liberation. The entire reserves of a family or *metcha* can be offered to a passing company of soldiers in a single evening. A family can lend its only donkey to carry a wounded fighter. And when several days later the owner learns the animal was gunned down by a plane he will not sling curses or threats. Instead of questioning the death of his donkey he will anxiously ask whether the wounded man is safe and sound.

Under a colonial regime, no crime is too petty for a loaf of bread or a wretched sheep. Under a colonial regime, man's relationship with the physical world and history is connected to food. In a context of oppression like that of Algeria, for the colonized, living does not mean embodying a set of values, does not mean integrating oneself into the coherent, constructive development of a world. To live simply means not to die. To exist means staying alive. Every date grown is a victory. Not the result of hard work, but a victory celebrating a triumph over life. Stealing dates, therefore, or allowing one's sheep to eat the neighbor's grass is not a disregard for property rights or breaking the law or disrespect. They are attempts at murder. Once you have seen men and women in Kabylia struggling down into the valley for weeks on end to bring up soil in little baskets you can understand that theft is attempted murder and not a peccadillo. The sole obsession is the need to fill that ever shrinking stomach, however little it demands. Who do you take it out on? The French are down on the plain with the police, the army and their tanks. In the mountains there are only Algerians. Up above, Heaven with its promises of an afterlife, down below the French with their firm promises of jail, beatings and executions. Inevitably, you stumble up against yourself. Here lies this core of self-hatred that characterizes racial conflict in segregated societies.

The criminality of the Algerian, his impulsiveness, the savagery of his murders are not, therefore, the consequence of how his nervous system is organized or specific character traits, but the direct result of the colonial situation. The fact that the Algerian patriots discussed this issue, that they were not afraid to challenge the beliefs inculcated in them by colonialism, that they understood each was a screen for the other and in reality they were committing suicide by pitting themselves against their neighbor, was to have an immense impact on the revolutionary consciousness. Once again, the colonized subject fights in order to put an end to domination. But he must also ensure that all the untruths planted within him by the oppressor are eliminated. In a colonial regime such as the one in Algeria the ideas taught by colonialism impacted not only the European minority but also the Algerian. Total liberation involves every facet of the personality. The ambush or the skirmish, the torture or the massacre of one's comrades entrenches the determination to win, revives the unconscious and nurtures the imagination. When the nation in its totality is set in motion, the new man is not an a posteriori creation of this nation, but coexists with it, matures with it, and triumphs with it. This dialectical prerequisite explains the resistance to accommodating forms of colonization or window dressing. Independence is not a magic ritual but an indispensable condition for men and women to exist in true liberation, in other words to master all the material resources necessary for a radical transformation of society.

Conclusion

Now, comrades, now is the time to decide to change sides. We must shake off the great mantle of night which has enveloped us, and reach for the light. The new day which is dawning must find us determined, enlightened and resolute.

We must abandon our dreams and say farewell to our old beliefs and former friendships. Let us not lose time in useless laments or sickening mimicry. Let us leave this Europe which never stops talking of man yet massacres him at every one of its street corners, at every corner of the world.

For centuries Europe has brought the progress of other men to a halt and enslaved them for its own purposes and glory; for centuries it has stifled virtually the whole of humanity in the name of a so-called "spiritual adventure." Look at it now teetering between atomic destruction and spiritual disintegration.

And yet nobody can deny its achievements at home have not been crowned with success.

Europe has taken over leadership of the world with fervor, cynicism, and violence. And look how the shadow of its monuments spreads and multiplies. Every movement Europe makes bursts the boundaries of space and thought. Europe has denied itself not only humility and modesty but also solicitude and tenderness.

Its only show of miserliness has been toward man, only toward man has it shown itself to be niggardly and murderously carnivorous.

So, my brothers, how could we fail to understand that we have better things to do than follow in that Europe's footsteps?

This Europe, which never stopped talking of man, which never stopped proclaiming its sole concern was man, we now know the price of suffering humanity has paid for every one of its spiritual victories.

Come, comrades, the European game is finally over, we must look for something else. We can do anything today provided we do not ape Europe, provided we are not obsessed with catching up with Europe.

Europe has gained such a mad and reckless momentum that it has lost control and reason and is heading at dizzying speed towards the brink from which we would be advised to remove ourselves as quickly as possible.

It is all too true, however, that we need a model, schemas and examples. For many of us the European model is the most elating. But we have seen in the preceding pages how misleading such an imitation can be. European achievements, European technology and European lifestyles must stop tempting us and leading us astray.

When I look for man in European lifestyles and technology I see a constant denial of man, an avalanche of murders.

Man's condition, his projects and collaboration with others on tasks that strengthen man's totality, are new issues which require genuine inspiration.

Let us decide not to imitate Europe and let us tense our muscles and our brains in a new direction. Let us endeavor to invent a man in full, something which Europe has been incapable of achieving.

Two centuries ago, a former European colony took it into its head to catch up with Europe. It has been so successful that the United States of America has become a monster where the flaws, sickness, and inhumanity of Europe have reached frightening proportions.

Comrades, have we nothing else to do but create a third Europe? The West saw itself on a spiritual adventure. It is in the name of the Spirit, meaning the spirit of Europe, that Europe justified its crimes and legitimized the slavery in which it held four fifths of humanity.

Yes, the European spirit is built on strange foundations. The whole of European thought developed in places that were increasingly arid and increasingly inaccessible. Consequently, it was natural that the chances of encountering man became less and less frequent.

A permanent dialogue with itself, an increasingly obnoxious narcissism inevitably paved the way for a virtual delirium where intellectual thought turns into agony since the reality of man as a living, working, self-made being is replaced by words, an assemblage of words and the tensions generated by their meanings. There were Europeans, however, who urged the European workers to smash this narcissism and break with this denial of reality.

Generally speaking, the European workers did not respond to the call. The fact was that the workers believed they too were part of the prodigious adventure of the European Spirit.

All the elements for a solution to the major problems of humanity existed at one time or another in European thought. But the Europeans did not act on the mission that was designated them and which consisted of virulently pondering these elements, modifying their configuration, their being, of changing them and finally taking the problem of man to an infinitely higher plane.

Today we are witnessing a stasis of Europe. Comrades, let us flee this stagnation where dialectics has gradually turned into a logic of the status quo. Let us reexamine the question of man. Let us reexamine the question of cerebral reality, the brain mass of humanity in its entirety whose affinities must be increased, whose connections must be diversified and whose communications must be humanized again.

Come brothers, we have far too much work on our hands to revel in outmoded games. Europe has done what it had to do and all things considered, it has done a good job; let us stop accusing it, but let us say to it firmly it must stop putting on such a show. We no longer have reason to fear it, let us stop then envying it.

The Third World is today facing Europe as one colossal mass whose project must be to try and solve the problems this Europe was incapable of finding the answers to.

But what matters now is not a question of profitability, not a question of increased productivity, not a question of production rates. No, it is not a question of back to nature. It is the very basic question of not dragging man in directions which mutilate him, of not imposing on his brain tempos that rapidly obliterate and unhinge it. The notion of catching up must not be used as a pretext to brutalize man, to tear him from himself and his inner consciousness, to break him, to kill him.

No, we do not want to catch up with anyone. But what we want is to walk in the company of man, every man, night and day, for all times. It is not a question of stringing the caravan out where groups are spaced so far apart they cannot see the one in front, and men who no longer recognize each other, meet less and less and talk to each other less and less.

The Third World must start over a new history of man which takes account of not only the occasional prodigious theses maintained by Europe but also its crimes, the most heinous of which have been committed at the very heart of man, the pathological dismembering of his functions and the erosion of his unity, and in the context of the community, the fracture, the stratification and the bloody tensions fed by class, and finally, on the immense scale of humanity, the racial hatred, slavery, exploitation and, above all, the bloodless genocide whereby one and a half billion men have been written off.

So comrades, let us not pay tribute to Europe by creating states, institutions, and societies that draw their inspiration from it.

Humanity expects other things from us than this grotesque and generally obscene emulation.

If we want to transform Africa into a new Europe, America into a new Europe, then let us entrust the destinies of our countries to the Europeans. They will do a better job than the best of us.

But if we want humanity to take one step forward, if we want to take it to another level than the one where Europe has placed it, then we must innovate, we must be pioneers.

If we want to respond to the expectations of our peoples, we must look elsewhere besides Europe.

Moreover, if we want to respond to the expectations of the Europeans we must not send them back a reflection, however ideal, of their society and their thought that periodically sickens even them.

For Europe, for ourselves and for humanity, comrades, we must make a new start, develop a new way of thinking, and endeavor to create a new man.

On Retranslating Fanon, Retrieving a Lost Voice
by Richard Philcox

I suppose I first met Frantz Fanon when I went to Africa, to Senegal in 1968 as an English teacher. At the age of twenty-three I was a naive young Englishman leading a sheltered life who was about to discover the meaning of underdevelopment and colonization. My vision of Africa was nil and I had as much insight into Senegalese society as a brochure at a travel agent. Rereading some of the notes I made at the time I appeared to be more interested in finding a fan, buying a moped and renting an apartment than what was going on around me. The fact that the school textbooks I had to use talked about daffodils and snow or that half of my forty pupils to a class fell asleep at three in the afternoon when the thermometer reached forty degrees Celsius seemed odd but it took me two years of teaching to put two and two together and confront the issues of underdevelopment and colonization. My political consciousness was aroused and I returned home with more questions than answers: one of them being, What on earth am I doing here? to paraphrase Bruce Chatwin. Eight years after independence Senegal still had all the trappings of a French colony and Dakar was a compartmentalized world, which Fanon described so vividly in the opening chapter on violence in *The Wretched of the Earth*.

This was the world I was destined to work in, live in, and play in, and the other sector, the "native" sector, could only be glimpsed through the windows of the embassy's chauffeur-driven car or perhaps when we strayed on our mopeds into areas where friends working for the American Peace Corps used to live. And when at embassy receptions or dinner parties the conversation would inevitably revolve around "them," the others, it was, as Fanon says, often couched in zoological terms, referring to the odors, the stink, the hordes, the swarming, seething, sprawling population vegetating under the sun.

The year was 1968 and, true to the assimilation of a French colony, Senegal mimicked the events of May 1968 in France. Except they lasted for an entire year and both school pupils and university students deserted their classrooms in a vague attempt to change the order of their world and forge ahead with a genuine decolonization. But this was no revolution in the Fanonian sense and the students were content merely to sit and wait, instead of "blowing the colonial world to smithereens" and creating an agenda for total disorder. Just south of Senegal's border, in Guinea, Sékou Touré's resounding "No" to France, which met with admiration and applause from Third World revolutionaries, evidently had little chance of repeating itself in Senghor's Senegal.

My second encounter with Fanon must have been on my return to France in 1971. One year before Britain joined the Common Market I was not only forced to apply for a work permit, but also undergo a series of medicals, mandatory for immigrants from nonmember European Union countries. Most of the immigrants, of course, were from North Africa, and Algeria in particular. And it was here I witnessed that very special relationship, based on humiliation and contempt, that exists between the French and the Algerians. We were all made to line up in front of a nondescript building near the boulevard périphérique and once inside, submitted to a series of humiliating medical examinations that would allow us to apply for a work permit at another line at the Paris Préfecture. It was obvious that all the clichés about the Algerian's criminal impulsiveness, his indolence, his thefts, his lies and rapes, which had been inculcated into the French bureaucrats' minds before, during, and after the Algerian war, rose to the surface and treatment was dealt out accordingly. There was a long way to go before that colossal task, described by Fanon, of reintroducing man into the world, a man in full, could be achieved with the crucial help of the European masses who still rallied behind the position of their governments and media on colonial issues.

My third encounter with Fanon came with my many visits to Martinique and Guadeloupe, the island contexts that were to shape and mold the young Fanon. The sheer assimilation to France's cultural, educational, and political penetration not only turned him into a French intellectual (*The New York Review of Books* in 1966 described him as a "Black Rousseau . . . His call for national revolutions is Jacobin in method, Rousseauist in spirit, and Sartrian in language—altogether as French as can be.") but also forced him to question and challenge the very nature of the colonized subject. The alienation of his black-skinned, white-masked fellow islanders made him realize that if colonialism was not fought and defeated, then the islands of Martinique and Guadeloupe would disappear, swallowed up by the tide of assimilation. He somehow sensed that the bravado of the Martinicans was a lot of hot air, that they would never rise up against their colonizers and he'd do better to put his ideas into practice in the French departement of Algeria where the men had the guts of their convictions. On his return from his final visit to Martinique in 1951, Alice Cherki (*Frantz Fanon: Portrait*, Paris: Editions du Seuil, 2000) quotes him as saying, "I met more milquetoasts than men." Commenting on the tragic events of 1959 in Martinique to his friend Bertene Juminer while in Tunis, he told him: "Let them pick up their dead, rip their insides out and parade them in open trucks through the town. . . . Let them yell out: 'Look what the colonialists have done!' But they won't do anything of the sort. They'll vote a series of symbolic motions and start dying of poverty all over again. In the end, this outburst of anger reassures the colonialists. It's merely a way of letting off steam, a bit like a wet dream. You make love to a shadow. You soil the bed. But the next morning everything is back to normal. And you don't think any more about it" (*Présence Africaine*, 1st semester 1962: "Hommage à Frantz Fanon," p. 127).

Any visitor from outside France visiting the French islands of the Caribbean is immediately struck by the overwhelming presence of a metropolis seven thousand kilometers away, the extraordinary alienation of a petite bourgeoisie more attuned to France than their own destiny, and he or she cannot but admire Fanon's lucidity. Perhaps this is one of the reasons why he is studied more in the universities of the English-speaking world than in France and the French Caribbean where the skeletons of the Algerian war and the color hierarchy, respectively, are too close for comfort. Perhaps this is one of the reasons why Fanon's latest biographer, David Macey, and his new translator are two Englishmen, two islanders, who not only understand Fanon's love-hate, off-again/on-again relationship with France, but are also fascinated by the only French-speaking Caribbean intellectual who, as Edouard Glissant says, "really matched action to words by espousing the Algerian cause" (*Le Discours Antillais*, Paris: Editions du Seuil, 1981, p. 36). As David Macey says, "It was his anger that was so attractive." After all we Brits have a long history of angry young men. And then there is the way he has been treated—pulled in all directions by postcolonial scholars, made to fit their ideas and interpretations—and a great sense of injustice comes to mind every time Fanon is mentioned.

So this brings me to why I have crusaded for a new English translation of Fanon. First of all I was tired of people asking me if I translated anyone else besides Maryse Condé. But more important, I felt the need to challenge my skills at translating another type of text, one that defined as a theory the subject matter of alienation, colonization, and the color complex in so many of the French Caribbean novels I had already translated. Secondly, I felt that Fanon's had not done him justice. I felt that his voice had got distorted and he should be given a second chance to be heard. John Felstiner wrote in his book *Translating Neruda: The Way to Macchu Picchu* that "perhaps the real 'original' behind any translation occurs not in the written poem, but in the poet's voice speaking the verse aloud . . . a translator may also pick up vocal tones, intensities, rhythms, and pauses that will reveal how the poet heard a word, a phrase, a line, a passage. . . . What translation comes down to is listening." I have the good fortune to be in possession of a tape of Fanon's address to the First Congress of Black Writers and Artists in Paris in 1956. I have listened to that tape over and over again, and although Fanon's voice is not particularly charismatic, in fact it is rather bland, I was struck by the way he uses language and the emphasis he places on many of the words. He hammers his thoughts home in a very precise, cut-and-dried manner. There is even the slightest hint of hysteria, a controlled anger, of someone who would not like to be contradicted, perhaps even the voice of an *écorché vif*, a tormented soul, as Francis Jeanson thought of him. Ato Sekyi-Otu, who wrote *Fanon's Dialectic of Experience* (Cambridge, Mass.: Harvard University Press, 1996) argues that we should read Fanon's texts "as though they form one dramatic dialectical experience" rather than considering his statements "irrevocable propositions and doctrinal statements." "With what immensely complex and compelling force Fanon's texts speak to us when we read their contents as speech acts in the moving body of a dramatic narrative!" And there is drama behind his voice born out of urgency as he worked against the clock. Knowing that *Les Damnés de la Terre* had been dictated to his wife during his final year, I used the oral tone I had captured over the tape in my translation of *The Wretched of the Earth* and endeavored to make it read more like an oral presentation with that earnestness of voice he was known for. In fact the many repetitions and lyrical, not to say delirious, digressions in *Les Damnés de la Terre* are proof of a man dictating his text with the knowledge that he has little time left to live and desperate to put his thoughts, every single one of them, down on paper.

In his Preface to the first edition of *Peau noire, masques blancs* Francis Jeanson tells how one day he wrote to Fanon asking for clarification of a particularly obscure passage in the book. An answer was duly furnished and Fanon added: "This passage is inexplicable. When I write such things I seek to touch my reader in his emotions, i.e., irrationally, almost sensually."

Further on in his letter Fanon goes on to confess how he is drawn to the magic of words and that for him language is the ultimate refuge, once it is freed from conventions, from its voice of reason and the terror of coming face-to-face with oneself. "Words for me have a powerful effect. I feel it impossible to escape from the sting of a word or the vertigo of a question mark." He went on to say that, like Césaire, he wanted to sink beneath the stupefying lava of words that have the color of quivering flesh.

When it came to translating Fanon I was constantly aware of the man as a doctor, as a humanist and an intellectual from the Third World. He would never let me forget it. His use of the human anatomy to illustrate the colonized's behavior can be seen throughout his work.

I now had to develop a strategy for my own translation. I had a choice of keeping the rather heavy, pompous style and language of the 1950s or deciding to update and modernize it without losing Fanon's voice. I had in mind a young reader who would be swept along by Fanon's thoughts in the language of the twenty-first century. Without betraying Fanon I decided to tighten up the text, update the vocabulary, and retrieve his lost voice.

One of the translation problems I had to settle, which came up time amd time again throughout the text, was the translation of "colon," the European inhabitant of a colony once the colonization process has got under way. I was tempted to use the word *colonizer* since it sounded right pitted against the word *colonized*. But a colonizer composes the original force that colonized the country and does not convey the meaning of the European who settled, lived, worked, and was born in the colony. *Colonial* has two different associations, one for the English, especially in East Africa, and one for the Americans, pertaining to the thirteen British colonies that became the United States of America or to that period; *settler* was being used by the media in the Mideast crisis to refer to the Jewish settlers and would be the immediate reference for a reader. I first decided on a compromise between the French word *colon* and the English *colonist* and coined "*colonist.*" My editor, however, decided otherwise, and we kept the word *colonist.* I felt that by keeping the word *colon* the term not only spoke to the English-speaking reader but also remained faithful to Fanon, for whom Algeria was the constant point of reference. *Colon, gendarme, metropole, maquis, indigène*; the Arabic terms of *çof, zar, djebel, douar, Roumi, razzia, fellah* and *djemaa.* All words from a French colonial context, all terms from an Algerian context which, however hard Fanon tries to universalize, bring us back to his country of origin and his country of adoption.

And finally there is that word dreaded by all translators of French Caribbean texts: *nègre*. Constance Farrington did not deal with the problem or perhaps she didn't have to at the time: she merely translated *nègre* and *noir* by the word *Negro*, which was accepted usage in the 1950s and '60s, and in the process lost a subtle difference. But if the translator decides to update and modernize his vocabulary, then he is faced with a sticky issue. In Randall Kennedy's fascinating book *Nigger: The Strange Career of a Troublesome Word* (New York: Pantheon Books, 2002) he cites Professor Clarence Major as saying that when it is used by black people among themselves it is a racial term with undertones of warmth and goodwill . . . reflecting a tragicomic sensibility that is aware of black history. It is also "the filthiest, dirtiest, nastiest in the English language." The word *nègre* would have been used in the same way by Fanon, the Martinican, whether referring to the black man in general or putting it in the mouth of the oppressor as an insult. It was a word rehabilitated by the black intelligentsia of the time and thrown back at the European as the supreme weapon. One of the great achievements of Césaire's epic poem "Notebook of a Return to My Native Land" is to reappropriate the negative term and give it a positive meaning. In *Pour la révolution africaine* (*Toward the African Revolution*), in the chapter "Antillais et Africains" Fanon describes how the word *nègre* was used for the Africans by both Europeans and French Caribbeans alike. He quotes the example of a boss in Martinique demanding too much from his employee and getting the response: "*Si vous voulez un nègre, allez le chercher en Afrique*" ("If you're looking for a nigger, go and find him in Africa"). To quote a more modern example of this, we only have to look at the opening lines of Chris Rock's signature skit: "I love black people, but I hate niggers. . . . Every time black people want to have a good time, niggers mess it up." It wasn't until Césaire came along that "for the first time, we saw a lycée teacher, and therefore an apparently worthy man, simply tell West Indian society that it is 'good and well to be a nigger.' Of course it was a scandal." And Fanon ends his chapter on national culture with the words: "There can be no such thing as rigorously identical cultures. To believe one can create a black culture is to forget oddly enough that 'Negroes' are in the process of disappearing, since those who created them are witnessing the demise of their economic and cultural supremacy." Now that the vocabulary has evolved it places the translator in a twenty-first-century predicament. I have updated the word *Negro*, when he refers to the peoples of Africa or the diaspora, to *black*, and used *nigger* when it is the colonizer referring to the same. In some cases, I have left *Negro* in its historical context. But I have lost something in the translation of the word *nègre*, for it has both a sting and an embrace, and that is irretrievable. I have modernized the word *indigène* to *colonized* or *colonized subject*, ridding it of today's pejorative sense of *native* although Fanon, in keeping with the colonial vocabulary of his time, uses both terms indifferently in the very same paragraph.

So how relevant is Fanon today? I can remember going into the FNAC bookstore in Paris last year to buy an edition of *Les Damnés de la Terre* and being asked: Fanon? How do you spell it? Oh yes, here we are, as the girl consulted her computer, *Les dames de la terre*! Fanon obviously hasn't left his mark here, I thought, and moved on. But how far can we move on and forget him? We cannot forget the martyrdom of the Palestinians when we read in Fanon's chapter "On Violence": "At the individual level, violence is a cleansing force. It rids the colonized of their inferiority complex, of their passive and despairing attitude. It emboldens them and restores their self-confidence." We cannot forget the lumpenproletariat, the wretched of the earth, who still stream to Europe from Africa, Iraq, Afghanistan, and the countries of the former Eastern bloc, living on the periphery in their shantytowns and refugee centers, waiting for a better life. The bourgeoisie in Africa still unreservedly and enthusiastically adopt the thinking mechanisms characteristic of the West, still has alienated to perfection its own thoughts and grounded its consciousness in typically foreign notions, still turns its back on the majority of its population, vacationing on the French Riviera and building colossal palaces for prestige sake, joining hands in "this huge caravan of corruption" and becoming, as Fanon says: "a bourgeois bourgeoisie that is dismally, inanely, and cynically bourgeois." And his thoughts on culture differentiating Africa from the Americas, visioning the disappearance of black culture in favor of national cultures, regarding traditions basically stifling whereas a culture is constantly changing, modernizing, and penetrated by other influences. He was wrong of course on many points, especially pan-Africanism, the role of the peasantry in leading a revolution, and the fate of Algeria. But at the time, his analyses of alienation and decolonization were extraordinary eye-openers, not only for a complacent Europe but for his fellow islanders, blinded to reality. It is his anger, conviction, and humanism that will always remain with us.

So this has been my fourth encounter with Fanon, and perhaps the most intimate. The other three were encounters with the others, the colonized, the colonial subjects. This time I had come face-to-face with the man himself and had to take on the extraordinary task of gaining access to the author's voice and meaning, and initiating communication with the target audience. The very fact that I had lived in Africa, France, and the French Caribbean helped enormously in understanding the society and culture that had shaped and influenced Fanon. But I no longer had the good fortune to be able to pop into the next room and ask him what exactly he meant in such and such a paragraph as I can when translating Maryse Condé. I had accompanied him on his life's journey, but the closest I could get to the man himself was being in the company of Bertene Juminer, Assia Djebar, Roland Thesauros, Edouard Glissant, Mme Christiane Diop of *Présence Africaine,* and Aimé Césaire, all of whom had crossed his path. You might think that translating the dead gives you a whole lot of freedom—there's nobody there looking over your shoulder or making rude comments. But in fact there are crowds of people looking over your shoulder—from the readers of the original translation to the postcolonial scholars who have staked their reputation on Fanon's ideas. Translating a dead man means stepping very warily through a minefield littered with the debris of another time and another translation. But the very fact of looking back was a driving force to modernize the text and look ahead. In Fanon's case, translating the dead was a case of translating life itself. I felt I had to bring a dead translation back to life. To quote John Felstiner on Celan, he hoped that in translating Celan's poems he felt something akin to what Celan felt writing them. Retranslating Fanon, rewriting Fanon almost gives me the same kick. As if I am the one writing down his thoughts in English for the first time.

And then there is that secret feeling that married to a writer from Guadeloupe, from the French Caribbean, I have always known Fanon and understood his dilemma and ambition as a Martinican. No one sums up this personality of the French Caribbean better than Aimé Césaire in "Hommages à Frantz Fanon" published in *Présence Africaine* in 1962:

Perhaps Fanon reached such heights and his vision was so broad because he was a French Caribbean, in other words he had started off so far down and from such a narrow base. Perhaps only a French Caribbean, in other words one so destitute, so depersonalized could have set off with such determination to conquer himself and plenitude; only a French Caribbean, in other words one so mystified to start off with, could manage to dismantle with such skill the most elusive mechanisms of mystification; only a French Caribbean, finally, could want so desperately to escape powerlessness through action and solitude through fraternity.

—Richard Philcox